Fables of Desire

Studies in the Ethics of Art and Gender

Helga Geyer-Ryan

Polity Press

Copyright © this collection Polity Press 1994
Copyright © each individual chapter Helga Geyer-Ryan 1994

First published in 1994 by Polity Press
in association with Blackwell Publishers

Editorial office:
Polity Press
65 Bridge Street
Cambridge CB2 1UR, UK

Marketing and production:
Blackwell Publishers
108 Cowley Road
Oxford OX4 1JF, UK

238 Main Street
Cambridge, MA 02142, USA

ISBN 0 7456 0642 3
ISBN 0 7456 1177 X (pbk)

A CIP catalogue record for this book is available
from the British Library and from the Library of Congress.

Typeset in 10 on 12pt Sabon
by Acorn Bookwork, Salisbury
Printed in Great Britain by Biddles Ltd,
Guildford and Kings Lynn

This book is printed on acid-free paper.

Contents

Acknowledgements

The author would like to thank the following for permission to reprint material that has previously been published elsewhere:

Manchester University Press for chapter 1, 'Counterfactual Artefacts: Walter Benjamin's Philosophy of History', from Timms and Collier (eds), *Visions and Blueprints* (Manchester University Press, 1988); John Benjamins B. V. for chapter 2, 'The Rhetoric of Forgetting: Brecht and the Historical Avant-garde', from T. D'haen, R. Grübel and H. Lethen (eds), *Convention and Innovation in Literature* (John Benjamins, 1989); The Macmillan Press Ltd for chapter 3, 'The Castration of Cassandra', from J. Birkett and E. Harvey (eds) *Determined Women* (1991); Johns Hopkins University Press for chapter 6, 'Abjection in the Texts of Walter Benjamin', which first appeared as 'Effects of Abjection in the Texts of Walter Benjamin' in *MLN*, German issue, *Walter Benjamin 1892–1940*, 107, 3 (1992); The University of Essex (Department of Literature) for chapter 7, 'Prefigurative Racism in Goethe's *Iphigenie auf Tauris*', from Francis Barker et al. (eds), *Europe and its Others* (1984); The University of Birmingham (Centre for Contemporary Cultural Studies) for chapter 10, 'Popular Literature in the Third Reich', from H. Geyer-Ryan, *Popular Literature in the Third Reich: Observations on the 'Groschenroman'*, General Series SP no. 60.

Tony Harrison and Peters, Fraser and Dunlop for permission to quote 'The Ballad of Babelabour'; Methuen London and Routledge, Chapman and Hall, Inc. for permission to quote Bertolt Brecht's 'Questions from a Worker who Reads' from *Poems 1913–1956* © Bertolt Brecht, translation © Michael Hamburger. Every effort has been made to trace all copyright

Chapters 6, 12 and 13 have been translated from the German by Andrew Winnard.

Introduction: Literature and the Ethics of the Other

The essays in this volume span a wide range of texts and topics, but they all revolve around the same central problems and are all shaped by the same broad objective. Their aim is to bring the challenge of post-structuralist and especially feminist theory into dialogue with the legacy of the Frankfurt School, with its unique blend of politics, philosophy, cultural analysis and hermeneutics.

A key concern of this debate is the attempt of feminism to blaze a trail between modernism and postmodernism, the twin peaks of twentieth-century cultural theory. As a political practice, feminism is deeply committed to the struggle against domination and exploitation. It therefore needs the analytical categories of the subject, of the individual, of consciousness, of value, of action and of liberation, all of which constitute the true heritage of the social and cultural semantics of modernity. Feminist theory, on the other hand, in its most radical form, dismantles every concept handed down by cultural tradition, seeking to expose the specific interests concealed by groundless claims to permanence and universality. But it thereby threatens to pitch the feminist project into an abyss of unheeding relativism in which no firm ground on which to choose and act can be found. It is this tension between the need for reconstruction, the need to tell a new tale, and the desire to deconstruct whatever masquerades as given, which lies at the heart of *Fables of Desire*.

If the book has a hidden agenda, it is to hasten the renewed rapprochement of ethics and aesthetics, whose historic uncoupling in the work of Kant has been reinforced more recently by the marginalization of ethical concern in cultural theories spawned by the linguistic turn. The return of ethics to contemporary theoretical debates is long overdue, and it has already helped transform earlier political notions of culture into a more flexible and open-ended enterprise. Under the impact of unforeseen, decisive shifts in global history and politics, such as the disappearance of the old communist regimes, the ensuing emphasis on nationalisms and ethnic demarcation, unexpected warfare and the massive migratory movements between nations and continents, the foregrounding of ethics responds both to the urgent need for a new programme of humanism and to the current crisis in political theory caused by the discrediting of the latter's claims to a securely grounded, quasi-universal validity.

In this respect the new ethics are an immediate result of international exchanges in the field of theory in the last two decades. They mark a distinct juncture between two eras of thinking. From the past they have inherited a deep aversion to any gesture of closure or totalization, which would risk conceptualizing reality in terms of fixed identities, binary oppositions or essences. From the present and the future the new ethics have absorbed the need for alternative modes of identity which would be constructed in such a way as to include from the start the notion of alterity, the place of the other.

The thinker most vital to the development of this project is the French philosopher Emmanuel Lévinas. This might seem surprising in the context of this book in as much as Lévinas, following a specifically Jewish tradition of privileging language over images, never sketched a comprehensive aesthetic theory comparable with those evolved by Adorno, Benjamin, Kristeva or Lyotard. But what makes him so important at this moment of our history is his endeavour to ontologize the ethical dimension as the basic condition of our human existence. Lévinas is able to do this, while avoiding the traps of essentialism and the transcendental ego, by founding his ethics on the asymmetrical quality of human intersubjectivity.

In Lacanian theory the unbridgeable distance of the Other contaminates all phenomena of psychic and cultural life with privation or lack; the mutual exclusion of being (presence) and sign (consciousness, thought, ego, language, representation) gives rise to alienation and death. But, according to Lévinas, the same predicament, conceived of as the origin of desire, situates the self in an attitude of obligation to the other. Because the otherness of my fellow human being can never be totally disclosed to me, this absolute alterity, which is nevertheless the very guarantee of my intersubjective identity, is the existential abyss out of which concepts of desire, transcendence and infinity emerge, forcing me to experience every individual as a singularity. This is the reason for what Adorno terms the incommensurability of individuals. Compared with this notion of identity, theories of intersubjectivity, communication or justice which are based on the idea of equality as the result of equivalences between individuals are bound to fall short and turn perversely into their opposites: loss of identity, empty communication and injustice.

Because the inner lives of individuals are constructed in different ways, the other always eludes the meanings with which I seek to fix her. The other person presents an excess of meaning, a secret, a thing-in-itself in Kantian terms, which surpasses my power of exegesis. The heterogeneity of the other, the consequence of her epistemological opacity, is enhanced by the psychoanalytic recognition of the split subject who does not even know herself and by the phenomenological perception of the gulf between being and meaning, which renders self-awareness perpetually belated.

The paradox of the simultaneous appeal and impenetrability of the other is expressed, for Lévinas, in the face. The face is an inscription of an import for which no code exists. The asymmetrical relationship between individuals cannot be adequately synchronized by mere identification or projection, but only by a surplus of unqualified attention, a response which Lévinas calls 'generosity'. Such a response can never be grasped in logical terms because by definition it is ethical from the very beginning.

The strangeness of others emerges as the exchange of language. Language or speaking only occurs in the realms of alterity. Though language presupposes notions of equivalence, identity, universality and abstraction, verbal communication does not necessarily repress alterity. According to Lévinas, it releases the other into intersubjectivity, offering alterity to apprehension. The contradictory message of the other's countenance, at once inviting and impeding interpretation, manifests itself in language as the entanglement of universality and heterology, as the disparity between the logic of the utterance and the heterology of uttering.

What holds the centrifugal compound of intersubjective alterity together as the ethical dimension is the transference of proximity in the linguistic act. The proximity of two individuals prevents the urge for fusion or communion, which are the products of principles of equivalence and sameness.

The alien quality of the other, which can never be recuperated, is described by Lévinas as a trace, as a sign of absence, a reminder of a past and irretrievable meaning. The face is such an inscription, but so also is a way of writing, the style of a text. Lévinas goes so far as to conclude that it is only the trace which is the true support of meaning in a text. The trace as face, as style, witnesses the impact of otherness and opens up any system, institution or supposed totality towards infinity, in other words towards contingency and subversion.

Literary texts, with their avowed production of mimesis and fictionality, their plethora of rhetorical strategies, constantly summon the faces of their authors and the generations of readers who contributed to their survival from the past. The author of a literary text might be dead, whether literally or metaphorically, but the faces conjured up by the work live on as the other of the text. These traces of the text can be readily translated into Lacan's famous statement that a signifier represents a subject for another signifier, or into Benjamin's notion of the aura of an artwork.

The literary text as face or trace of an other, as an intimate means of scripting the fable of my identity and yet separated by an unbridgeable abyss of desire, sabotages not only the coercive routines of everyday language but also our conventional perceptions of the world and its practices. Both the work of literature and its critical interpretations always betray the visage of the other, manifest in the impossibility of producing a final, closed meaning. The irreducibility of any speech act, which is magnified in the literary text, but provisionally subdued by the logic of institutionalized utterance, gives rise to the insatiable desire for fresh signification. This desire is really our desire for the other, and, since it can never be fulfilled, the sign of infinity.

Fables of Desire takes issue with the excess of meaning of literary artefacts and their critical texts. This surplus of signification is read as the other's expression of her otherness and as the instigator of our desire for meaning. At the same time *Fables of Desire* engages with the narratives of alterity, the tales of the quandaries of otherness and of the coercions of identity.

As otherness is, in psychoanalytic terms, the Real of the subject, that which eludes signification and therefore even one's own consciousness and language, it can never be said, but only demonstrated, staged, brought towards the point of perception in the imagination of the recipient. Because this blurred zone of inner experience can never be fully transposed into language, it generates that space of desire in the fable which resists interpretation. It is the pivot around which the spiral of commentary revolves, shaping and re-shaping literary history.

The same desire can be detected in the fables spun by literary critics and theoreticians in their allegories of reading. It can be detected in the endless repetition of the hermeneutic and semiotic enterprises, which the literary text, the fable of desire, exacts from its amateur and professional readers alike. The desire of the reader for otherness and as otherness re-emerges in the difficulty, obscurity or hermeticism of the text's critical commentary and is institutionalized in literary criticism and theory. What we call difficulty, convolution, over-abstraction, originality or obsessiveness in privileging certain issues can be read as the insistence of the unconscious in the supposedly objective text of the professional reader.

Within the framework of such a literary ethics, the present study tries to bring the voices of the European Enlightenment, the still unfinished project of modernity, into dialogue with the demands of what we now call post-modernism, the critical self-reflection of modernity, as it turns against its own temptation to totalize an atrophied discourse of reason designed to eclipse all instances of otherness.

The power of this perspective to challenge prevailing discourses of history, representation, gender, race and hierarchy opens up new dimensions of dissent in the field of symbolic production. *Fables of Desire* draws heavily on a theory of reading developed by Walter Benjamin. In his 'Theses on the Philosophy of History' Benjamin points out that 'every image of the past that is not recognized by the present as one of its own concerns threatens to disappear irretrievably';[1] but he also observes in his *Passagen-Werk* that our capacity to recognize these proleptic images is itself historically conditioned, that it is the changing horizon of the present which allows hitherto mute works from the past to speak, previously cryptic texts to become legible, for the first time.

The present collection of essays thus (re-)reads central texts from a broad European literary and theoretical tradition in the fresh light of radical cultural theories of the present, including feminist theory, psychoanalysis, the Critical Theory of the Frankfurt School, the concept of orientalism and the Bakhtinian hermeneutics of polyphony. These reconstructive readings are perceived as having always been latent within the multivocal textuality of the literary artefact, but as only now susceptible of realization. The process of realization and reappropriation must constantly confront and contest, however, the canonized forms of interpretation through which conservative cultural institutions have sought to repress or erase the radical configurations of meaning stored within the text.

This volume of essays is written directly against the politics of forgetting. The strategy of reading it deploys is rooted in the conviction that the struggle against domination is never decided once and for all, but must be continually staged and waged anew. In the field of culture this struggle can be defined as a battle between the reactionary drive to subdue the site of symbolic production to the imperialistic sway of a unified cultural discourse, and the democratic liberation of an indefinite plurality of disparate voices, committed to the indivisibility of communicative reason and social difference.

In this sense *Fables of Desire* involves a running argument against both the arbitrariness of current forms of relativism and the stifling soliloquies of cultural pessimism and nihilism. Consequently, a number of closely related preoccupations inform all the essays: identity, sexual difference, gender politics, textuality, violence, power and voice. These are the crucial territories upon which the strife between unification and polyphony, violence and desire is played out.

The first two essays deal with problems of continuity and rupture in theories of narrative. The essay on Benjamin elaborates the connection between his philosophy of history as a non-linear historiography and his

Marxist engagement with the aesthetics of the European avant-garde. 'The Rhetoric of Forgetting' begins with a critique of basic postmodern assumptions and proceeds to explore the vital bearing of past and present notions of memory and its suppression on the poetics of modernism and the avant-garde.

The following four essays examine representations of the relationship between sexual difference, power and signification. They show how symbolic significance depends on the violent repression of the female body, sexuality and voice ('The Castration of Cassandra', 'Female Reason and Symbolic Violence', 'Adultery as Critique' and 'Abjection in the Texts of Walter Benjamin'). How this repressive syndrome is secretly linked to ethnocentric, nationalistic or racist attitudes is shown in the next three essays ('Prefigurative Racism in Goethe's *Iphigenie auf Tauris*', 'Sexuality in Robert Musil's *Young Törless*' and 'Space, Gender and National Identity').

The last five essays overthrow deeply entrenched views of fundamental importance to the continuance of the present cultural-political regime. 'Popular Literature in the Third Reich' refutes the idea that popular romance has always necessarily served the interests of the right, by attacking it in a context which would seem to make it incontestable. The next three essays take up again the problem of the repressed (female) body, but this time on the level of the theoretical text, in order to establish the connection between this phenomenon and the privileging of purely linguistic theories of literature by certain dominant poststructuralist and postmodernist critics.

'Enlightenment, Sexual Difference and the Autonomy of Art' contends that the concepts of art as either autonomous or socially engaged are not mutually exclusive, as traditional criticism, the New Historicism or Cultural Materialism would have it, but simultaneously active on different planes of artistic experience. The exclusion of a whole body of committed or sentimental literature from the canon can be revealed as a ruse of cultural hegemony. Against de Man's notion of 'undecidability' of the literary text and its corruption by aesthetic ideology, 'Unreal Presences: Allegory in Paul de Man and Walter Benjamin' amplifies the hitherto muted case for a demonstrably valid interpretation, rooted in the reader's position in the real.

'Writing, Image and Reality' shows how the acknowledgement of the sensuous spectacle of a text in the reader's imagination is indispensable to any comprehensive theory of literature and how at the same time the subversion of visual fixity is activated by the reflexivity of the text's polyphonic structure. Finally, the theory that the project of modernity was doomed to perish by the inherently corrupt, instrumental character of reason since the Enlightenment, the argument which found its most persuasive advocates in Adorno and Horkheimer, is undermined through an allegorical reinterpretation of Homer in 'From the Dialectic of Force to *The Dialectic of Enlightenment*: Re-reading the *Odyssey*'.

NOTES

1   Walter Benjamin, 'Theses on the philosophy of history', *Illuminations*, ed. Hannah Arendt (Collins/Fontana Books, London, 1973), pp. 255–66, esp. p. 257.

Part I

Narratives of History

1

Counterfactual Artefacts: Walter Benjamin's Philosophy of History

Throughout Benjamin's work between 1920 and 1940 there runs one major preoccupation: the sketching of a modernist theory of history. Closely linked to this are Benjamin's explorations of how human subjectivity might be reconstructed in a way which would meet the demands of cultural modernism without at the same time dissolving the capacity for political action. Thus his texts contain the basic elements for a new theory of the subject and a new theory of history; and, since history is itself a text, they also include a new hermeneutics of reading and writing.

As a modernist philosopher of history, Benjamin called into question such notions of traditional historical discourse as continuity, development, process, progress and organism. As a modernist theoretician of historiography, he was critical of traditional narrative with its rosary-like chain of cause-and-event stories. Inspired by the practice of the literary avant-garde, he developed his own theory of textual production or signification, which was based on the principle of fragmentation and montage: the central features of Benjamin's own texts are thus the quotation, the thesis, the fragment, the arrangement and the compilation.

It was the vision of nineteenth-century Paris, with its refracted and ruptured archaeology, which provided Benjamin with the material imagery out of which he strove to fashion his new conceptions. Paris was both the epitome of capitalism and a wellspring of the forces which opposed it, and as such it represented for him a mythological microcosm of modern times. Above all, Paris inspired Benjamin with its catalytic fusion of what he saw as the two most advanced developments in twentieth-century politics and culture: Marxism and Surrealism. In Benjamin's writing the two movements enrich and transform each other. The abstract language of Marxist theory becomes more concrete and sensually perceptible by being infused with the images of mythology (*Bilderschrift*). As Benjamin says:

> There is a central problem of historical materialism and it is about time it was recognized: that is, whether the Marxist understanding of history is only possible at the cost of reducing the concrete presence of history before our eyes. Or: how is it possible to enhance this concrete presence of history and to combine it with the application of Marxist methods? The first stage will be to adapt the montage principle in history; that means to erect the large constructions from the smallest, precisely and pointedly manufactured units.[1]

At the same time the tendentially ahistorical mythologization of Paris in avant-garde writing is revealed as a phantasm unless it is demystified by underpinning it with historical and political awareness. In this respect Benjamin explicitly sets his *Passagen-Werk* apart from Aragon's *Paysan de Paris*:

> Whereas Aragon stays within the realm of dream, the aim in this case is to find the constellation of awakening. Whilst in Aragon there remains an element of impressionism – the mythology – and this impressionism is to be held responsible for the many formless philosophemes in the book, in this case it is a question of dissolving mythology into the realm of history. Of course, this can only happen by awakening an as yet unconscious knowledge of what has been.[2]

The concept of dream and awakening are of crucial importance in Benjamin's writing. Dream is the juncture of the imagery of physical concreteness and exuberant materialism with the structures of desire. But this dream-world is furnished by objects which in capitalism are necessarily commodities, and consequently the structures of desire are made up of desire and fear (*Angst*) at once. In contrast, awakening is the moment where the spell or illusion of reconciling a desire for fulfilment with a structure of exploitation and alienation can be broken. In this dream, under the spell of capitalism, desire and objects of fulfilment are authentic and distorted at the same time. The task of the new historian is to set free the forces and drives of authentic liberation without giving up a materially better life and the more refined structures of desire which go with it.

Benjamin's starting-point is to 'read' Paris. He says: 'The topos of Nature's book shows that it is possible to read reality like a text. So this will be done here with the reality of the nineteenth century.'[3] Benjamin's reading of nineteenth-century Paris constitutes the deciphering of the primal landscape (the *Urlandschaft*) of twentieth-century capitalism and mass psychology. It is only better-informed later generations who will be able to look at the past in such a way as to produce a reading of it which illuminates the present like a flash of lightning. Conversely, Benjamin's specific reading of Paris can only come about at a historical moment where a fusion between Marxism and Surrealism is possible and where such an *idiosyncratic* reading is vital for the politics of Benjamin's own time.

> It is not the case that the past sheds its light on the present or the present its light on the past, but the image is that in which, what has been, enters into a constellation with the 'Now' [*Jetzt*] in a sudden flash. In other words: the image is dialectics at a standstill ... The image read, i.e. the image in the 'Now' of the potential realization, is most clearly marked by that critical and dangerous momentum, the basis of all reading.[4]

And, even more important: 'the historical index of the images not only tells us that they belong to a certain time, above all it tells us that only at a certain time do they become readable'.[5]

Thus we can detect two important implications for his philosophy of history. Firstly, to read the *world* in order to find out about history means that history becomes spatialized. The transformation of a temporal concept into a spatial one implies that a view of time as process or progression has been supplanted by a sense of time having stopped, of history having come to an end. This radical shift of perspective becomes a dominant theme of cultural production during the period opening around the turn of the century and culminating in the First World War and the proletarian revolutions which grew out of it. Secondly, to *read* the world assumes that history is seen as a text, as an artefact, as something constructed, the encoding and interpretation of which are always to be understood as socially and ideologically conditioned.

Both of these ideas, the spatialization of time and history as text, emerged from the historical constellation from within which Benjamin began to write, and of which he was acutely aware from the beginning. With the First World War, history as *bourgeois* history, hitherto legitimized and sustained by the notion of 'progress', did indeed come to an end. Imperialism stood fully unmasked at last. At the same time an alternative force, whose political perspective opened up a whole new way of writing history, had seized power successfully in Russia. Nevertheless, after the defeat of the proletarian revolutions in Europe, the ruling classes reinforced their hegemony by satisfying certain demands for social and political reform. The Social Democrats increased their influence, but paid the high price of adapting themselves ever more to bourgeois modes of thought and action, a development facilitated by a deterministic interpretation of Marx's theory since the Second International.

Marx's analysis of capitalism had established on a theoretical level the proposition that capitalism necessarily produces the forces of its own destruction. But what he did not say was whether those counter-forces would inevitably triumph before capitalism had the chance to turn its own particular collapse into a universal catastrophe. It was on just such an assumption of inevitable triumph, however, that the social-democratic theory rested: the unconsidered supposition that the decline of capitalism would mean the ineluctable progress of socialism. This in turn made it possible to evolve the theory of the peaceful, because automatic, transformation of capitalism into socialism; a theory designed (not necessarily consciously) to still the desire to fight actively against bourgeois imperialism.

One social formation where this problem was perceived and tackled with increasing idiosyncrasy was the cultural avant-garde. Not only had bourgeois culture done nothing by 1914 to abolish ossified patterns of life, to eradicate social injustice and to prevent the First World War, but some artists had greeted and glorified that bloody spectacle in which a morally bankrupt capitalism flagrantly betrayed the humanist values to which it had hitherto claimed to subscribe. The reason for what looked like art's submission to the interests of the ruling class, and its function as a means of ideologically shoring up a crumbling society, was found in art's separation from life: by defining and institutionalizing art as autonomous, bourgeois society had rendered it ineffectual. Thus the attempt to reintegrate art and life, to aestheticize life, in other words, was the common aim of avant-garde movements such as Dadaism, Futurism and Surrealism. It is the aim summed up in Breton's phrase 'pratiquer la poésie'. This reintegration was not, however, meant to take place within the existing society. Rather, the aesthetic way of perceiving and producing reality was seen as a means of changing society: a society dominated on all levels by abstraction, instrumentalism and technical rationality, and by an ideal of progress which concentrated wholly on the development of science and technology in order to maximize exploitation and profit.

Drastically oversimplified as it is, this outline of the situation around the time of the First World War needs to be borne in mind for a proper understanding of the historical and cultural trends which informed and shaped Benjamin's writings from 1920 to 1940. His whole *œuvre* centres upon the same dominant issues, constantly weaving them together into the complex texture of his conception of history. Benjamin's idea of the pregnant or charged moment of historical recognition, whereby one can find condensed in a work a whole life, and in a life a whole epoch, applies equally to his own texts. Whichever of them we might select for closer analysis, and however remote it might seem at first sight from his main interests, it will turn out in the end to be one point in a magnetic field: a unit complete in its own specific thematic purpose, but directed at the same time towards a more fundamental and comprehensive concern which exists only in the total formation of its different units.

In this respect Benjamin's 'Theses on the philosophy of history', written shortly before his death in 1940 and (significantly) not meant to be published, are only the very tip of the iceberg. This becomes clear when we recognize that the themes treated here recur in the *Passagen-Werk*, his most ambitious intellectual project. Benjamin's 'Theses' are dictated by the drive to rewrite history from the perspective not of the victors of history, i.e. the ruling classes, but of their victims. Such an alternative reconstruction of the past does not mean, however, just another version of traditional historicism, a mere chronicle of past events and great figures supposedly unconnected with the present, though in fact, of course, shaped by the historian's conscious or unconscious alliance with the ruling class. On the contrary. The writing of an oppositional history is doubly rooted in the social formation of the writer's own time. On the one hand only an alliance with the victims of, and potential liberators from, social and political oppression in the present can provide the vanishing-point towards which the counter-history is projected. And on the other hand, this salvaged history, wrenched from the grasp of collective amnesia, is necessary for the abolition of the status quo, because, as Benjamin puts it, each generation has been vested with the messianic power to redeem all those who suffered in the past.[6]

This rewriting of history is not an easy task, and it is constantly threatened by failure. There are three main reasons for this. The first is that the witnesses of the other history are continually disappearing. They are only to be found in what the dominant process of history has secreted as waste, as the superseded and outmoded which can thus, by definition, have no function within the 'advancing' capitalist order. Once free of its use-value, this waste has once again the potential to indicate a counterfactual history. For what is left is a pure form – pure because it is defunct – into which new meaning can be deposited, an activity performed by the artist, the historian and the collector alike. 'Anything which you know won't be existing much longer becomes an image', says Benjamin with reference to Baudelaire's way of finding material for his urban poetry, and he draws the comparison between the artist of the capitalist city and the ragman:

> The poets find the refuse of society on their street and derive their heroic subject from this very refuse. This means that a common type is, as it were, superimposed upon their illustrious type. This new type is permeated by the features of the rag picker with whom Baudelaire repeatedly concerned himself. One year before he wrote 'Le vin des chiffoniers' he published a prose presentation of the figure: 'Here we have a man who has to gather the day's refuse in the capital city. Everything that the big city threw away, everything

it lost, everything it despised, everything it crushed underfoot, he catalogues and collects. He collates the annals of intemperance, the stockpile of waste. He sorts things out and makes a wise choice; he collects, like a miser guarding a treasure, the refuse which will assume the shape of useful or gratifying objects between the jaws of the goddess of Industry.'[7]

The loss of that which is outmoded is the loss of the dream material, the very stuff of mythological and symbolic resonance. For what is disappearing are those objects of our own past, in which the connection between technology and mythology had been created. Such a connection can only be achieved by children, says Benjamin.

> Task of childhood: to bring the new world into the realm of the symbolic. The child can do what an adult is totally incapable of doing: recognize the new once again. Railway engines already have the character of symbols for us because we saw them in our childhood. For our children cars – of which we ourselves see only the new, elegant, slick side – have this character ... for every truly new natural formation [*Naturgestalt*] – and basically, technology is one such – there are corresponding new images. Each generation of children discovers these new images to incorporate them into mankind's treasury of images.[8]

So the second point is that this disappearance of the objective material of a counter-history is paralleled by an ever-increasing loss of experience on the part of the subject. Experience depends upon the capacity of personal memory to interrelate the biographical past and present. For Benjamin, biographical memory and historical memory are analogous procedures, and one cannot exist without the other. From this follows the third factor jeopardizing the project. I have said that the medium in which the epistemological moment, the flash-like identity of subject and object, transpires is for Benjamin no longer the language of theory but the language of images; but the mimetic powers are constantly being eroded and reduced by the demands of instrumental rationality, the philosophical backbone of capitalist technology.

These three points outline the material conditions for an alternative production of historical meaning. Benjamin's central stress on the mimetic and the imaginative as basic factors in changing the world of the status quo links him directly with Surrealism and has also given rise to various attempts to claim him as a Judaic religious thinker. But what Benjamin found in the imagery of the Messiah or in the ecstatic moment of what he emphatically defines as '*profane illumination*' are precisely the emotional and pictorial foundations of sensuous perception, of an alternative way of seeing; in short: of creativity.

Until then the mimetic and imaginative faculties had not been made productive for scientific, political and historical practice, but had survived mainly in areas where inspiration, vision and revelation as elements of mystical discourse paraphrased the moment of recognition. As these fields of application were themselves concerned with the production of imaginative material, especially in religion or art, the general validity of the mimetic faculty for all kinds of epistemological activity had been overlooked. But if we recall, for instance, that Kekulé, the founder of organic chemistry, had visualized the structure of the benzine ring while dreaming of a snake swallowing its own tail, it may not be altogether fanciful to consider whether the mimetic – the aesthetic – might indeed be the general organon in which theory and practice are linked.

Modern psychology still speaks of the 'desirable and proper mystery which surrounds the creative act', and adds modestly but significantly: 'the best that can be said is that certain uniformities do seem to characterize highly original scientists and artists'.[9] Even today we have only taken the very first steps towards establishing a psychology of the imagination, which neuro-physiologists do not hesitate to define as 'the highest level of mental experience', its processes inextricably bound up with those of 'the lower level of sensuous experience, imagery, hallucination and memory'.[10]

I am quoting this not least because it points up the remarkable insights of Benjamin and the Surrealists nearly forty years before the quoted essay was written. Imagination, hallucination and memory are the key categories deployed by them in order to grasp a framework of epistemological production which is by definition aesthetic because it is always mimetic. In the epistemological process correspondences are discovered between objects which hitherto had appeared unconnected. Benjamin's key witnesses on this point are Baudelaire, Proust, Aragon and Breton's *Nadja*. We develop these faculties only because nature itself is full of correspondences. Therefore the Surrealists, for instance, gave accounts of everyday life in the confidence that its aesthetic character made any artistic procedure superfluous. *Le hasard objectif* ('objectified chance') is an aesthetic feature of reality. It is only because correspondences exist between past and present that we can bring the two together, both on the personal biographical level and on the communal plane of history. Only in this way can true experience, that is, the investment of otherwise inert and isolated fragments with meaning, be achieved. It is precisely at this stage that Benjamin brings the philogenetic and the ontogenetic to the point of conflation. For authentic experience is always the salvaging of something in danger of being forgotten or repressed: the ever-vanishing traces of the historically defeated who did not write history, or the engrams of the unconscious described by Freud in *Beyond the Pleasure Principle* and by Proust as the content of the *mémoire involontaire*; especially when the chances of finding the right mimetic object for reactivating those fading traces are so slight and fleeting.

But for Benjamin it is not only the difficulty of still finding the right corresponding objects. The modern individual has also undergone a process of psychological reconstruction whereby unconscious engrams are increasingly less encoded. In mass society, especially in the cities, the main psychological stimulus is shock, but in order to avoid trauma the consciousness is continually on guard to protect itself against such an unforeseen flooding by high rates of impulse. According to Freud the psychic energy of conscious events disappears without trace. *Mémoire involontaire* and *mémoire volontaire* – memory and consciousness – are mutually exclusive. Thus Benjamin argues: 'Experience is indeed a matter of tradition, in collective existence as well as in private life. It is less the product of facts firmly anchored in memory than of a convergence in memory of accumulated and frequently unconscious data.'[11] But the more people are exposed to shocks, the less material is laid down in the *mémoire involontaire* as the reservoir of authentic emotional and sensuous experience. People in capitalist mass society find it more and more difficult to make sense of their own lives as a result of the impoverishment of their store of mimetic material and emotional energy. The shattering of the matter of memory into disconnected episodes and events, out of which the individual desperately strives to distil real experience, is epitomized in Baudelaire's notion of 'spleen'. Spleen is the condition produced by the running wild of isolated happenings which can find no place in the context of a personal – or social – history which would render them meaningful.[12]

Experience, understood as the reactivation of memory through its fusion with the present, is thus endangered by two factors. Firstly there is the diminishing possibility of accumulating unconscious data, which through correspondent structures would conflate and deepen the existing engrams or traces of memory in the cortex, as John Eccles has argued:

> The engram postulate accords well with the experience of remembered imagery. By far the most vivid memories are evoked by some closely similar experience. Here the new, evolving spatio-temporal pattern must tend to correspond closely to the old, congealed pattern: the impulses of the new pattern flow into a channel of the old and trigger its replaying.[13]

The second factor is the total randomness of the principle by which one finds the object or situation which might trigger the old memory. For Benjamin this, too, is due to radically changed patterns of perception in modern society. Through the separation of private and public interest and the consequent atomized existence of the individual, public matter can no longer be assimilated so readily to the personal life. As Benjamin observes:

> According to Proust, it is a matter of chance whether an individual forms an image of himself, whether he can take hold of his experience. It is by no means

inevitable to be dependent on chance in this matter. Man's inner concerns do not have their inescapably private character by nature. They do so only when he is increasingly unable to assimilate the data of the world around him by way of experience.[14]

This is the reason for the disappearance of true story-telling, the oldest form of communication. In contrast with the modern mass media, in story-telling

> it is not the object of the story to convey a happening *per se*, which is the purpose of information; rather, it embeds it in the life of the story-teller in order to pass it on as experience to those listening. It thus bears the marks of the story-teller as much as the earthen vessel bears the marks of the potter's hand.[15]

What appears in the marks of the story-teller and the potter's hand is Benjamin's concept of the aura. The aura is that emanation surrounding something, in which the most subjective, that which can only be perceived through an identification triggered by the senses, converges with the factual. We really can speak of the *unio mystica*, the inextricable blending of 'the nearest and the most remote': 'Experience of the aura thus rests on the transposition of a response common in human relationships to the relationship between the inanimate or natural object and man ... To perceive the aura of an object we look at means to invest it with the ability to look at us in turn.'[16]

It is the aura of Combray, the village which is so poignantly recalled by Proust's narrator in *Du côté de chez Swann*, which appears in Proust's *mémoire involontaire*, in contrast to the merely factual Combray of the reflexive, discursive *mémoire volontaire*. From here we can see introspectively the connection between the outmoded and the aura. But beyond the utterly private acts of memory of the private gentleman Proust, the most authentic experience, the strongest aura is evoked in the coincidence of private and collective experience. The calendar, with its public feast-days, provides a concept of time whereby such coincidences are socially organized. But until such time as a new calendar might be conceptualized, capable of really preserving individual memory through the collective memory of a liberated society, it is necessary to sustain a memory of history instilled with the desire for liberation. The struggle to conserve that alternative memory of history can be compared to the difficulty of evoking the *mémoire involontaire*. The conscious, discursive memory of fact, void of sensuous re-enactment and tending to stifle any experience truly pregnant with subjectivity – that is, with unconscious, mimetic, imaginative material – functions in the same way as the official bourgeois writing of history. Furthermore, both the paradigm of historicism and the paradigm of progress are closed to the possibility of imparting meaning to the collective memory. For historicism there is no link between past and present. For progress neither past nor present really exists, because they are perceived highly selectively and always as transitional: time there is empty. But apart from that, in the official version of history the sheer facticity of things seems to acquire the self-evidence of the necessary and ineluctable. The once-existing possibility of alternative paths of collective action disappears.

But how can the repressed and the forgotten be restored? As regards the perceiving subject, new ways of seeing have to be activated. As regards the object, the refuse and detritus of history have to be examined for their alternative potential. Benjamin twice gives the same example of the kind of fresh historical vision that needs to be acquired and, significantly enough, they are spatial scenarios. It is not alien to the perceiving subject, but has been superseded by automatized, functional modes of perception. The non-automatized mode of vision existed in the past at the point of learning something. Once that process is finished, however, the attitude towards the object is almost fixed forever. Benjamin uses the image of the city in order to clarify these different ways of relating to history. In 'Städtebilder' he speaks about his experience of orientation in Moscow. At first the city was a phantasm created by the imagination around the names of streets, squares and buildings. This creation resists reality for a long time, unyielding. Then, in the clash between imagination and reality, the city becomes a labyrinth and the visitor falls victim to innumerable topographical traps. Now the city resists identification, it tries to mask itself, escapes and hatches plots. But finally the abstract schemes of maps will carry off the victory, and the vivid, sensuous encounter between man and city will be buried beneath a concept which is purely functional. And in *One-Way Street* Benjamin says:

> What makes the first glimpse of a village, a town, in the landscape so incomparable and irretrievable is the rigorous connection between foreground and distance. Habit has not yet done its work. As soon as we begin to find our bearings, the landscape vanishes at a stroke like the facade of a house as we enter it ... Once we begin to find our way about, that earlier picture can never be restored.[17]

In order to reacquire that estranged vision, the mimetic and imaginative faculties must be developed and expanded through practice. The use of intoxicating drugs like opium or marijuana and the state of dreaming are only extreme forms of such practice, which can be pursued likewise in ordinary everyday activities such as reading, thinking, being alone or the strolling of the *flâneur* in the city. All these activities imply the discharge of consciousness. This intensified state of imaginative perception will then be able to recognize in certain outmoded objects and constellations those 'dialectical images' which can release material for an alternative, counterfactual history. The moment of recognition when the object 'opens its eyes beneath the gaze of the historian' is Benjamin's *profane Erleuchtung* ('profane illumination'). These moments are rare; they occur suddenly and fleetingly, like flashes of lightning.

The objects which are able to provide 'dialectical images' for an alternative historical signification are, on the one hand, the relics of an objectively scattered totality; and on the other, the fragments which the historian blasts out of what appears to be a coherent totality of historical meaning. What Benjamin recognizes as the essence of modernist artistic production, the deconstruction of questionable totalities and the remounting of the fragments into artefacts, the meaning of which has no resemblance to their former function, is again fully applicable to the practice of the historian himself. The destruction of the organic artwork and its replacement by a form of art based on the montage principle is systematized in Benjamin's theory of allegory. The theory of allegory, the result of Benjamin's position as a modernist, but demonstrated fully in terms of the baroque drama, provides a general theory of the production of textual meaning.[18]

If we deconstruct Benjamin's concept of allegory we find the following determinants, which describe the main aspects of textual production and reception:

1 The allegorist breaks an element out of its normal context. By doing so he isolates it, deprives it of its original function and meaning. An allegory is therefore a fragment in contrast to the organic symbol. As Benjamin puts it: with allegory 'the false illusion of totality is extinguished'.
2 The allegorist reassembles his fragments and creates a new meaning. This sort of meaning is constructed and derives in no way from the original context of the fragment.
3 Benjamin interprets the allegoric procedure as an expression of melancholy. Under the eyes of the melancholic (the one who turns his back on life and social activity, thus interrupting the coherence of his own totality of existence) objects are stunned. They lose the capacity to communicate meaning.

The relation between allegory and melancholy leads to a further point:

4 Allegory represents history as decay. It exposes the image of a fragmented, paralysed history in the form of a frozen primal landscape.

The comparison of the organic and non-organic text on the level of production shows the convergence between allegory and what is known as montage. While the 'classicist' (which I use as shorthand for the organically or symbolically producing artist) respects the traditional meaning of his material and tries to create a new totality in accordance with it, the avant-gardist kills off his material by blasting it out of its context, and mounts the fragments anew, regardless of their tradition. The classicist tries to cover the fact that his product is constructed, and wants to create a second nature. The avant-gardist exposes the materiality and technicality of his work, thus stressing its character as an artefact.

In so far as the avant-gardist assembles his work out of fragments, destroying the category of totality, montage can be seen as the basic principle of all modernist texts. This has consequences for the mode of reception too. In the organic work every part received its ultimate meaning through its relation to the whole. In contrast, the non-organic work releases its parts into utter freedom from the whole. They can be read individually or in groups and they make perfect sense in themselves.

The montage principle as a mode of alternative historiography exactly reflects the decline of bourgeois history. Historicism and the theory of progress are both organic concepts of history. The different epochs, which 'are all equally near to God', as the historicist Ranke put it, are seen as mature, fully developed totalities closed off against each other. The notion of progress underlies the concept of evolution, which is likewise based on the image of an organic body still developing towards its final mature state. But after the First World War the function of these concepts is concentrated exclusively on the affirmative aspect of ideological constructs. Objectively the history of the bourgeoisie has fallen apart into isolated fragments. The once totalizing force of its signification as progressive, humane and ascendant over feudal society has turned openly into mechanisms of domination and exploitation at all costs. A whole mode of history has come to an end, and this is widely reflected in cultural production during the opening decades of the twentieth century.

History has been transformed into a space where all its fragments are stored in chaotic disorder. What finally lurks beneath the veneer of history as progress is history as continuous catastrophe. Hence Benjamin's famous angel of history:

> His face is turned towards the past. Where we perceive a chain of events, he sees one single catastrophe which keeps piling wreckage upon wreckage and hurls it in front of his feet. The angel would like to stay, awaken the dead, and make whole what had been smashed. But a storm is blowing from Paradise; it has got caught in his wings with such violence that the angel can no longer close them. This storm irresistibly propels him into the future to which his back is turned, while the pile of debris before him grows skyward. This storm is what we call progress.[19]

In the angel we see the allegorist, the melancholic who is paralysed in the face of the catastrophic destruction of the world and its meaning. But for the dialectical historian and those who are interested with him in the reconstruction of an alternative world, it is precisely the wreckage, the debris out of which the new foundations can be constructed.

For Benjamin the treasure-house of such historical debris was the city: Berlin, where he grew up, but especially Paris, where he lived for a long time and which was for him the capital of the nineteenth century. We can see now that the centrepiece of his theory of textual production, the allegoresis, is completely determined by the ever-accelerating wastage of commodities and their contextual structures, which could best be experienced in the metropolis. But it is also to be found in that marginal literature and art which was never appropriated by the official canon of high culture; and indeed it can be discerned in high culture itself once the deconstruction of bourgeois modes of interpretation has opened up the possibility of alternative ways of reading. It is contained likewise in objects salvaged from oblivion by the collector – Benjamin himself being an avid collector of books, especially children's books. If we recall that the German word for 'to read' is *lesen*, which is directly related to the Latin word *legere*, meaning 'to collect', we can see the close connection between textual reception/production and the collecting of vanishing items. Benjamin's ultimate aim is 'to read what has never been written' ('lesen, was niemals geschrieben wurde').

In this paradox we find the essence of his methodology. Firstly there is the conflation of the two meanings of *lesen*. When Benjamin says, 'History is a text of images', those images can be products of the imagination and they can be concrete objects, both not written in the strict sense of the word. And secondly, there is the endeavour to read in a way which destroys the text in question as a written document of its *own* time. To read a text from the past in the light of a present perspective dissolves our notion of 'the original', of the 'genetic'. At the same time the idea of correspondences, which makes possible the charging of the past with a *Jetztzeit* constructed by the concern to emancipate society from repression, prevents such historiography from total arbitrariness or relativism. The concept of correspondences is at once the link between different periods and the avoidance of another powerful holistic and organic conception of history in the service of bourgeois society: Nietzsche's theory of eternal recurrence. In his collection of aphorisms entitled 'Central Park' Benjamin states:

> For the idea of eternal recurrence the following fact has its significance: the bourgeoisie no longer dared face the approaching order of production which it had set in motion. Zarathustra's idea of an eternal recurrence and the motto

on pillow anti-macassars 'Nur ein Viertelstündchen' (Just a quarter hour) are complementary.[20]

NOTES

1 Walter Benjamin, *Das Passagen-Werk*, in *Gesammelte Schriften*, ed. Rolf Tiedemann and Hermann Schweppenhäuser (Suhrkamp, Frankfurt/M, 1972–89), vol. 5, ed. Rolf Tiedemann (1982), esp. pt 1, p. 575.
2 Ibid., p. 571.
3 Ibid., p. 580.
4 Ibid., pp. 576–7.
5 Ibid., p. 577.
6 See Walter Benjamin, Über den Begriff der Geschichte', in *Gesammelte Schriften*, vol. 1, ed. Rolf Tiedemann and Hermann Schweppenhäuser (1974), pt 2, pp. 693–4; tr. 'Theses on the philosophy of history', in Walter Benjamin, *Illuminations*, ed. Hannah Arendt (Collins/Fontana Books, London, 1973), pp. 255–66, esp. p. 256.
7 Walter Benjamin, 'Das Paris des Second Empire bei Baudelaire', in *Gesammelte Schriften*, vol. 1. 2, pp. 582–3 (author's translation).
8 Benjamin, *Das Passagen-Werk*, p. 493.
9 Frank Barron, 'The psychology of imagination', *Scientific American*, 9 (1958), pp. 150–60, esp. p. 135.
10 John Eccles, 'The physiology of imagination', *Scientific American*, 9 (1958), pp. 135–46, esp. p. 135.
11 Walter Benjamin, 'Über einige Motive bei Baudelaire', in *Gesammelte Schriften*, vol. 1. 2, p. 608 (author's translation).
12 Benjamin, drawing heavily on Bergson's theory of memory, emphasizes that Bergson never tried to analyse memory and experience as historically shaped phenomena. Benjamin himself seems to be very close to the theory of Maurice Halbwachs as developed in his study *Les cadres sociaux de la mémoire*, though his name is not mentioned in Benjamin's writings. Compare also the essay 'The Rhetoric of Forgetting: Brecht and the Historical Avant-garde', ch. 2 in this volume.
13 Eccles, 'The physiology of imagination', p. 141.
14 Benjamin, 'Über einige Motive bei Baudelaire', p. 610.
15 Ibid., p. 611.
16 Ibid., pp. 646–7.
17 Walter Benjamin, *Einbahnstrasse*, in *Gesammelte Schriften*, vol. 4, ed. Tillman Rexroth (1971), pt 1, p. 119; tr. *One-Way Street and Other Writings*, intro. Susan Sontag, tr. Edmund Jephcott and Kingsley Shorter (Verso, London, 1979), p. 78.
18 The relationship between the notions of modernism, montage and Benjamin's concept of allegory has been excellently analysed by Peter Bürger, *Theory of the Avant-Garde* (Manchester University Press, Manchester, 1984). See also the essays 'Abjection in the texts of Walter Benjamin' and 'Unreal presences: Allegory in Paul de Man and Walter Benjamin', chs. 6 and 12 in this volume.

19 Benjamin, Über den Begriff der Geschichte', pp. 697–8/'Theses on the philosophy of history', p. 259 (n. 6 above).

20 Walter Benjamin, 'Zentralpark', in *Gesammelte Schriften*, vol. 1. 2, p. 677; tr. Lloyd Spencer: 'Central Park', *New German Critique*, 34 (1985), pp. 32–58, esp. p. 46.

2

The Rhetoric of Forgetting: Brecht and the Historical Avant-garde (*with Helmut Lethen*)

In Roman law there was a punishment known as 'damnatio memoriae'.[1] Any representation of the condemned person was symbolically wiped out: from coins, inscriptions and memorial statues. The name, the individual physiognomy and the person were to be consigned to oblivion. Even in the age of psychoanalysis, which discovered deeper levels where that which had been wiped out remains etched in the mind, these procedures of forgetting are not yet a thing of the past. For a democratic public, retouching the past may seem rather dubious, yet access to the collective consciousness comes in for closer scrutiny than ever before. Given this situation, contemporary avant-garde art somewhat surprisingly makes use of the old techniques of 'damnatio memoriae'. Images are painted over, statues wrapped up, mythologies distorted in order to save them from the oblivion into which the collective memory has thrust them. These are some of the complications to be dealt with in considering the rhetoric of forgetting.

Under the influence of a new reading of Nietzsche the rhetoric of forgetting is once again a contemporary issue.[2] Forgetting is now positively reappraised as a productive activity, often under the banner of 'postmodernism'. In contrast to this trend, those theoreticians who regard the project of modernity as still incomplete retain their polemical insistence on the counterforce of remembering. Forty years after the fall of the Third Reich, Jürgen Habermas still finds the following to be true: 'The dominance of the past, which returns like a nightmare to hang over the unredeemed present, can only be smashed by the analytic power of a form of remembering which can look calmly at what has happened as history without seeing it as morally neutral.'[3] But does this quotation really contradict the reappraisal of forgetting? After all, it only states that remembering is necessary in order to break the compulsion to repeat the past blindly. For Habermas, it is memory which can annul the conventions of repression by analytic acuteness. The sentence does of course imply that forgetting is what allows the nightmare to dominate. At the same time Habermas sees himself compelled to distinguish his concept of analytic memory (which in this case he does not place within a psychoanalytical framework) from a kind of scientism of memory, which believes that it is only possible to achieve precise recall of the past by not taking a moral standpoint on it. But it is precisely this moral perspective which for Habermas is indispensable for the analytic acuteness of memory.

This last aspect of Habermas's argumentation should serve as a warning for us not to be too quick to prefer the obvious solution to the problem of remembering and forgetting. Because at first sight it would seem obvious to suspect that what appears to be a contradiction could easily be solved by clarifying our terminology. The commonplaces of the study of history would be all too tempting here:[4]

- that there can be no methodically disciplined memory without selective forgetting;
- that much must be forgotten if essential things are to be retained;
- that the sense of history is characterized by the fact that it can forget;
- finally, that the traditions of memory are only preserved if they are permanently subject to a process of forgetting which serves to rejuvenate them.

These arguments could lead to the assumption that, in the final analysis, there is a 'dialectic' between remembering and forgetting. Yet the concept 'dialectic' – if it is hastily employed to reconcile a contradiction, as in our case – obscures the problem more than it throws light upon it. Moreover the truths set out here are by no means necessarily universally valid. They are historically coloured by the thinking of the first third of the twentieth century. The theoreticians who based themselves upon them have absolved the school of Nietzsche and now wish to reconcile the school of historicism with an aggressive theory of forgetting. The representatives of this theory had for a while – in a quite undialectical way – praised the destructiveness of forgetting: 'History's fountain of youth is fuelled by Lethe. Nothing renews as effectively as oblivion.'[5] Walter Benjamin's phrase, combining elements of Nietzsche with elements of Proust, clearly shows the opposition to historicism. Historicism itself was a product of the nineteenth century, yet even at the beginning of the twentieth century it forced that whole generation of the avant-garde who experienced the full force of historicism as a nightmare into unreserved appreciation of forgetting.

Modernists versus Avant-gardists

The criterion of forgetting

Let the dead poets make room for the living ... the time for masterpieces is past.

Antonin Artaud

'The dialectical relationship between avant-garde and post-modernism', says Umberto Eco in 1985, 'is similar to that which exists between forgetting and remembering. At certain moments in history a polemical break with the past is necessary. At other times we need to pause for breath.'[6] We are in agreement with this statement in so far as it attaches the keywords 'break' and 'forgetting' to the historical avant-garde of the period 1910–40. We shall call into question their relationship to 'postmodernism.' For the members of the avant-garde, for their part, stood in opposition to contemporary modernists – Proust, Rilke, Mann, Gide, Musil, Joyce, Svevo – by virtue of their rhetoric of forgetting.[7] The work of the modernists was devoted to memory. It was in the medium of memory that the dilemma of individual identity was to be explored in their great novels. The avant-gardists, on the other hand, devoted themselves in their own polemical way to the exact opposite. They were not willing to tackle a task which, as far as they could see, would be never-ending: that of reconstructing the subject within the process of remembering. Their attack aimed to obliterate the unity of the subject, something which in their view – contrary to all appearances – was still the organizing force behind the pluralizing of the individual to be found in the work of the modernists. This opposition seemed irreconcilable for both factions of the modern movement. Forgetting, as propagated by the avant-garde, was supposed to break the feedback effect of memory on identity, an effect which idealistic philosophy had made appear inevitable.[8] This link between memory and identity was reinforced by historicism and left untouched by psychoanalysis. Moreover, forgetting allowed political action to be justified on a voluntaristic basis.

A movement which was so determined to abandon the 'institution of art',[9] in order to become involved in day-to-day political decision-making, had to insist on forgetting, as forgetting is, according to Nietzsche, the prerequisite for vital action. In the work of the modernists they found only thoughts on the dilemma of action itself. The portrayal of the decline of the individual and the attempt to regain identity within the process of memory were difficult to reconcile with the decision to act. For the modernists a decision of this kind would have required some kind of authority which might have given patterns of feeling and acting general validity even in a post-bourgeois time.

   In this historical situation where the avant-garde saw no further place for the bourgeois individual, by appealing to forgetting they sought to replace it with an archaic, pre- or extra-bourgeois 'typus'. The background for these conceptions of forgetting was formed by the idea that it was necessary and possible to bring about a great break in history and cultural convention. It was precisely this background idea which aroused scepticism among the modernists. At the beginning of the twenties, Robert Musil regarded ideas of a sudden radical change in mental conventions in the wake of political breaks as 'mythologizations'.[10] In his opinion such thinking underpinned historical events with a kind of catastrophe theory which would not be in keeping with the evolutionary speed with which morals and mentalities were developing. Ironically, modernists like Thomas Mann and Robert Musil suspected that their younger adversaries, the avant-garde, represented the last bastion of the concept of a self-defined subject created in a voluntaristic act. (Georg Lukács was to confirm this suspicion.) It could therefore turn out to be the case that in contrast to the claims made in modernist programmes, modernist writing forgets the unity of the subject in a more decisive way than that of the avant-garde. For the modernists themselves did not believe unquestioningly in the feedback effect between memory and identity. Rather they sought to portray to what extent man does not hold sovereign sway over his memories; to show that the effort of remembering must destroy the conventions of the memory which form the habitual framework of identity in order to ensure experience of a 'self'; that this 'self' is not found to be intact as a unit but only split or pluralized into many fleeting images; and that even these fleeting images are still threatened by the 'sea of forgetting', from which they are saved only by objective chance.

Samuel Beckett: a tableau of forgetting

In 1932 Beckett's essay on Proust was published.[11] It came at a time when the energies of the European avant-garde were largely spent and the various groupings within the movement had broken up. At that moment Beckett had recourse to Marcel Proust's labyrinth of memory. From reading *A la Recherche du temps perdu* he would come in his later work to portray the waste landscapes of forgetting.[12] Within these landscapes he places various kinds of small vessels and cavities, the last *vases clos* of remembrance. Shut inside them are beings who try in vain to see over the rim of the vessels. From the fragments of memory which they bring to light or play to themselves on tape we may conclude that they could once have been subjective individuals.

   At first sight, these landscapes of forgetting seem more like parodies of Proust's spheres of remembrance. In the spheres which Beckett depicts,

Proust's attempt to establish some kind of identity within the medium of remembrance is carried through virtually to the point of nothingness.

In his essay on Proust, Beckett drew attention to the extent to which the avant-garde concept of forgetting may be seen to be a continuation of Proust's work. It would nevertheless be true to say that the formulations used by Beckett in describing Proust's explicit theory of remembering clearly show the subsequent influence of the functionalist school of the twenties and American pragmatism.

Beckett emphasizes that for Proust memories form a kind of programming code for the machinery of perception. Memory works as part of a kind of 'synthesizing team' which is set up on labour-saving principles by habit.[13] Habit is the practical form in which the memory functions. For habit consists of a system of automatic correlations between remembering and justifying which a 'self' constructs around itself to relieve and stabilize itself. The memory only conveys the schematic ideas which are imposed upon the person by her/his habitual patterns of action. If past reality is to be grasped 'vividly' this automatic memory mechanism must be made to break down. The unforeseeable risk involved in destroying it comes from the fact that the 'old self', this 'agent of security and dullness', is in danger of giving up its role as coordinator of habits. Such an experiment, therefore, could only really be carried out in the realm of the imagination. However, the automatic feedback effect of memory–perception–identity–memory can at times be broken by chance memories.

This mixture of Proust, Bergson, and twentieth-century functionalism may sound rather vague. It has nevertheless been pointed out in research work, and rightly so, just how close these arguments come to scientific discourse on the nature of memory, particularly in the theories which Maurice Halbwachs, a pupil of Bergson and Durkheim, published in his book *Les cadres sociaux de la mémoire* in 1925.[14] We shall return to these later, but first we would like to deal with the question of whether Beckett was right to cite Proust when emphasizing the need to destroy the automatic memory mechanism.

Marcel Proust: forgetting and its power to preserve

In fact, in the wake of Bergson, Proust had emphasized the functional aspect of the everyday workings of memory. The memory eliminates, i.e. forgets anything which is not of use to everyday habit. The rules of the memory are therefore governed by pragmatic conventions. Habit is thus at once the guarantor of the memory and the cause of forgetting. Those who have grown accustomed to seeing Proust's *Recherche* as an opera of remembrance may be surprised to see the emphasis which Proust gives to the factor of forgetting; for forgetting he employs the classical metaphor of the sea.

Proust emphasizes again and again that 'what we call remembering a person consists really in forgetting him'.[15] Things must be seen as 'emerging from the dust of memory', washed clean by the waters of forgetting to present themselves in a 'vivid' form.[16] Proust develops an anti-psychological concept of memory which thus differs both from Bergson's conceptions and that of psychoanalysis.

> If it is true that the sea was once upon a time our native element, in which we must plunge our blood to recover our strength, it is the same with the oblivion, the mental nothingness of sleep; we seem then to absent ourselves for a few hours from time, but the forces which have gathered in that interval without being expended measure it by their quantity as accurately as the pendulum of the clock or the crumbling hillocks of the hourglass.[17]

Metaphors from physics are used to explain his anti-psychological concept of forgetting. Safe from the usages of daily habit, that which is forgotten accumulates energy which cannot flow away in remembering. It is still possible to detect some traces of a correspondence to psychoanalysis in these metaphors. But by looking at where Proust deposits forgotten matter we can see the differences. Forgotten things are not preserved in some strange space in the psyche but in the material world outside. In Proust, memories of manifestations in time are transformed into separately preserved reserves which are spatially distributed. They remain – as if shut in jars – in various places distributed through the years of our lives. 'That is why the better part of our memories exists outside us, in a blatter of rain, in the smell of an unaired room or of the first crackling brushwood fire in a cold grate.'[18] Yet these three images point to a paradox: it is the most fleeting, transitory and precisely non-materially fixed perceptions which remain 'preserved' outside the psyche. (The same idea is found later in the most diverse avant-garde documents, ranging from Brecht's early lyrics to Walter Benjamin's 'Theses on the Philosophy of History'.) For Proust these perceptions of transitory sensations remain committed to the realm of the forgotten, since at the time of the sensation they had no elemental function, i.e. for him they remain 'in reserve'. Forgetting seals them off and keeps them fresh.

Above all, forgetting serves as a protection against the vast indifference of the conventions of memory. The more inaccessibly these vessels containing memories are stored under the protection of forgetting, the greater the effect of defamiliarization on the person who remembers episodes in her own past life, and the less that person presumes to hold sway over her memories, the more rewarding is the impression which re-encountering these preserves can provoke.[19] This is the basis of Proust's critique of Bergson. Nowhere in Proust do we find recall in the medium of the *mémoire pure*. Proust's *mémoire involontaire* is *not* subject to a freely made decision, as Benjamin's commentaries on Proust have pointed out again and again.[20] No free act of will can bring about recall. In Proust, things past are outside the jurisdiction of the 'self'. It is pure chance if we encounter them. Paradoxically, the avant-gardists redefine this jurisdiction: for them, the act of forgetting becomes the point of sovereign decision. The connection between Proust's reflections on the relationship between forgetting and remembering and his observations on innovation in art is rather revealing from our point of view. Proust stood in conscious opposition to the dictates of innovation imposed by the avant-garde. In view of the contemporary trends – the pentatonic system, Cubism and Futurism – he could see little hope of the sudden break which purported to wipe out all trace of convention at one fell swoop. For him, art tends rather to develop by lengthy processes of assimilation in the course of which the earlier conventions are incorporated into the new circumstances, creating new forms of perception. During this process of change those clichés of perception which only serve to preserve stable habits are eliminated. They are replaced by new figurative systems which have not yet taken on the function of regulating action.

If we apply Proust's concept of remembering and forgetting to the problem of convention and innovation, the result is as follows: breaking through the convention of memory involuntarily by means of the *mémoire involontaire* does not lead to the creation of something entirely new but rather allows us to re-experience things forgotten. *Likewise in art, it is not a sudden, conscious and forceful renewal which leads to a new truth, but only repetition.*[21] The converse would of course be equally true: only the repetition of things forgotten effects a lasting break with convention but it does not bring about something entirely new. However, that which is repeated must first pass through the forgetting stage, as Proust said, in order to gain energy.

By emphatically accepting the category of repetition, Proust was unmistakably in opposition to claims for a radical break in the programmes of the avant-garde. Had he, like that other modernist Robert Musil, recognized a mythologizing element inherent in this talk of a 'break'? At least Proust's construct did not rest on innovation alone. By exploring the dialectic of remembering and forgetting he switched into that powerful cycle formed by the feedback effect[22] of habit–memory–identity–memory in order to explode it from within.

Maurice Halbwachs: Les cadres sociaux de la mémoire

When Maurice Halbwachs published his attack on Bergson's theory of memory, Proust's work was already complete. Bergson had based himself on the theory that the whole of past experience remained present in the subterranean caverns of the memory. Like the pages of a book which can be turned up, complete systems of signs from the past are stored up. By managing to recall the stored images the individual becomes aware of her identity. This is the starting-point of Halbwachs's critique: he suspects that Bergson obviously needed to introduce the idea of a complete image kept in storage *because* he wanted to regain a concept of *personal identity*.[23] But as the image of personal identity could not be found in the physical or social sphere, it had to be concealed in the repository of the psyche. From the point of view of the sociology of the memory Bergson's theory of memory seemed like a final vain attempt to safeguard the unity of the subject despite experience to the contrary.

In his theory of memory Halbwachs rehabilitates the category of space from which Bergson had tried to detach the *mémoire pure*. The individual capacity to remember is dependent on the social background upon which it draws and the extent to which it participates in the collective memory. Nestling in the conventions of patterns of action, habitual rituals and physical shells, a person remembers. In this process local *tradition* and, above all, *verbal convention* form the most elementary and at the same time most durable framework for the collective memory. Up till now we have found nothing to contradict Bergson's critical view of the workings of the memory, which are firmly entrenched in the pragmatics of everyday life. But Halbwachs shows that people are unable to escape from this social shell. Even memories of childhood remain 'within the network of domestic thinking'. The *illusion* of freedom of memory comes about at those points when a person finds herself at the intersection of different currents in collective thinking.

It is only a high degree of complexity in an individual's relationship to the social frame which brings about the illusion of autonomous procedures of remembering. By constructing *mémoire pure*, purely personal memory, Bergson succumbs to this illusion, according to Halbwachs. For the so-called individual memory is only the 'recording apparatus' which is set in motion by collective factors.[24] External stimuli (the 'buildings in the town', re-encountering members of an earlier group) are necessary in order to reconstruct memory images from vague and fragmentary particles in a process of combining. According to Halbwachs there is no one place, be it physiological or mental, where complete memory-images could be stored. And thus the last refuge of personal identity also disappears.

Halbwachs does not develop a dramatic concept of remembrance, and consequently his theory does not provide an emphatic concept of forgetting. Mary Douglas has pointed out that, through studying Leibniz's writings, Halbwachs adopted the principle that 'between clear and obscure, there are little transitions'.[25] For Halbwachs, the transitions between remembering and forgetting are equally smooth. Since remembering involves the task of reconstruction, that which cannot be reconstructed remains forgotten because the social framework offers no stimuli. If forgetting is ever experienced as a painful process then it is when this framework is taken away from a person (by separation from the group, leaving the country, being placed in a foreign-language environment or by the death of a close friend or relative).[26]

Shifting the problem as Halbwachs does has far-reaching consequences. Since for him the subjective individual is a point of interference in the social network, in his theory the opposition between individual and society as set out in the philosophy of life breaks down. At first sight, this theory appears to be one-dimensional compared with Bergson's. But it achieves a considerably higher degree of complexity on the very point where Bergson's theory puts up a mere backdrop: in the postulation of a collective framework. For Halbwachs, the collective memory ceases to be the completely transparent, straightforward and therefore hostile construct against which only the 'individual' can revolt in order to create 'pure' life. Instead, the social spheres themselves are full of contradictions, and traces of social resistance are also to be found in the collective memory, which are still waiting to be reconstructed into complete images by historians. Halbwachs's statistical surveys on the conditions of the working class in the nineteenth century are evidence of his positivist commitment to find these traces without claiming to be able to extract an overall picture by spontaneous or intuitive means.

This look back at the theories of Bergson, Proust and Halbwachs may now serve as a counterfoil to the rhetoric of forgetting to be found in the work of the avant-garde. A comparison shows the relative simplicity of the latter. The rhetoric of the avant-garde does not get caught up in a dialectic of remembering and forgetting. Compared to its complex interweaving in Proust, we find a dramatic reduction of complexity in the first manifestos of the avant-garde: 'Everything in art is convention, and yesterday's truths are the lies of today' was one line in a speech by the Italian Futurist Marinetti in 1910.[27] The avant-garde made an obvious attempt to undercut the complexities normally associated with the term 'dialectic'. In so doing they appear to modify Nietzsche's phrase: in order to act it is necessary to forget complexity. Their attack was directed first and foremost against the storerooms of the collective memory: museums, libraries and academies. 'Set light to the libraries! Direct the canals to flood the museums!'

Museum landscape and areas of total mobilization

Glücklich ist, wer vergisst,/was nicht mehr zu ändern ist.
                                        Johann Strauss, *Die Fledermaus*

In 1871 Carl Jakob Burckhardt and Friedrich Nietzsche encountered each other in Basle. The scene is well known: the two men had been desperately seeking one another after receiving news of the fire in the Louvre during the Paris Commune. (The gallery was not damaged, while the Commune was destroyed.) It was the fear that one of the great storehouses of cultural memory might have been encroached upon which motivated the two scholars. It is worth reminding ourselves of this scene, because just four decades later the avant-gardists were advocating burning down the museums as part of a revolution in art – inspired by Nietzsche's critique of the paralysing historicism of his time and his positive reappraisal of forgetting.

By 1910 the proponents of historicism were no longer theoretical authorities like Leopold von Ranke or Droysen, to whom Nietzsche stood in opposition. Cultural spheres had been permeated by a kind of trivial historicism. We shall briefly mention four aspects of this historicism from the viewpoint of the opposition:

- fleeing from the present historicism overcomes the crisis of the subject by dressing itself up in borrowed historical identities;
- contrary to the experience that the process of history takes place behind the backs of the individual, historicism suggests that 'history' as an overall process can be controlled; that in all expressions of it a central point can be deduced;
- of most interest to historicism in cultural expression is the citation of tradition as the productive core. For historicism, innovations form only the topmost layer of a palimpsest. True 'depth' can only be achieved if the more traditional layers below are brought to light;
- this means for the work of art that historicism cuts off the expressive dimension. The analysis of the expressive is replaced by the reconstruction of genesis.

While Nietzsche could still find a kind of radicalized enlightenment in historicism, the generations which followed him merely saw it as inappropriate for capturing contemporary experience and as an obstacle to intervening action. For historicism not only validated the judgement uttered by Marx in *The Eighteenth Brumaire of Louis Bonaparte*, but even seemed to be the realization of Marx's warning: 'The tradition of the dead generations weighs like a nightmare on the minds of the living.' It is no coincidence, then, that the rhetoric of forgetting was to develop in the same period which saw the 'crisis of historicism'. The appeals to forget were given their first emphatic formulation in the manifestoes of Italian Futurism. The objects under attack were described principally in spatial categories: a landscape characterized by the cult to the monuments of a dead memory. Intellectuals were seen as slaves of antiquated rites, museums as cemeteries, libraries as burial chambers, a town like Venice as a hospital. This landscape paralysed the avant-garde's readiness to act. To act we must first forget. The first action of the avant-garde was a symbolic act: 'We must forget external reality and our knowledge of it in order to create new dimensions.' It is a slogan which follows on immediately from Bergson. 'The new dimension' which is to be achieved by symbolic acts of destruction is turned inward. For a person stepping out of the museum-like façades of historicism, real reality is dynamic: 'Everything moves, everything flows, everything takes place at high speed. A figure never remains motionless before us but is constantly appearing and disappearing.'[28]

However, the imagery used by the Futurists shows that this positive reappraisal of the transitory aspect is in no way due to Nietzsche. In contrast to Nietzsche, they declare their approval for the rapid process of modernization. As the custodians of culture traditionally distance themselves in exclusive spheres as a protest against modernization, the avant-garde were moving away from the conventional attitudes of artists by expressing their approval of progress. Here lies the element of opposition and at the same time affirmation in the Futurists' revolt. They allied themselves to progress, that powerful machinery of forgetting. Architects expressed it as follows in their Futurist manifesto in 1914:

> We have lost the sense of the monumental, the monolithic, the static, and we have enriched our sensibilities with a taste of the light, practical, short-lived and rapid. We feel we are no longer the people of cathedrals, palaces and convention halls but instead the people of large hotels, stations, broad streets, huge arches, covered markets, illuminated tunnels, straight motorways, salutary urban renovation.[29]

While the Futurists extolled the sphere of their future as a sphere of total mobilization, it was generally filled with events which happen anyway: from urban modernization to war. All technical achievements mentioned in the quotation were not new. They had already been brought about under the aegis of historicism. Historicism was merely the compensatory complex which served to conceal the destruction of civilization and to compensate for the damage done with non-material values. The productive element in the rhetoric of forgetting lies in stripping away this compensatory veil which had been placed over the normal processes of destruction as a kind of ideological reconciliation. But the Futurists were wrong to assume that historicism really restricted the development of productive powers. They were taken in by a façade. Behind this façade society was plunging forth into modernization. Some of the great department stores of the German *Gründerzeit* may be regarded as symptomatic of this state of affairs: seen from the outside, the dressings of the past; inside, largely functionalist.

Almost two decades later, when the energies of the avant-garde seemed to be exhausted, there appeared in 1932 one last avant-garde polemic against the 'museum-landscape', Ernst Jünger's broadsheet 'The Worker: Dominance and Form'.[30] It is a monstrous work, which had the misfortune to be adopted precisely within the sphere for which it was written: in the political force field at the end of the Weimar Republic. Thus the book had the dubious good fortune – to be envied by many of the avant-garde – of being read outside the institution of art. But in the field of politics where it ended up readers extracted only what was in accordance with the political tendencies of the time. It was then no longer perceived as the avant-garde manifesto which it undoubtedly was.

For Ernst Jünger, the museum-landscape of bourgeois society had assumed grotesque proportions twenty years after the Futurist manifestos. A 'historical fetishism' restricted mobility with its leaden weight as it had always done. Historicism was still in the dock. In Jünger's view, it weakened the power of production, alienated man from the elemental level of life, and acted merely as a kind of anaesthetic concealing the decline of the individual. Of course, individualism was only being defended by a small band of people anyway. The 'museum business' was no more than an anachronistic oasis of bourgeois security. Its function was limited to offering a plausible refuge from political decision-making to the last self-appointed individuals. But this could not last. Jünger observed that the process of storing up and conserving cultural assets went hand in hand with the development of 'magnificent means of destruction'. The discrepancy was considerable. 'There is no way out, no way to the side, no way back; it is much more important to increase the growth and the speed of the process we are caught up in.'[31]

The direction of the process is at first a negative one: it is the 'dying-process' of bourgeois culture. Against this background, forgetting bourgeois cultural values can be seen as 'throwing off baggage' on the march into the future, as Jünger put it using military jargon. This 'throwing off' allows us to enter the sphere of 'total mobilization'. The two strategies of forgetting outlined here go nowhere near far enough in showing up the complexity which may be involved in looking at other writers. But first we would like to bring in a theory to which the avant-gardists liked to refer and which, in the course of our investigation so far, has only been mentioned briefly without systematic explanation. A look back at Nietzsche's theory of forgetting may help to clear up some of the contradictions encountered so far.

Friedrich Nietzsche: the paradoxical nature of forgetting

But history's fountain of youth is fuelled by Lethe. Nothing renews as effectively as oblivion.

Walter Benjamin

The positive reappraisal of forgetting in the avant-garde is combined with a positive reappraisal of the transitory element, a celebration of dynamism and glorification of the new. The aim is for an immediacy which is able to disrupt the conception of history as a process of decline. The principles of this 'presentism' were formulated by Nietzsche, and in Nietzsche's work this longing for a continuous present came to be expressed in his emphatic theory of forgetting.

Were the avant-garde directly influenced by Nietzsche's writings when they emphasized the 'benefits of active forgetfulness'? Paul de Man gives a central place to the motif of forgetting in modern literature in his study of the rhetoric of contemporary criticism, *Blindness and Insight*. In his opinion, this question is asked in the wrong way. For him, it is not a question of adopting Nietzsche's texts. For him, the various voices advocating forgetting are rather an indication of the 'authentic spirit of modernity' in general. His argument is weakened by a significant omission, a frequent occurrence in the present debates. To avoid contradictions, he does not take account of the second major branch of the modern movement, i.e. the modernists. For de Man, Nietzsche's essay *Of the Use and Misuse of History for Life* constitutes the *founding* document of the modern movement. At the same time he analyses it as a *symptom* of modernity. In his commentary on the founding document he reconstructs Nietzsche's form of argumentation; in analysing the symptom he shows up the paradoxical nature of modernity. For Paul de Man the rhetoric of forgetting is part of the core of modernity:

> Modernity exists in the form of a desire to wipe out whatever came earlier, in the hope of reaching at last a point that could be called a true present, a point of origin that marks a new departure. This combined interplay of deliberate forgetting with an action that is also a new origin reaches the full power of the idea of modernity.[32]

In Nietzsche's writings, de Man finds the origin and justification of the obsession with the idea of a *tabula rasa* which we come across in the first third of this century in both the writers of the avant-garde and in the work of avant-garde architects and town-planners. In so doing de Man picks out a motif which has not yet been considered in the context of literature. There was one idea formulated by Nietzsche which played a part in all the theories of forgetting formulated in this period. 'Forgetting is a part of all action!' De Man applies this proposition to the way writers write. In the cause of forgetting this symbolic action should be justified as a free act. 'Literature has a constitutive affinity with action, with the unmediated, free act that knows no past.'[33] An avant-garde writer sees his work more than ever before in the history of literature as 'the product of his own action'.[34] The power to carry out this action is undoubtedly dependent on losing the memory. For the memory might remember that the slate already had writing on it before the authors took up their chalk. It is odd that at a historical moment when other turn-of-the-century writers were first noting down their feeling of being mere appendages of an anonymous linguistic process, the idea of a *tabula rasa* should come about upon which it was possible to leave an original mark.

Paul de Man also draws attention to the fact that Nietzsche's justification of forgetting never neglects the opposing face of historicism. For a justification of forgetting is automatically linked to that which it negates: historicism. De Man points to a paradox as a constitutive part of Nietzsche's presentism.

Let us now consult Nietzsche's work itself. It covers a large number of arguments with which we are already familiar. But there is also a warning against drawing false conclusions: fleeing the school of convention to embrace spontaneity is by no means an innovation as far as Nietzsche is concerned.[35] Instead we now insist in semi-forgetfulness on what we formerly copied consciously. When a person gives himself over to spontaneity by virtue of forgetting, he usually proceeds through the medium of convention. In this case Nietzsche is decidedly in favour of a conscious appropriation of convention rather than a blind plunge into the sphere of action. We shall see, however, that this scepticism with regard to spontaneity is not maintained in the closing passages of the work. In his appeal to 'youth' he largely forgets his own warning.

Anyone who remembers Nietzsche's essay as a justification of forgetting will be surprised to discover that there are many sentences which emphatically extol the virtues of memory. Nietzsche looks at the various views of history put forward by his contemporaries from the point of view of action, of how far they convey the power to break free from the fetters of the past. In those cases where remembering is only possible if no action is taken in the present time, he is dismissive. In all three types of history – antiquarian, monumental and critical – he pinpoints both crippling and productive elements. He advocates a discipline of history which records not established facts but which discovers a transitory element within the fact, or which uses the fact to argue for radical change. His plea for forgetting is a conscious act of opposition to history as the history of established facts. At this point we find a first inconsistency. His idea of forgetting is based on a static image of the unconscious present of animal existence. At a second glance, it is based on the reconstruction of an equally static historical precedent: the absolute presence of the Greeks in their 'non-historical sphere', in which freedom to act in the present time is not hindered by any attachment to the past. We can see how quickly Nietzsche's text leads to paradox if it is read as a series of instructions. This is usually the case with appeals like 'be spontaneous!', 'be forgetful, remember the Greeks!' Since such paradoxes are known to have the effect of hindering action rather than promoting it, those who have adopted Nietzsche's view have had to forget the paradoxical structure of his argumentation in order to find a concept of action within it.

Moreover, Nietzsche does not use the term 'forgetting' in a clearly positive sense by any means. On the contrary. In *monumental* historiography Nietzsche criticizes the fact that it forgets large sections of the historical context (typically enough the overall social context of the monumental effects). According to Nietzsche, this gives rise to a fatal idealization of the real course of history. When dealing with the *critical* view of history, Nietzsche points out that if destruction is not to be random but aimed at a specific target, then it is necessary to remember. Nietzsche describes critical remembering as a 'cruel' process sparing no convention, because only in this way can remembering emphasize 'the injustice of the existence of a thing' and explain historically, by virtue of remembering, why this thing deserves to perish (a viewpoint closer to the heart of the socialist historians of his time).

But it is not only remembering which, sitting in judgement over history in the name of justice, is obliged to destroy the conventions of the memory. Even the forensic work of *antiquarian* history can serve the dynamics of modern life. By bringing to light the traces of past struggles through archaeology, it can serve as an encouragement to go against the blind power of facts. Reading the essay *Of the Use and Misuse of History for Life* tends to leave the reader faced with contradiction when she reads that 'the same life which requires forgetfulness requires the temporary destruction of this forgetfulness.'[36] What matters for Nietzsche is clearly the right time, the right amount and the correct application of forgetting. But since Nietzsche's concept of 'life' goes substantially beyond the realm of the possibility of knowledge, no single rational criterion is offered against which the amount, function or time can be measured. It is not surprising therefore, that under the shelter of this concept of life, all the refinements which Nietzsche put forward had to be forgotten. Nietzsche's arguments are – at least in this work – more complex than the avant-garde rhetoric of forgetting would lead us to suspect. If Nietzsche's concept was to be acted upon, its complexity would have to be undercut. The opponents of the avant-garde, modernists such as Thomas Mann, Robert Musil or André Gide went much further in plumbing the depths of this complexity; after all, it was not the will to act which governed their reading of it. The avant-garde did not merely accept the reduction of complexity which was scorned by the modernists in order to remain able to act. They consciously applied this reduction in their idea of the *tabula rasa* in order to provoke those who were sophisticated to the point of being unable to act and who yet longed for a vital decision. While the modernists played out the paradoxes into ever more varied constellations in an attempt to establish the possibilities of useful behaviour which defy even the most extreme pressure to make a decision in the political sphere, the avant-garde attempted to move directly into the field of political decision-making. As has been pointed out before, the decisive difference lay in the fact that the avant-garde were convinced that a radical break (in history and literary convention) was possible, while writers such as Proust, Thomas Mann, Musil and Joyce regarded this idea as a myth – a myth which was certainly powerful enough to provide the impulse for revolutionary action, but which was unsuitable as a means of setting in motion and maintaining the dynamism which had already partly been achieved in all areas of life.

In his closing passage Nietzsche had appealed to 'youth'. He had prescribed forgetting as the prerequisite for vital action. As far as the time for this was concerned, Nietzsche was in no doubt: it had come *now* (and even four decades later, Nietzsche's readers were the last who would have qualified his writing by historicizing it). Yet even at the right time, he was still unclear on the right amount of forgetfulness. He was aware that it is a 'poison'.[37]

Drug-induced forgetting

By setting up a close interrelation between the theme of forgetting and the categories of decision-making and action, we are in danger of suppressing another viewpoint with a venerable tradition. In addition to the active variety of forgetting, there is a more tranquil variety which can also be traced back to Nietzsche (and far beyond). As in the active version, drug-induced forgetting also serves to rupture history, a history conceived as one of decline. Yet, instead of anticipating a future to be built by action, the more tranquil variety turns back. This type of forgetting is constantly governed by the myth of origin. We go back to the childhood of life. It is only by forgetting the conventions of civilization which govern our daily lives that we can remember more archaic grounds of existence. These are presented as 'original'. This tranquil variety of forgetting was articulated in the work of Gottfried Benn – a far cry from the forgetting which is bound up with action. However, the case of Gottfried Benn demonstrates that in times of extreme political decisions, as in 1933, this tranquil regressive manoeuvre was carried blindly along with the action of others. Benn puts the decadence of history down to the overdevelopment of the brain on the physiological level, leading to the instincts being blunted. Thus for him forgetting serves to 'remove the brain'. The process of forgetting is to allow us to remember more original vegetative forms. The metaphors of forgetting are the sea, the poppy, the blue. The poppy is the flower of forgetting (opium). The stages of immersion experienced by Benn's hero Rönne in

Gehirne (the so-called *Rönne-Prosa*) are short-lived. They are self-induced productions which can come down to earth at any moment. They do not go beyond the framework of positivist science upon which Benn retained such a negative fixation, much as the avant-garde had done with historicism. In many poems immersion in forgetting is consciously celebrated as an artistic act and the 'archaic' origins appear, ironically enough, in the colours of the historical decadence of the late nineteenth century. Sometimes there are hints of comedy and sarcasm in the awareness of how unmistakably modern, even fashionable, this plunge into the sea of forgetting really is. Sometimes the heroic tone is dominant – without the optimism with regard to progress demonstrated by the Futurists. Sometimes Benn's texts are embedded in the political movement of Fascism which promised to forget humanist values once and for all.

Brecht's Rhetoric of Forgetting

Carnivalesque forgetting

Innocence is a child and forgetting a new beginning, a game.
Nietzsche, *Also sprach Zarathustra*

If it is correct to say that the 'authentic spirit of modernity' finds its expression in the positive reappraisal of forgetting, as Paul de Man suspects[38], it is surprising how little this view has been applied to a writer in whose work the theme of forgetting is ever-present. Bertolt Brecht crystallized Rimbaud's praise for the completely new in verses in which he transfers Rimbaud's already venerated watchword into the jargon of the New Sobriety:

This superficial rabble, crazy for novelties
Which never wears its bootsoles out
Never reads its books to the end
Keeps forgetting its thoughts
This is the world's
Natural hope.
And even if it isn't
Everything new
Is better than everything old.[39]

Since Brecht's emphasis on the productive power of forgetting was seen as scandalous already by his Marxist contemporaries, little research has been done into it to date.[40] If it was considered at all, it was either as a symptom of the nihilism in his early work or as teething troubles in his pre-Marxist phase. For most critics this was one and the same thing anyway. For this reason there has been no explanation of why Brecht connected a 'weak memory' of all things with the possibility of revolution. Nor has there been any explanation of why the concept of forgetting put forward by the young Brecht came to be a favourable disposition to his own particular interpretation of Marxism.

The scenery of Brecht's early lyrical works is largely constructed around the motif of forgetting; destructible towns, circulating currents, decaying bodies – beneath a sky from which have been banished all the mythological agencies which once had their place there. In this lyrical work forgetting is an element of the carnivalesque:[41] forgetting brings about detachment not only from the family context but also from social distinctions in general. Even the strict division between private and public life, a constitutive element of modern-day morality, is dissolved in the realm of the carnivalesque.

By schematically isolating these motifs, we can now distinguish six different aspects of this carnivalesque forgetting:[42]

1. The first thing to be forgotten is *moral control* by external and internal agencies. Brecht treats these moral persecutors as if they were bugging devices, psychological or religious 'ticks' which even control dreams ('Report on a Tick'[43]). In carnivalesque forgetting he seeks to create areas without 'ticks', areas where there is no fear. Thus he says in 'The Great Hymn of Thanksgiving':

Worship with fullness of heart the weak memory of heaven!
It cannot trace
Either your name or your face
Nobody knows you're still living.[44]

It is not only the burden of the dead memory of the commandments which is consigned to oblivion. The internal regulators of the conscious are also to be neutralized at the same time.

2. An adjunct to this is the other aspect of forgetting. Forgetting is inseparably tied to the motif of *carpe diem*.

Don't be led astray!
There will be no return
Through the doors will vanish the day
Nightwind is on its way.
Morning will not come.[45]

3. The amoral element in forgetting is linked in these lyrics to Brecht's *acceptance of transitoriness*. It is only this acceptance which liberates from

the fear of the punitive agencies of the future. The biblical metaphor of 'smoke' thus takes on a double meaning in Brecht's work. The smoke of transitory things mingles with the smoke of pleasure. It is inhaled. (Smoke from opiates, but chiefly that of 'Virginia'.) Brecht's acceptance of transitoriness from the very beginning forms part of his view of time flowing in the way described by Heraclitus. During the twenties, however, this basic position is increasingly influenced by Brecht's approval of the raging torment of modernization, a motif we are familiar with from the Futurists. This becomes a particular characteristic of Brecht's new functionalist phase. A directorial force is written into the 'stream of oblivion'.

4. In Brecht's rhetoric of forgetting, however, there are also surprising points of contact with both Proust and Freud. In his poem 'Remembering Marie A.,' Brecht explains *forgetting as being the prerequisite for the ability to experience*, which consists not of fixing an identical moment but of experiencing the passing of this moment.[46]

5. Combined with this is a further motif. The carnival of forgetting has, as we saw in the stanza from 'The Great Hymn of Thanksgiving,' the advantage that a person plunging into it cannot be identified in any way. Since both the person's name and individual physiognomy are blotted out, *the person loses her legally liable identity*. The process of blotting out individual distinctions extends as far as forgetting the differences between the various specimens of the human species and 'other animals.' The eponymous hero *Baal* is just such a borderline case of forgetting. In the case of both Ophelia in the poem about the drowned girl and the past love Marie A., the first things to be forgotten are those features in which – according to the traditional view – the signature of the individual has been most indelibly printed: the face.

6. In addition to these five motifs of carnivalesque forgetting, Lehmann has drawn attention to an aspect which was already conspicuous in Nietzsche's work and which would have a lasting effect in Brecht's work right up until his aesthetics of materialism in later years.[47] In his *Genealogy of Morals* Nietzsche had set up a notable connection between forgetting and eating, incorporation and digestion. For Brecht this was no simple etymological joke (*vergessen* – 'to forget' contains the word *essen*, 'to eat'). The play on words revealed the fact that the conversion of energy necessarily presupposes a process of destruction such as forgetting/eating. For him, forgetting was part of the metabolism of his version of dialectics. Nietzsche's *Genealogy of Morals* had not gone so far. This is what he had to say:

> Forgetfulness is not just a *vis inertiae*, as the superficial among us believe. Rather it is an active and in the strictest sense positive hindrance which is responsible for the fact that things which are experienced or taken in are as unlikely to reach our consciousness in the process of digestion ('Ein-

verseelung') as in the myriad processes by which physical nourishment, so called incorporation ('Einver leibung') takes place ... A little quiet, a little *tabula rasa* of the consciousness, so there is room for new things ... – that is the benefit of active forgetfulness, a doorkeeper as it were, an upholder of mental order, peace, etiquette, from which it is immediately evident that there can be little happiness, little present without forgetfulness.[48]

Brecht then formulates this as follows:

Of those cities will remain what passed through them, the wind!
The house makes glad the eater: he clears it out.
We know that we're only tenants, provisional ones
And after us there will come: nothing worth talking about.[49]

Forgetting and resistance

About ten years after the *Hauspostille* poems Brecht wrote a poem with the programmatic title 'In Praise of Forgetfulness'. Brecht's concept of forgetting had changed. The time was not right for purely carnivalesque forgetting. Since many elements of democratic convention had been 'forgotten' in the new state created by Fascism with nothing short of 'futuristic' élan, there was no counterweight to the extolling of a diffuse destructive power. Forgetting now clearly required a subject and a purpose to base itself upon if it was still to remain an attitude of opposition.

Forgetfulness is a good thing
How else would
The son leave the mother who has fed him?
Who gave him the strength in his limbs
And keeps him from trying to use them?

Or how could the pupil leave the teacher
Who gave him knowledge?
Once knowledge is passed on
The pupil must go his own way.

New inhabitants
move into the old house
If those who built it were still there
The house would be too small.

The stove is working well. The stove-fitter
is long gone. The ploughman
Does not recognize the loaf.

Without forgetting how could the
Man get up in the morning after the night has wiped out all traces?
How could a man after being knocked down six times
Rise a seventh time
To plough the stony ground, to fly
Towards the dangerous sky?

The weakness of memory
Gives man strength.[50]

Five different versions of forgetting are presented here. The first stanza shows forgetting as a variation on the motif of the cold shock, the necessary separation from the symbiotic relationship with the mother.[51] Brecht emphasized – as did contemporary psychoanalysis, by the way, for example Ferenczi's – that this sudden loss of warmth to which the child is exposed at birth itself is necessary if the child is to develop a sense of reality.[52] Peter von Matt drew attention to Brecht's memorable secret motto: a person who cannot tear herself away from the warmth of the mother-and-child relationship remains stupid. Conspicuously, the son who is addressed in the poem is without a father unless we assume that the father appears in the second stanza in the shape of the teacher. But by this time the son has already come through the family drama formulated by pschoanalysis (if he was ever subjected to it in Brecht's conception). The second version of forgetting takes up 'the praise of doubt'.[53] Knowledge learned makes us able to separate ourselves from the authority of whoever disseminated it. In this case, forgetting guarantees the freedom to live without mentors. Does the third version take up again the old anarchistic refrain 'the house makes glad the eater: he clears it out?' Hardly. For in contrast to the earlier urban poems the destructive element here is not directed at the 'house'. There is no demolition of the old shell in the manner of Futurism, and no eating bare. Instead it is only the absence of the old inhabitants which gives the new room to move. In the house of tradition the new people must have enough scope of their own in order to be able to assimilate the old conventions at all.

At the same time there is an important shift in this verse which we have not yet considered. It deals not with old inhabitants but with the architects. At this point – in contrast to the earlier lyrics of forgetting – the images of incorporation give way to the producers. It is this viewpoint of the producer which is then dominant in the fourth version of forgetting too. This three-line verse expresses two views of the process by which the producer becomes estranged from his product. The second of these alludes to the Marxist concept of alienation. In the fifth stanza the various versions of forgetting presented in the preceding verses are bound up with the ability to resist with a certain amount of pathos. The poem ends with a kind of conclusion:

The weakness of memory
Gives man strength.

Since this strength too – embodied in the figures of subsequent mothers,
teachers and conventions – is subject to the same law of forgetting, the
praise of forgetfulness has a paradoxical effect: it preserves the *memory* of
what continues to happen in the course of generations between the 'stony
ground' and the 'dangerous sky' – as long as the ground is still stony and
the sky still dangerous. The poem does take up several aspects of forgetting
from the early lyrics; yet the carnivalesque aspect is unquestionably functio-
nalized in the direction of inexhaustible resistance. There is still an echo of
the avant-garde motif in the poem written between 1933 and 1938, but here
couched in arguments. In 'Praise of Forgetfulness' there is the justification
for what in the carnival of forgetting did not even require justification.

Wiping out the traces

If you have anything else to say
then tell me, I'll forget it.
Brecht, *A Reader for Those Who Live in Cities*

'If I cannot rely on my memory,' wrote Freud in his 'Treatise on the Magic
Block' in 1924, 'I can supplement and assure its function by making a
written note. The surface upon which these notes are kept, the slate or the
sheet of paper, is then as it were a material piece of the apparatus of
memory.'[54] You then only have to remember where you made the note to
be able to reproduce it again at any time. This has the advantage that what
you remember is not subject to the distortions which it clearly undergoes
in the memory. Even so, this technique of noting things down involves a
problem. How lasting is the note made? Is there enough room for everything
we write down? If the note is written in ink on a sheet of paper it will be
preserved for the foreseeable future at least. I thereby retain a permanent
trace of the memory. The disadvantage of this procedure, however, apparently lies in the fact that the writing surfaces are limited. One page is soon
full, further pages must be added. The result is a memory archive made up
of boxes and boxes of notes, a repository of permanent traces. The disadvantage of this kind of archive is that it has recorded vast amounts of
data which are of no interest now or which I do not want to remember.

In view of this complication Freud points to another procedure which
does not have this disadvantage. When one writes on a slate with chalk,
one is working on a surface which can be used over and over again.
Anything superfluous can be rubbed out straightaway without changing the

surface itself. The disadvantage here is that there is no firm or reliable record of any permanent trace. And as soon as the slate is full, some of the old notes have to be rubbed out to make room for new ones. Freud concludes that neither of these models is appropriate for illustrating the performance of the mental apparatus of perception and the memory systems connected to it as a whole. In his search for a device to illustrate the nature of the memory apparatus, Freud hits upon something which today is only found as a toy for children: a magic slate. There is a light grey cover-sheet on top of a black wax stencil. The top layer is protected by a plastic sheet. When one writes on the plastic sheet with a special pencil the light grey sheet sticks to the wax stencil producing a visible mark. By sliding the slate in and out the lighter sheet is separated from the dark wax and the mark is erased. However, the engravings on the wax remain. It is in this particular characteristic that Freud saw remarkable correspondences with the way he supposed the apparatus of perception and memory were constructed. It can make the marks disappear without erasing the permanent traces entirely. Thus it can be written on time and time again indefinitely.

For the light grey cover-sheet the strong plastic sheet offers 'protection', which absorbs and tempers the powerful stimuli which bombard the apparatus of perception. The engravings in the wax are legible when the light falls on them in a certain way. The workings of memory and perception are thus distributed over two different systems. Of course, Freud is aware that an analogy of this kind, between a toy and the apparatus of mental perception, should not be taken too far. For instance, the magic slate cannot reproduce the writing from within once it has been erased. Nevertheless Freud ventures to demonstrate by reference to this little toy how the system of perception, consciousness and protection from stimuli (plastic layer and light grey sheet) works in relation to the unconscious level (wax stencil). He equates the appearance and disappearance of the writing with the awakening and fading of consciousness.

But Freud extends the analogy in another way. As explained before, the writing disappears each time the intimate contact between the paper receiving the stimulus and the wax layer retaining the impression is broken. With this Freud illustrates his psychological theory of how the apparatus of perception works. The murky system of the unconscious periodically energizes the system of perception and consciousness. Only in this state is the latter system capable of receiving perceptions which are accompanied by consciousness, and to convey the stimuli further into the unconscious system of remembering. If this energy is withdrawn and the contact broken, the consciousness is also extinguished. Thus the whole system of perception is periodically closed to stimuli. The system of perception only works when the memory systems send out 'feelers'. This reference to Freud breaks into our discussion of Brecht and may seem out of place. But we introduced it not only to show the wide variety of ways in which remembering and forgetting were tackled in the first thirty years of the twentieth century. We also wanted to demonstrate just how complicated a model Freud constructed to explain the system of retaining and eradicating traces.

In comparison to this the avant-garde's rhetoric of forgetting seems almost simplistic. The important factor in connection with Brecht is that Freud uncovered a new dimension to the problem: the separateness of perception/consciousness from memory. The separateness of the perception system from that of memory, which Freud had promoted to the level of a physiological statement, came up again in the work of Bergson and Proust as a necessary assumption. If man wishes to experience herself as being 'alive' then she must remove perception from the control of memory. Brecht radicalized this demand for separation still further. His characters see it as necessary for their sheer survival to cease to allow their perceptions and actions to be guided by the memory system.

An example from Dadaism on the 'wipe out the traces' theme may serve to illustrate the relationship between the avant-garde and Brecht: it is said that Francis Picabia would pointedly erase the drawings he made on a blackboard at the end of his happenings. This may be seen as a gesture relating to Nietzsche's presentism 'a little quiet, a little *tabula rasa* of consciousness, so there is room for new things!!! – that is the benefit of active forgetfulness.'[55] Before the drawing has the chance to enter the collective memory of the cultural museum, preserved to no effect, it is erased. In Brecht's *A Reader for Those Who Live in Cities* which we will now look at, this *tabula rasa* gesture is so completely transformed that even traces of Nietzsche seem to have been completely wiped out.

The rhetoric of forgetting and Brecht's Marxism

Marxist scholars have repeatedly felt compelled to recognize a curious defect in Brecht's form of dialectics. For them this defect was chiefly apparent in the undue emphasis which Brecht placed on the destructive element. Why were the benefits of synthesis so seldom displayed in his work? The reason for this lies in the fact that the central motif of forgetting in Brecht's early work did not disappear – as scholars have often suggested – when Brecht read Marx in the mid-1920s. Yet it did shift to other problem areas. The defect which scholars have pointed to is apparent at those points where the motif of forgetting persists. And it was precisely this motif to which Brecht ascribed revolutionary power.

Brecht's reading of Marx was undertaken with a susceptibility created in part by his reading of Nietzsche.[56] We can apply the watchword of his early work to his incorporation of the edifice of Marxist theory: 'The house makes glad the eater: he clears it out.' Brecht's reading of Marx went beyond conventional interpretation in the reforming tradition of Kautsky (on this point he is guided by Lenin's critique). Yet this interpretation is just as markedly distinct from the humanistic reading which Georg Lukács propagated on the basis of the early writings which saw Marx as the theoretician of reification. Brecht's occasionally antihumanistic reading shows the influence of Nietzsche. His praise for Heraclitic flux and his suspicion with regard to teleological models of history might have tempted him to subscribe wholeheartedly to the interpretations of Marx put forward by his teacher Karl Korsch. But Korsch wanted to introduce a distinction between Marxism and the communist concept of action, and so his reading too was rejected in part. We can see that there is no point adding up the influences and rejections to arrive at the result that Brecht's Marxism consists of 20 per cent Nietzsche, 15 per cent Korsch, 40 per cent Lenin, 10 per cent Behaviourism, 5 per cent Soviet reflexology and 10 per cent Hegel or Heraclitus or Chinese philosophy. We have to accept the fact that Brecht's Marxism is a genuinely new creation. And within this creation the motif of forgetting plays an important role. Certainly, the paradoxical nature of forgetting suddenly acquires well-defined political contours which were not so easily recognizable in the early phase.

On the basis of Nietzsche's text, Paul de Man defines this element of paradox in the following way: 'The more radical the rejection of anything that came before, the greater the dependence on the past.'[57] The radical rejection of the old concept of the subject clearly involved harking back to an even older concept. It is easy to find evidence of this within the orbit of the avant-garde. Artaud harks back to Balinese theatre; the Expressionists are influenced by African art; the Surrealists long for pre-Columbian times or for regression to the childhood stages of development: Picasso is interested in pre-Christian Iberian art and the Russian Constructivists are inspired by icon painting.

In all cases we can recognize a desire to regain a less complicated status for the subject than that which the bourgeoisie had conferred upon it. Even in his early lyrics Brecht's concept of forgetting is also aimed at the concept of the subject which is to be eradicated. But there is not immediately a new agency to take the place of the old individual. For a while there is merely a *tabula rasa*. It is a stencil upon which various names can be recorded, pre- and extra-bourgeois. Even the name of the proletariat.

By the mid-1920s we may observe a new name slowly being written on this *tabula rasa*. By way of a document which reveals how this slow transformation takes place we shall comment here upon a poem which once again displays all the elements of the avant-garde rhetoric of forgetting. The text demonstrates – and is in this respect comparable to Beckett's play – how the feedback effect of memory and identity is interrupted with the purpose – in contrast to Beckett – of finding forms of action which will fulfil a minimum requirement: survival. The poem is called 'Wipe Out the Traces' and it was put together with other poems written around 1926 in the collection entitled *A Reader for Those Who Live in Cities*:[58]

Part from your mates at the station
Enter the city in the morning with your coat buttoned up
Look for a room, and when your mate knocks:
Do not, O do not, open the door
But
Wipe out the traces

If you meet your parents in Hamburg or elsewhere
Pass them like strangers, turn the corner, don't recognize them
Pull the hat they gave you over your face
But
Wipe out the traces

Eat the meat that's there. Don't stint yourself.
Go into any house when it rains and sit on any chair that's in it
But don't sit long. And don't forget your hat.
I tell you:
Wipe out the traces

Whatever you say, don't say it twice
If you find your ideas in anyone else, disown them
The man who hasn't signed anything, who has left no picture
Who was not there, who said nothing:
How can they catch him?
Wipe out the traces

(That is what they taught me)

The history of this poem's reception has something to do with the *tabula rasa* structure produced by the rhetoric of forgetting. There has therefore been a fatal temptation to read the poem in all sorts of different ways depending on the rapidly changing historical moment. The fact that the subject figure presented here is itself *empty* seems to have misled its readers in various situations into reading the name of a *heroic* subject into the poem.

Walter Benjamin suggested three different readings for Brecht's poem. In 1932 he illustrated Nietzsche's watchword 'positive barbarity' in a favourable way by referring to this poem. In it he saw the motions of the 'destructive character' which checks everything to see if it merits destruction.[59] He observed an avant-garde gesture, yet he did not perceive the paradoxical nature of it: burning the ships in order to reach the shores. (The ships were burned. People remained on the old coasts of capitalism.)

During his years of exile Benjamin rejected this reading. In response to Arnold Zweig, who saw in the 1926 poem a prophetic prefiguration of the fate of the emigré in exile in foreign towns, Benjamin put forward a different version: he now saw the poem as giving instructions to the communist cadre which operated illegally during the Weimar Republic.[60] The tendency toward this interpretation is still seen in today's commentaries. (For example, in the sixties Franco Buono identified rules of conduct for underground fighters in an occupied town within the text.[61]) In 1940 Benjamin ventured in his diary to put forward a new, more topical reading for the *Reader for Those Who Live in Cities.*[62] He now saw the poem in the context of the activities of the GPU (the State secret police, forerunner of the KGB). So the chain of interpretations of the poem over a ten-year period gives an insight into the biography of an intellectual in the thirties.

But none of these published readings has kept in mind the absurd or comic or suicidal consequences which the text would have if it were seen as a code of conduct. Not one considers the iconographic scale of the figures shown, which goes as far as the slapstick tramp of Chaplin. It is the figure of the person who seeks to avoid objects with a will of their own by making himself disappear as an identifiable subject, yet by doing so exercises a magnetic attraction for such intractable objects. Thus the seventh poem has quite an amusing beginning:

> Don't talk about danger!
> You can't drive a tank through a man-hole:
> You'll have to get out.
> Better abandon your primus
> You've got to see that you yourself come through.[63]

If in *A Reader For Those Who Live in Cities* the person addressed obeys the instructions given in the poem, this means in no way that the difficulties become less but just that the person goes from one reduction to the next. As the years passed Brecht himself clearly became aware of the fact that the *tabula rasa* structure of the subject was leading in his plays and poems of the mid 1920s to the dangerous phenomenon whereby people saw his characters as heroes. The most marked example is the history of his play programmatically entitled *Man Equals Man.*[64]

When Brecht discovered that his hero, who from being a private person was reassembled into a war machine, was completely in tune with the pathos of the New Sobriety, he tried to undermine this tendency by producing the play as a comedy. This explains why there are also comic passages in *A Reader for Those Who Live in Cities* which have the function of leading away from heroic readings. At the end of the twenties Brecht tried to substantiate the transformation of his hero into a revolutionary fighter. Yet the chief obstacle to this was the fact that the plot of the play had the hero as a member of the English Colonial army. By the middle of the thirties he finally realized that the reassemblage of his hero could also be seen as an account of the transformation of a petit-bourgeois into a national socialist. (Today we rather tend to read Brecht's play as the story of the reassemblage of a man who has fallen amongst the soldiers. This reassemblage is due to the fact that this human being is male. According to the point of view this story can be read either as a tragedy or a comedy.) Here we have a remarkable parallel to the various interpretations which Benjamin undertook with 'Wipe out the Traces'. What is the result of all this?

The *tabula rasa* structure of the subject described here did not permit any number of different names to be inscribed. For this stencil may well have allowed a collective type of varying origin to be entered, yet one name it would not accept: that of the individual. The consequences of the antihumanistic concept which formed the basis of this structure was that contemporary Marxist criticism handled the plays and poems from this phase with extreme suspicion.

The iconography of the subject who was instructed to move in various ways in 'Wipe Out the Traces' may well be more complicated than the descriptions offered so far might suggest (émigré, guerrilla, communist cadre, partisan, positive barbarian). Thus the figure of survival presented here could also be derived from the 'intellectual nomad' types which Nietzsche set up in opposition to the 'firmly rooted intellect' in a sudden upgrading of a word used disparagingly. until then.[65] The image of the nomad is bound up with the myth of Ahasuerus the Wandering Jew, who in the nineteenth century had also been described as 'the angel of doubt' (Andersen) and who accompanies Zarathustra as a shadow. Benjamin had in fact linked the image of the nomad with that of the communist cadre.[66] When he was in Moscow in 1927 he described with fascination the apartments kept by communist officials. The bourgeois interiors had been removed from the rooms, and they lived a temporary lifestyle in bare rooms as if they were camping out. They seemed ready to pack up at any moment should the hour or the party require.

The iconographic tradition behind this agent of forgetting is thus more colourful than the one-dimensionality of the figure suggested: the Ahasuerus of legend, the intellectual nomad type, the tramp, the image of the Soviet official, the typical figure of a character who behaves futuristically. All these figures have one thing in common: they are specialists in separation; and they all stand in opposition to an ideologically basic figure which was dominant in cultural criticism of every hue: the figure of an individual that looks for contact with purer origins in being rooted (in tradition or to an area) in order to escape from the history of decline taking place in civilization.

In contrast Brecht's poems extol the virtue of uprooting oneself. Our poem is also unable to wipe out the traces of another influence: the traces of Dadaism. After all, as a Dadaist pamphlet expressed it in 1919: 'Being a Dadaist means being opposed to any kind of sedimentation; sitting for one moment on a chair means having risked one's life.'[67] It is thus hardly surprising that the instructions which Brecht's poem issues for an anonymous figure bear a confused resemblance to the instructions which Walter Serner gives his criminal types in his *Conman's Handbook*.[68]

Paradoxes of a one-dimensional poem

What happens to the figure in this poem who is forced to conceal his identity step by step? Or to be more precise: what stages must the person addressed be forced to go through until he is finally lying in an unmarked grave?

Brecht's poem is a notable commentary on the traditional poem covering a life history which follows the course of life from the cradle to the grave. He had made his own attempts at this genre ('Of the Friendliness of the World'). In 'Wipe Out the Traces' entry into the world is through the station, the separation from the parents comes a little later, after separation from the mates. With biblical pathos, the rule of solidarity is neutralized.[69] Departure from the world is marked by a gravestone with no name on it. The road covered along the way is a route through the town. But Brecht has removed any trace of urban scenery. The progression through this terrain is governed by codes of conduct set down by an unnamed authority. They are designed to prevent any other authority which may be on the tail of the central figure from identifying this figure. The figure described here, whose conduct is anonymous, survives – we know not what for – in a chain of separations. There can of course be no question of self-realization. The only thing we can say with any certainty about this fleeting figure is that he appears to be without any profound structuring of the psyche; he has had to throw off the baggage of memory; his internal mental control is suspect and is replaced by the external control imposed by the instructions. The figure becomes the object of behaviourist observation. Buttoning up his jacket and putting down his hat, the figure shuts itself off. The principles of survival are given out by the external authority like stimuli. The correct reflexes are expected. The psychological remainder is nothing but a black box. Even though this poem may appear to be one-dimensional and flat, it nevertheless confronts the reader with a series of contradictions:

- the laws of the urban terrain in which the figure is moved around seem *transparent* to the speaker; the figure himself is shut off: from the point of view of modern pragmatic anthropology an 'ensemble of functions' (Helmut Plessner) which is *impenetrable* even to itself;

- the *mobility* of the figure seems to be *unlimited* and unaffected by any convention (of memory, loyalty, settledness, morality or property) as long as he *obeys the instructions* given. But on this *planned* course he is in the final analysis merely following a *fateful cycle* which leads to death;
- anyone who is that determined to *forget his origins* must clearly expect to meet *his parents* around the next corner in that town.

The most ironical paradox, however, is the fact that the instructions reflect back on the author himself: if you sing the *praises of anonymity* with such consistency you develop such an *individual trademark* that from it it is possible to *identify* the *unmistakable voice* of the author.

Education or the classic example of cynicism

In Poem 10 in *A Reader for Those Who Live in Cities* Brecht's verses are seen by critics as setting out the programme and justification of his writing. They can be interpreted as being pedagogical:

When I speak to you
Cold and impersonally
Using the driest words
Without looking at you
(I seemingly fail to recognize you
In your particular nature and difficulty).
I speak to you merely
Like reality itself
(Sober, not to be bribed by your particular nature
Tired of your difficulty)
Which in my view you seem not to recognize.[70]

Researchers today tend to interpret these lines as a fortunate indication that Brecht intended his writing to be merely a simulation of coldness. It was meant to make the 'receiver' shiver a little in order to illustrate the degree of alienation. Critics in the twenties refused to involve themselves in this kind of pedagogical attempt to render Brecht's work harmless. In 1932 Rudolf Arnheim argued on a political level that reality did not 'speak' in cold and general terms; it 'spoke' in warm and specific terms in order to reconcile man to the degree of the cold.[71] Arnheim undoubtedly meant the ideological reality which surrounds people. Its 'speech' is not revealing: Arnheim was right on that point. Brecht *constructs* the phantom of a cynical reality. If even Poem 10 met with scepticism from Marxist contemporaries, then it is plausible that none of the other poems could exactly be seen to contain a code of conduct for the communist cadre. The reaction of socialist critics to Brecht's *A Reader for Those Who Live in Cities* is interesting from the point of view of remembering and forgetting. Béla Balász saw the cold tones of the poems as merely the top layer of a palimpsest.[72] Beneath this layer he noted the murky origins of a discourse which annihilated the subject. In his view the poems had not succeeded in wiping out the traces of genealogy: the traces of Nietzsche. Balász noted the 'Dionysian frenzy of self-denial'. For Balász this was the hidden basis of the text. The more obvious jargon of functionalism seemed only to be grafted onto it.

Would it not have been more obvious to look for synchronic correspondences in Soviet Constructivism, Bekhterev's reflexology and theories of the Bauhaus? It would probably have been more productive. Instead socialist criticism concentrated on looking for the hidden genealogy *behind* the avant-garde attitudes of authors who sympathized with the workers' movement. This was a valid and informative approach to take; but in the end it always led back to the trivial realization that none of the combatants was born with a clean slate. Those who raise 'the proletariat' to the rank of a homogeneous subject apparently have the tendency to judge intellectuals who subscribe to the same view on the criterion of homogeneity. Instead of looking into how productive a mixture of different influences may be in a concrete situation, this kind of criticism appeared to work on the assumption that 'pure theory' could be etched into a clean stencil with no writing on it. But obviously no reading of Marx would be received by an empty slate unless the person had Marx sung to her as a lullaby. Let us remember Freud's 'Magic Block'. The protection against stimuli already served to prevent the invasion and razing of the old cognitive and emotional strongholds of the subject. The new mark met with the old systems of memory. Just because the older marks were not visible did not mean that they had not left a permanent trace. Correcting ideological mistakes is not the same as wiping clean a blackboard covered with chalk-marks.

Thus the criticism which came from comrades knew no mercy. In the rhetoric of forgetting it saw merely the style of older enemies. Anyone who ran with the pack to that extent would inevitably end up being eaten by the same pack. That was the prediction. Anyone who approved of reification in that way would inevitably end up bringing down on themselves the curse which Karl Marx had pronounced upon it. But true to his principle of 'treating harsh reality in an even harsher way', Brecht was content for a while to show that this language could outdo reality. The consequence of this was that the poems of the *Reader for Those who Live in Cities* are rejected even today as classical examples of cynicism – if they are not immediately rendered harmless by didacticism.

Forgetting as a productive flash back

Our starting-point for the analysis of forgetting in this poem by Brecht was Paul de Man's theory that in the desire to wipe out the structures handed down by tradition there is a strong possibility of regression to even older structures. We would like finally to illustrate from another point of view the fact that these poems by Brecht posit a social sphere which appears to come before the period when the bourgeois individual was constituted. This can be explained further by means of a comparison with the contemporary theories of Norbert Elias and Sigmund Freud.

Let us recapitulate: Brecht's poems present a figure who requires advice from outside for every move it makes because clearly guidance from within itself or spontaneity would have led to both insanity or premature death. The behaviourist view points out that the authorities which have been internalized by the individual as part of bourgeois society have now ceased to function. The individual presented here has to be taught the basis of survival in a violent environment by an outside specialist. As the construction of a pacified bourgeois society gradually turns out to be a phantom, so the internal counterbalances begin to fail. Thus Poem 8 in the cycle reads as follows:

> Give up your dreams that they will make
> An exception in your case.
> What your mother told you
> Binds no one.
> Keep your contracts in your pockets
> They will not be honoured here.[73]

Once the image of a pacified society has disappeared any kind of social contract is banished to the realm of dreams. In the spheres posited by the poems there prevails an atmosphere of permanent danger. There are at most small, fleeting islands of a mere shattered existence present in them (the friendliness of a whore for one night, for example in Poem 9). But physical violence can burst in at any moment. This is why Brecht advocates leaving behind the areas protected by loving care. Before the individual is caught out in the cold by violence, she should toughen herself up for the survival struggle in the cold areas of the imaginary.

Brecht's images thus stand in conspicuous contrast to the images sketched by Sigmund Freud and Norbert Elias in their theories of the process of civilization in the twenties and thirties. For them, the very situation which Brecht saw as the norm for the bourgeois state was a pre-bourgeois warrior-society. Elias's basic assumption had been that the capacity to govern oneself only develops in a pacified community where physical force is concentrated in monopolies such as the police and the army. 'Force is confined to barracks and it only comes out of storage, out of the barracks, and directly into the life of the individual in the most extreme cases, in times of war and in times of social upheaval.'[74] The day-to-day round of civilization is then largely freed from the burden of this force. Force becomes the responsibility of special troops who stand guard at the edge of the daily round but who are seldom obliged to intervene, since in modern society acts of physical force are largely replaced by mental self-direction. 'This force stored up behind the scenes,' as Elias put it so memorably, 'exercises a constant pressure on the life of the individual which in many cases he is scarcely aware of since he has become completely accustomed to it.'[75]

Brecht's urban poems present the 'pacified spheres' in such a way that the figures portrayed in the poems are made so acutely aware of the pressure exercised by this stored-up force that they believe they are living in the old pre-bourgeois warrior-society. It is certainly true that Brecht removed the explicitly political and military traces of civil war from the urban scenery in this cycle of poems. But the spheres he portrays are constituted by violence and they force the individuals who wish to survive into the cycle of total mobilization. Judged by Norbert Elias's criteria such spheres come before the construction of a bourgeois state. This is why mental self-determination does not yet function within them (or no longer functions). The behaviourist view consistently excludes the inner 'voices', which no longer exercise their orientational function (or do not yet exercise them); in other words, it merely demonstrates how the individual is led into some fatal course of action by the inner voices (as in the *Lehrstück* or didactic play form). The outer voice is in control. The self which speaks is its sounding-board.

By introducing the flashback to pre-bourgeois spheres in such a conscious way, Brecht shows up the unstable ground of the constitutional state, which not only is based on violence but allows areas which are constitutionally outside the rule of law. This is one reason for the obsession which Brecht has with these spheres – the criminal underworld or the world of soldiers. Brecht's flashbacks to images of pre-bourgeois spheres are mediated by the rhetoric of forgetting. But he also presents a state of affairs which is all too easily forgotten: the extent to which violence lies at the basis of bourgeois legal systems like the Weimar Republic. Brecht's flashback thus reveals a situation which had a terrible relevance at the end of the twenties. Marxism taught him that this situation was nothing new.

Epilogue: The Débâcle of Forgetting

What remains. Solitary text waiting for history. And the memory full of holes, the fragile wisdom of the masses, threatened by forgetting.

Heiner Müller, 'Absage'

In the mid-thirties when criticism of the motifs of avant-garde thinking became more acute in the light of current historical experiences, Max Horkheimer once again tackled Bergson's metaphysics of time.[76] There is no trace of the emphasis placed on forgetting. Horkheimer advocates a consciously guided active process of remembering. In so doing he rejects the value placed on forgetting. The vehement criticism directed at the official memory-work of historians by the avant-garde was always linked to a relapse into the stream of 'life' or into the dynamics of the real process. 'Forgetting' had once been the name for an act carried out by intuition on its own authority which breaks through the memory framework in order to come into contact with the subterranean stream (of life, the unconscious, of pure time). In 1934 Horkheimer clearly sees that the reason for criticizing the memory lies in the shape of historicism. But he sets up a model of the 'didactic view of history' to counter the concept of forgetting. For him this view of history has the power to listen to those forgotten in the continual workings of a remembering consciousness.

We should take note here of a seemingly harmless shift of viewpoint which nevertheless has far-reaching consequences. It is no longer a question of *that which* has been forgotten (childhood stages, origin, unconscious, pure stream of time) but of *those who* have been forgotten (those oppressed by the suffering of the past) whose fate Horkheimer regards as merely reinforced by official historiography: to be forgotten.

This takes up one of Maurice Halbwachs's motifs. The collective memory is not homogeneous, it contains contradictions. Horkheimer insists that the work of the historian is conscious selection. The criteria of selection are derived from the vision of the future which the historian has. Thus there are two activities involved in the work of the historian which are inextricably linked to one another: the more the historian uses memory to serve a better future, the more his memory images will become a 'mirror of past injustice'. Nietzsche had already seen the critical science of history as such a 'tribunal'. But what use is this kind of memory to those who have been forgotten? Horkheimer remains anti-metaphysical in opposition to Bergson:

No kind of future can put right what has happened to the people who have perished. They will never be called upon to enjoy happiness in eternity. Nature and society have done their work on them and the idea of the Last Judgement, into which the oppressed and dying poured all their longings, constitutes nothing more than a leftover of primitive thinking, which failed to recognize the empty part played by man in natural history and which humanized the universe. Amid this vast indifference it is only the human consciousness which can constitute a place where the disaster experienced can be alleviated, the only authority which is not content to put up with it ... Now that any confidence in eternity must inevitably be shattered, history is the only hearing which the present transitory generation of humanity can still give to the accusations of past generations.[77]

What immeasurable disasters were to follow in the years to come before the powers of understanding of the materialist view of history could no longer get by without the odd moment of theology, before the dialectician could draw strength from the 'primitive thinking' of Messianic hope! (In the forties Horkheimer was also to turn towards religion.)

1938 came Benjamin's late reply to Horkheimer's anti-metaphysical critique of Bergson. In his 'Theses on the Philosophy of History' he tries to combine various aspects of the concept of remembrance and forgetting in such a way as to give a new justification for a materialist view of history.[78] He links the critique of the concept of memory offered by historicism with Proust's concept of *mémoire involontaire*. In a positive reappraisal of the collective element in the spirit of Halbwachs and the socialist tradition, he introduces the Messianic hope of redemption for those forgotten. This should take place not only with the consciousness of the critical historian where Horkheimer had situated it, but in a better reality which must be fought for.

Benjamin too had once joined in the avant-garde chorus of praise for forgetting. His essay on 'The Destructive Character' contained the most extreme images of the fascination for the *tabula rasa* and there are clear traces of this in the 'Theses'. Two pioneers of the concept of forgetting also appear, albeit in brief quotations which are given as headings for theses VII and XII: Nietzsche and Brecht. But he does not adopt theories here as in earlier writings but images which supplement each other in a provocative way. Brecht's biblical lines from *The Threepenny Opera*, 'Don't forget the darkness and the cold / In this vale which resounds with misery', are answered with the image of the 'Garden of knowledge' in which Nietzsche allows the spoilt idler of historicism to indulge himself.

The critique of historicism is thus a constant motif from Nietzsche through to Benjamin. Benjamin intensifies this criticism of affirmative remembering. For him it is always 'empathy with the victor'.

Whoever has emerged victorious participates to this day in the triumphal procession in which the present rulers step over those who are lying prostrate. According to traditional practice, the spoils are carried along in the procession. They are called cultural treasures.[79]

Thus any aspect of culture becomes at the same time an aspect of barbarity. The dominant form of historiography attempts to wipe out the traces of this barbarity; not because of the sight of the barbarity but because of the sight of its victims.

Other motifs from the tradition of forgetting appear in notably modified forms:

The emphasis on the transitory element, which in Brecht's work was concentrated on the present time, is transferred by Benjamin to the 'image' of the past. In the moment when it is discernible the image of the past comes briefly to light. At any moment it is in danger of being distorted by the conventions of the memory.

While Benjamin bestows the status of transience upon the images of the past he attempts to construe a concept of the present as coming to a standstill. Benjamin's time of the 'Now' has nothing carnivalesque about it. It is the place which is blown out of the continuum of historical time and which is charged with images of the past for a split second. By construing this concept of a stationary time of the 'Now', Benjamin sets himself apart from the concepts of the avant-garde. For the avant-garde could only imagine this standstill in the regression mode (back to a child-hood stage). At the same time he sets himself apart from the constructions of a historical time which is based on the model of progress. This he sees as a notion of time similar to that of Newtonian science; on this point he is in agreement with Bergson.

The element of 'action' is also present. (Though it was no longer present in Horkheimer's work in 1934.) The continuum of history can be broken by action as Benjamin illustrated in the image of the shots fired at the clocks during the French Revolution (already an extremely symbolic and surrealistic form of action!). And in contrast to Horkheimer, Benjamin sees grounds for incorporating theological aspects into his theories. Whether Marxist vocabulary was inadequate for him to formulate a hope which was not directly linked to a subject of history; or whether he was mindful of early socialists who were not afraid of adding the odd theological element; or whether the bitterness of experience caused him to look back to perspectives of childhood – this is not for us to decide. He is not afraid of being blamed for 'primitive thinking', the term Horkheimer used in 1934 to describe the pretension to redemption. For the materialist historian who succeeds in halting historical time in the moment of danger (and this had now come) the images of past suffering appear in a faint Messianic light. Those forgotten are snatched out of the caverns of subterranean history into which the triumphal procession of official historiography had banished them. Materialist historiography has a share in this work of redemption. While such diverse elements of the concept of forgetting continued to have an effect in 1938, others were decisively eliminated. In the meantime the dramatic demand to forget humanistic conventions had been superseded by a power system which had no pretensions to humanity. In the face of the real barbarity, praise for 'positive barbarism', which Benjamin still subscribed to at the beginning of the thirties, seems like a Dadaist bluff, like a child playing with fire. At a time when the memory of humanistic values was to make possible the various alliances against fascism, the rhetoric of forgetting seems no longer to have any function.

Consequently the thirties saw the revival of an old genre: the historical novel. But the form of remembering induced by the political break came about too abruptly. Its sudden onset made it incapable of organically assimilating the avant-garde writing techniques which had been developed as part of the concepts of forgetting. The historical novel was an innovation which had to fall back behind the standards of form imposed by avant-garde literature. (Only the postmodernists were to attempt to combine the genre of the historical novel with avant-garde writing techniques.)

We have illustrated the different historical stages and varieties of the concepts of forgetting and observed two decades of the modern trend in literature during which a second rhetoric of forgetting developed after Nietzsche: the Italian Futurists, Benn, Jünger, Brecht and Beckett; Horkheimer and Benjamin. The rhetoric of forgetting is back in fashion today. It has been necessary to examine its historical development in order to recall what the current revival of this rhetoric seems to have forgotten.

NOTES

1   See F. Vittinghoff, *Der Staatsfeind in der römischen Kaiserzeit. Untersuchungen zur 'damnatio memoriae'*, Ph.D.diss. (Speyer, 1936).
2   See Burghart Schmitt, *Postmoderne – Strategien des Vergessens* (Luchterhand, Neuwied and Berlin, 1986).
3   *Frankfurter Allgemeine Zeitung*, 22 Nov. 1985.
4   See Uwe Japp, *Beziehungen. Ein Konzept der Literaturgeschichte* (Europäische Verlagsanstalt, Frankfurt/M., 1980).
5   Walter Benjamin, *Gesammelte Schriften*, ed. Rolf Tiedemann and Hermann Schweppenhäuser (Suhrkamp, Frankfurt/M., 1972–89), vol. 3, ed. Hella Tiedemann-Bartels (1972), pp. 287–8.
6   Umberto Eco, quoted by Dieter Zimmer, in *Die Zeit*, 6 Dec. 1985.
7   See Douwe Fokkema and Elrud Ibsch, *Modernist Conjectures: A Mainstream in European Literature 1910–40* (C. Hurst, London/St Martin's Press, New York, 1988).
8   See Hans Hagen Hildebrandt, *Becketts Proustbilder* (Metzler, Stuttgart, 1980).
9   Peter Bürger, *Theory of the Avant-Garde* (Manchester University Press, Manchester, 1984).
10 Robert Musil, *Gesammelte Werke*, ed. Adolf Frisé (9 vols, Rowohlt, Hamburg, 1978), vol. 8, p. 1419.

11 Samuel Beckett, *Proust and Three Dialogues* (Calder & Boyars, London, 1970).
12 See Hildebrandt, *Becketts Proustbilder.*
13 Ibid., p. 62.
14 Maurice Halbwachs, *Les cadres sociaux de la mémoire*, Travaux de l'année sociologique. Bibliothèque de philosophie contemporaine (Paris, 1925).
15 Marcel Proust, *A la recherche du temps perdu*, ed. Pierre Clarac and André Ferré (3 vols, Gallimard, Paris, 1954), vol. 1, p. 978.
16 Ibid., p. 992.
17 Ibid., p. 876.
18 Ibid., p. 692.
19 Hildebrandt, *Becketts Proustbilder*, p. 64.
20 Walter Benjamin, 'Zum Bilde Prousts', in *Gesammelte Schriften*, vol. 2, ed. Rolf Tiedemann and Hermann Schweppenhäuser, pt 1, pp. 310–24, esp. pp. 311, 323.
21 Cf. Marcel Proust, *Remembrance of Things Past*, tr. C. K. M. Scott-Moncrieff, Terence Kilmartin and Andrea Mayor (3 vols, Chatto & Windus, London, Random House, New York, 1982), vol. 1, p. 978.
22 Hildebrandt, *Becketts Proustbilder*, p. 1.
23 Mary Douglas, Introduction, in Maurice Halbwachs, *The Collective Memory* (Harper Colophon Books, New York, 1980), pp. 3–15, esp. p. 5.
24 Halbwachs, *The Collective Memory*, p. 32.
25 Douglas, Introduction, ibid., p. 5.
26 Halbwachs's theory is crucial for the understanding of the identity crises in the former communist countries, but especially in East Germany which, after being taken over by West Germany, was forced economically and politically into 'forgetting' its past.
27 Christa Baumgarth, *Geschichte des Futurismus* (Rowohlt, Hamburg, 1966), p. 181.
28 Ibid., pp. 181, 187.
29 Ibid., p. 219.
30 Ernst Jünger, *Der Arbeiter. Herrschaft und Gestalt* (Hanseatische Verlagsanstalt, Hamburg, 1941).
31 Ibid., p. 198.
32 Paul de Man, *Blindness and Insight: Essays in the Rhetoric of Contemporary Criticism* (Methuen, London, 1983), p. 148.
33 Ibid., p. 152.
34 Ibid., p. 161.
35 Cf. Friedrich Nietzsche, *Werke*, ed. Karl Schlechta, 2nd edn (3 vols, Munich, 1960), vol. 1, p. 234 (author's translation).
36 Ibid., p. 229.
37 Ibid., p. 281.
38 De Man, *Blindness and Insight*, p. 148.
39 Bertolt Brecht, *Poems 1913–56* (Eyre Methuen, London, 1976), p. 159.
40 See Hans-Thies Lehmann, 'Text und Erfahrung (Vom ertrunkenen Mädchen)', in Hans-Thies Lehmann and Helmut Lethen, *Brechts 'Hauspostille'. Text und kollektives Lesen* (Metzler, Stuttgart, 1978), pp. 122–45; Hans-Thies

Lehmann, 'Das Subjekt der Hauspostille. Eine neue Lektüre des Gedichts "Vom armen B. B."', in *Brecht Jahrbuch 1980*, ed. Jost Hermand and Reinhold Grimm (Suhrkamp, Frankfurt/M., 1981), pp. 149–71.

41 Rainer Grübel, 'Zur Ästhetik des Worts bei Michail Bachtin', in Michail Bachtin, *Die Ästhetik des Worts*, ed. Rainer Grübel (Suhrkamp, Frankfurt/M., 1979), pp. 21–79.

42 See Lehmann, 'Text und Erfahrung' and 'Das Subjekt der Hauspostille'.

43 Brecht, *Poems 1913–56*, p. 34.

44 Ibid., p. 74.

45 Bertolt Brecht, *Gesammelte Werke* (8 vols, Suhrkamp, Frankfurt/M., 1967), vol. 3, p. 260.

46 See Lehmann, 'Text und Erfahrung'.

47 Lehmann, 'Das Subjekt der Hauspostille', p. 40.

48 Nietzsche, *Werke*, vol. 2, p. 799.

49 Brecht, *Poems 1913–56*, pp. 107–8.

50 Brecht, *Gesammelte Werke*, vol. 9, pp. 628–9.

51 Peter von Matt, 'Brecht und der Kälteschock', in *Die Neue Rundschau*, 87 (1976), pp. 613–29, esp. p. 614; Lehmann and Lethen, *Brechts Hauspostille*, pp. 257–61; see also Helmut Lethen, 'Zwei Barbaren – Ernst Jünger und Bertolt Brecht', *Anstösse* 1 (1984), pp. 17–28.

52 See Helmut Lethen, 'Lob der Kälte. Über ein Motiv der historischen Avantgarde', in *Moderne versus Postmoderne*, ed. Dietmar Kamper and Willem van Reijen (Suhrkamp, Frankfurt/M., 1987), pp. 282–325.

53 Brecht, *Poems 1913–56*, p. 333.

54 Sigmund Freud, 'Notiz über den Wunderblock', in *Studienausgabe* (10 vols + 1 suppl. vol.; (Fischer, Frankfurt/M., 1969–79), vol. 3 (1975), p. 363 (author's translation).

55 Nietzsche, *Werke*, vol. 2, p. 799.

56 See Reinhold Grimm, *Brecht und Nietzsche oder Geständnisse eines Dichters* (Suhrkamp, Frankfurt/M., 1979); Hans-Thies Lehmann and Helmut Lethen, 'Verworfenes Denken', in *Brecht Jahrbuch 1980*.

57 De Man, *Blindness and Insight*, p. 161.

58 Brecht, *Poems 1913–56*, pp. 131–2.

59 Benjamin, *Gesammelte Schriften*, vol. 4, ed. Tillman Rexroth (1971), pt 1, pp. 396–8.

60 Walter Benjamin, *Versuche über Brecht* (Suhrkamp, Frankfurt/M., 1966), pp. 66–9.

61 Franco Buono, 'Nachwort', in Bertolt Brecht, *Gedichte für Städtebewohner* (Suhrkamp, Frankfurt/M., 1980), pp. 143–58.

62 Benjamin, *Gesammelte Schriften*, vol. 6, ed. Rolf Tiedemann and Hermann Schweppenhäuser (1985), p. 540.

63 Bertolt Brecht, *Poems 1913–56*, pp. 137–8.

64 See Michael Giesing et al., 'Fetisch Technik – Die Gesellschaft auf dem Theater der Neusachlichkeit', in *Theater in der Weimarer Republik* (Kunstamt Kreuzberg, Berlin, 1977), pp. 818–22.

65 Nietzsche, *Werke*, vol. 1, p. 817.

66 Benjamin, *Gesammelte Schriften*, vol. 4.1, p. 327

67 Peter Sloterdijk, *Kritik der zynischen Vernunft* (2 vols, Suhrkamp, Frankfurt/ M., 1983), vol. 2, p. 716.
68 Walter Serner, *Letzte Lockerung. Handbrevier für Hochstapler* (Renner, Munich, 1981).
69 See Peter Whitaker, *Brecht's Poetry: A Critical Study* (Oxford University Press, London, 1985), pp. 45–50; Edmund Licher, *Zur Lyrik Brechts. Aspekte ihrer Dialektik und Kommunikativität* (Peter Lang, Frankfurt/Berne/New York, 1984), pp. 163–73; Jan Knopf, *Brecht-Handbuch. Lyrik, Prosa, Schriften* (Metzler, Stuttgart, 1984), pp. 55–8.
70 Brecht, *Poems 1913–56*, p. 140.
71 Quoted in Ernst Schumacher, *Die dramatischen Versuche Bertolt Brechts 1918–33* (Rütten und Loehning, Munich, 1953), pp. 542–3.
72 Béla Balász, 'Sachlichkeit und Sozialismus', *Die Weltbühne*, 51 (1928).
73 Brecht, *Poems 1913–56*, p. 138.
74 Norbert Elias, *Über den Prozess der Zivilisation. Soziogenetische und phylogenetische Untersuchungen* (2 vols, Suhrkamp, Frankfurt/M., 1977), pp. 324–30. (All quotations are author's translations.)
75 Ibid., pp. 325–6.
76 Max Horkheimer, 'Zu Bergsons Metaphysik der Zeit', *Zeitschrift für Sozialforschung*, 3 (1934), pp. 321–43.
77 Ibid., pp. 340–1.
78 Walter Benjamin, 'Über den Begriff der Geschichte', in *Gesammelte Schriften*, vol. 1. 2 (1974), pp. 691–704 'Theses on the philosophy of history', pp. 255–66 (see ch. 1 n. 6 above).
79 Ibid., p. 696.

Part II

Sexual Difference, Power and Signification

3

The Castration of Cassandra

A little while ago, the following short item appeared in the British press. A family from Hull was on holiday at a seaside resort. The husband set about building a deep tunnel into the dunes. When he had got so far that he had completely disappeared inside the hole, his wife began to warn him of a possible accident. The man did not listen, of course, but carried on burrowing all the more determinedly, as his honour obliged him to do. Just as you would expect, the hole collapsed at a certain point and the man was suffocated.

The incident provides a perfect example of what I would call the Cassandra syndrome. It is certainly not restricted to Britain. It is ubiquitous in the Western world, and it has a classical history. Cassandra, the prophetess whom no one believed, is carried prisoner by Agamemnon to Mycenae. There she is put to death – ironically, as a symbol of the same male power which had seized her as its prize. Clytemnestra, Agamemnon's wife, who killed them both, is unable to see this irony. She is herself blinded by hatred for the patriarchal power structure, which had first claimed the life of her daughter Iphigenia, then placed her for ten years in the vulnerable position of royal wife without a husband, and had finally returned in the form of an estranged husband bringing a barbarian into her home as his concubine.

In Mycenae Cassandra is finally silenced, but not because of what she says, which the Achaeans do not believe and no longer even understand. The complete absence of understanding and response is the final point in the process of silencing to which she has always been subjected. What is also destroyed at this point is the language of her body, which signals the same message as her speech: mutilation and silencing by male violence. In the Mycenaean context Cassandra's body is no longer her own. It has become merely a sign of Agamemnon's phallic power.

But this is not yet the full story. In addition to the tragedy there is the satirical version. It is well known that mockery follows close on the heels of affliction, not least in the case of women. The Sicilian vase-painter Assteas, who lived in the fourth century BC, could not resist the opportunity to replace Cassandra's expropriated voice with the equivalent of a male speech-bubble. A clay fragment found in Buccino parodies the famous scene in which Ajax rapes the Trojan princess and priestess of Athene in the goddess's shrine, after the conquest of Troy. To do this, Ajax must first tear Cassandra away from the statue of Athene to which she is clinging in search of protection (see plate 2). In Assteas's version it is Ajax who seeks protection from the goddess and Cassandra who is trying to steal him away. The parody demonstrates a cornerstone of male fantasy, namely that a woman would like nothing better than to be raped. In other words, our Sicilian artist supplements sex scenario number one – overpowering the woman without further ado – with the much more flattering sex scenario number two, in which the woman declares that to be overpowered by the man is her deepest desire. It is not just from the word of de Sade that this lethal strategy is familiar. The silencing of Cassandra, which might otherwise be interpreted as the stigma of the violence she has suffered, is translated into the humorous discourse of the macho male.

Scenarios one and two are the most basic backdrops to the expropriation of female speech, and the Cassandra figure is the archetypal illustration of this, where the silencing of woman is bound up with the mutilation of her body. But Cassandra is not the only one. The phenomenon is reiterated in the figures of Philomela, Echo and Xanthippe, who similarly portray the destruction of female speech on various levels of communication by the symbolic and physical violence of men. The images we have of these women are important because they have come down to us unquestioned and sacrosanct as part of our cultural tradition. They represent social patterns of perception by which we organize our allocations of power and gender, body and voice. It is only when we deconstruct these allocations and dismantle their logic of violence that we are able to bring the dead voices back to life.

There is a proverb which says 'Speech is silver, but silence is golden'. This is the very essence of logocentrism. For if we are silent, the purity of our thoughts is unsullied by the swarms of signifiers. But it is also the very essence of phallocentrism. For if we are consciously silent, we still have the power to speak and, at the same time, the power to control access to speech through the ethics of silence. Observances of silence are power strategies.

When Bakhtin describes speech as always 'in an alien mouth, in alien contexts, in the service of alien intentions'[1] and recommends that 'it must be taken from there and made one's own'[2] or when Lyotard says 'to speak is to fight ... and speech acts fall within the domain of a general agonistics',[3] what they are saying is that women must win back the speech which has been systematically *expelled* or *exorcized* from their bodies since antiquity.

Philomela

The figure of Philomela provides a bloody and therefore even more graphic example of the violence that men practise on women's bodies and words. Tereus, king of Thrace and husband of the Athenian princess Procne, falls in love with Procne's sister, Philomela. He is especially enamoured of her beautiful voice. Instead of bringing her straight to his wife when she comes to visit, he hides her in a hut on the way and rapes her. To stop her telling anyone what has happened, he simply cuts out her tongue. Philomela weaves a message into a robe for her sister. Procne sets the mute woman free, and in revenge slays Itys, the son she bore Tereus, who bears a strong resemblance to his father. She cooks the boy and then serves him up to Tereus to eat.

In an essay written in 1924, J. Flügel describes the close connection between tongue and phallus, speech and sexual power.

> The unconscious equations, speech = sexual power, dumbness = castration or impotence, are clearly shown in the numerous customs connected with the cutting out of tongues. Excision of the tongue would appear to have been practised occasionally as a form of punishment at the same time as there were practised other punishments easily recognizable as castration displacements, such as blinding and the cutting off of hands (as well as castration itself).[4]

These interrelationships rooted in violence, in which silencing means taking away the *right* to speak, as well as the ability, and implies the castration and enforced impotence of women, are illustrated in the story of Philomela. Flügel points to a strong tradition of enforced silence, which principally applies to women. 'A woman's greatest virtue is her silence,' says a Sicilian proverb. 'Nothing is as unnatural as a woman who likes to talk,' says a Scottish one. 'Only silence makes women truly charming,' writes Sophocles in *Ajax*; and German popular wisdom tells us that 'Women who whistle and hens that crow should have their necks wrung without further ado.' Current studies in linguistic pragmatics and feminist linguistics confirm the universal validity of Flügel's findings.

Flügel underlines the fact that Philomela is indeed castrated in the process of mutilation – and this I think is the most exemplary demonstration of the interrelation between silencing and castration – by drawing attention to the punishment of Tereus upon whom the castration is repeated. His son is slain – the son being the symbol of the father's phallic power. The resemblance between father and son is given special emphasis. The son is dismembered: fantasies of dismemberment are also fantasies of castration.

Flügel comes to the conclusion that 'The whole story seems thus to constitute . . . a series of variations on the general theme of castration.'[5] He reminds us of *Titus Andronicus* where, in a similar way, Lavinia, after being raped, has her tongue cut out and her hands chopped off. In addition, the dismembered bodies of her sons are served up to the queen of the Goths, Tamora. These observations also clearly reveal the techniques of *damnatio memoriae*,[6] where the defacement of the statues of disgraced rulers constitutes a castration ritual which is intended not so much to wipe the persons concerned from the public memory as to divest them of their power.

Ovid, who tells the story of Philomela in the sixth book of the *Metamorphoses*, mentions yet another symptomatic detail. According to his version, Tereus raped Philomela several more times and with particular pleasure after he had cut out her tongue. It is this bloody consolidation of power over the silent, helpless body of the other – in this case and almost always the woman's body – which increases Tereus's sexual excitement.

The *Metamorphoses* are full of incidents of rape, mainly perpetrated against virgins, priestesses and fugitives. The obstacles increase the level of violence used; but they also increase that outrageously inflated self-esteem which forms the basis of sexual pleasure for those who have power over others.

When Flügel says, 'a violent sexual assault on a woman may easily be associated unconsciously with the idea of her castration (in the last resort the castration of the mother)',[7] it can be concluded that the ever-present threat of rape hanging over women in patriarchal societies and the speech controls to which they are no less continually subjected are part of a desire to castrate the female which can be seen as the wish to destroy her autonomous individuality and sexuality. Language and sexuality, tongue and gender are the points of intersection between psyche and soma. That is why they are the preferred settings in the drama of the battle of the sexes. Within that drama, the Philomela story is one more variation on the fundamental conflict: the clash of female and male power in a patriarchy.

In Philomela's case, the material conditions of her speech, the speech organs, are mutilated. Compared with other practices used to silence women, this is somewhat ineffective. As it is, Philomela merely requires a different set of signifiers to intimate what has been done to her. She manages to outwit the logocentrist Tereus by using a system of notation which itself is markedly female: her weaving, or *text*, which is the original sense of the word. In a violent context where the spoken word is in the control of the powers-that-be, subversion comes through text, the written word.

Tereus falls victim to his own ideology. He forgets that the woman he thinks he has reduced to nothing more than a sign, a sign of *his* sexuality, is herself a creator of signs, an author. Tereus's view of reality is inadequate because it is distorted by his own self-centred will to power. His view of women is wrong, as is his evaluation of the relationship between speech and reference. The logocentrist viewpoint (the confirmation of the truth and authenticity of what is said by the presence of the speaker) always contains an element of physical violence. The violence lies in a presence in which space is seized, penetrated and incorporated, in short usurped, in speech acts.

Echo

In the story of the nymph Echo we encounter another episode of female mutilation by male power. In the *Metamorphoses* again there is an account of the destruction of Echo's voice by jealous Hera, the goddess of patriarchal marriage. From then on, Echo can only imitate what others say before her. She falls in love with Narcissus, who loves only himself, and when this egomaniac *par excellence* rejects her, refusing to return the image of her ego by feeling desire for her himself, her body turns to stone.

In *Daphnis and Chloe*, Longus offers a more radical variation on the theme of woman withering into silence and the confirmation of male power.[8] Pan, rejected by Echo, is angry at the nymph 'because he envies her her singing and may not enjoy her beauty', as Longus puts it. In other words, he is required to respect her as a subjective being – she will not sleep with him – but, as a subjective being himself, he must immediately envy her, since her transformed status makes her a competitor, a threat to his ego. So he has her torn to pieces by crazed shepherds, upon which echoes rise from the scattered members of her body. Pan completes and surpasses the task of annihilating the female, begun by Hera and Narcissus in the name of male supremacy.

Xanthippe

Xanthippe's speech too is handed down by tradition in a fragmented form. There is no record of her body. The pictorial tradition does not normally extend to the physical aspect of the bodies of wives and mothers. The only type of female body which is put on display is the sexualized body, which falls within the sphere of influence of the phallus. It is the body which still denotes resistance, which has not yet given up its mystery, which gives a narcissistic boost to the male ego in the act of discovery and appropriation.

Xanthippe's body is already the battlefield of what men have imputed to it in writing and has disappeared amid these scrawlings. Only her voice comes down to us, her shrill voice. In her book *Thinking about Women*, Mary Ellmann describes a rhetorical trick of male criticism of texts by women: whatever these men do not like about the texts they describe as 'shrill', especially when they sense signs of female rebellion behind it.[9] It is precisely because this reproach, when levelled against the written medium, has a comic effect, that one recognizes it all the more readily when it is levelled against the spoken word. Here the purely acoustic difference between the female and male speech organs is conflated with the content of the utterance, and through such overemphasis on the expressive form what is actually expressed, the content, is completely obscured.

From the male point of view, Xanthippe and Socrates are the epitome of the classic arguing couple. He is the great sophist and maieutic philosopher, she the shrew, the opinionated, quarrelsome hysteric. This negative evaluation of female argumentation is one of the most effective means of cutting off the speech of women. The real target here is the phenomenon of *contradiction*. Whenever we encounter hierarchies of power, subordination and codes of obedience, we find that contradiction from the lower ranks is excluded. In the process of contradiction an individual will assumes that it has equal rights and is free. Children, pupils, servants, soldiers, prisoners, slaves, members of the lower orders, petty officials, employees and women: they are not to argue, for they are not to contradict.

Xanthippe is a woman who contradicted her husband, one of the greatest talkers of Western civilization. The means by which her voice is silenced in the collective memory is more subtle than the brute force employed by mythical figures. It is a means more appropriate to the refined customs of a culture centred upon language and its trustees, the philosophers, philologists, psychologists, hermeneuticists, theoreticians and historians.

The main focus of Xanthippe's speech is shifted away from the arena of criticism and rationality (which is reserved for men) into the sphere of psychological pathology – the traditional stamping-ground of female figures. The female critic becomes a grouse, the woman who sticks to her guns is labelled insane. This strategy of reducing what is said to the way it is said, the process of restricting a referential utterance to the expressive dimension, has remained the most effective method of castrating female speech to this day.

Cassandra

What has been said about Xanthippe is even truer of Cassandra. For in this case a female figure establishes her linguistic sphere not in private life but in public. Apollo had bestowed the gift of prophecy upon the Trojan princess on the condition that she sleep with him. Cassandra would thus have been promoted to the status of a public figure, a seer. According to an older version of the myth, however, both Cassandra and her twin brother Helenos were born with this power. The later version asserts that Cassandra must earn by high-class prostitution that which is given to Helenos as a man for nothing. Women who want to get on in their professional lives are not unfamiliar with this phenomenon.

The Trojan woman refuses to pay this price, so Apollo punishes her. But he does not simply take away the gift of prophecy. Far worse than this, he robs her of the power to convince others, leaving his victim forever torn between subjective and objective reality. This is the classic picture of hysteria and insanity, which are both meant to signify the split between the logic of the patient's personal world and the logic of her social environment.

Apollo here represents the male usurpation of the public sphere, which is denied to woman. She is held to embody the private sphere, and therefore is excluded from the public world. Indeed, public life is such *because* women are removed from it. Women do not simply *exist within* the private sphere; they *are* the private sphere. To move from there into the public sphere would not only constitute a blurring of demarcation lines but would also make it impossible to distinguish the division between reality and sign. Women would become more fully alive. It would be a return from their representational status as the private sphere to the presence of public life.

Women who displace these demarcation lines are deemed insane. Cassandra's speech, which uncharacteristically deals with affairs of state and war, in short with men's affairs, is made to appear nonsensical. Xanthippe brings aspects of public speech, that which is reserved for men who enjoy certain rights, into the private sphere: logic, argument, dialogue. Cassandra imbues the public code of heroism, war-mongering and depredation with private motives: peaceableness, fear of violence and death, anti-heroism. For, as Helene Foley writes in 'Sex and state in ancient Greece', 'left to himself the male will destroy his domestic life in the name of military glory'.[10]

Cassandra's ambiguous position between two spheres makes her sensitive to transgressions. In Troy, these are the intrusions of the outside upon the inside, of foreign bodies filled with brutality upon the internal sphere of women and children. The seer gives an accurate warning against the return of once-banished Paris to Troy, against the arrival of Helen from Sparta and against bringing the Wooden Horse inside the walls of Troy. Later in

Mycenae, she alone knows that her transition from outside to inside, her entry into the fortress of Agamemnon, spells death for her.

The offence Cassandra has committed as a *female* seer is to undermine the male discourse of power with a woman's voice and with her life-saving critique of the deadly narcissism that lies behind the ideologies of honour and fame. As Phyllis Chesler writes, 'it is clear that for a woman to be healthy she must adjust to and accept the behavioral norms for her sex, even though these kinds of behavior are generally regarded as less socially desirable ... The ethic of mental health is masculine in our culture.'[11]

By being deemed insane, Cassandra is robbed of the most important component of her speech as a communicative act: its performative force. This combination of speech deprivation and psychological anguish is well expressed in the German word *Entmündigung*, which corresponds to the English legal term, incapacitation. In Xanthippe's case, there is merely an attempt to shift the focus of her speech on to the means of its expression in order to obscure the content of what she says. It is precisely the deliberate occlusion of this content which serves as proof of its unimpaired validity. In the case of Cassandra, on the other hand, the content itself becomes the evidence of insanity. Thus there is no longer a differential aspect within the speech act from which it can be made clear that the loss of the criteria of validity results from a violent distortion from outside.

The linguistic dehumanization of the prophetess is accompanied by the control and domination of her body. It is not only possible to plot the stages of her degeneration temporally through her successive connections with Apollo, Ajax and Agamemnon. The dramatic monologue *Alexandra* (= *Cassandra*) by the Alexandrian poet Lycophron, dating from the third century BC, presents us with an arrangement in which the destructions of Cassandra are gathered in a synchronic plane. She is shut in a cave, in the dark. Her body has as good as disappeared, rendered motionless and invisible. Only her voice can still be heard. She prophesies the destruction of Troy, the suffering of the Greeks, the conflicts which will rage between Asia and Europe before settlement is reached. This monologue is heard by no one. Only Priam himself has been secretly informed by the guard of what his daughter predicts, and thus reveals the duplicity of political power in the field of ideology.

The graphic split within Cassandra, between voice and body, and between wisdom and madness, is reproduced by cultural tradition even today. The Cassandra figure crops up in two separate areas, either as a voice in text or as a body in pictures. But it is a voice and an image within the bounds of male appropriation and control. The voice is fragmented, the body shot through with sexuality to appeal to male eyes and hands. Thus Cassandra is entered into the traditional register of female representation. Full female voices, such as those of the Sphinx, the Sirens and Sappho, or

Plate 1 In this early picture on an Attic amphora from the sixth century BC we can recognize on the left side Ajax who threatens Cassandra in the centre. She is sheltered by the goddess Athene who is holding the Aegis (the famous shield of Zeus with the emblem of the Gorgon) above her body. (British Museum, London)

a sight which repels male sexuality, such as that of Medusa, are banished by the dominant cultural discourse into the shadowy realm of the abnormal and inhuman. The fact that the woman in the world of patriarchy is never a full voice, indeed not a voice at all but always a sexualized body – Helen of Troy is a prime example – is apparent in the following paradox. In the textual tradition Cassandra is dominant principally as a voice. So much so that even today men use this pseudonym. Journalists and feature-writers have adopted the name in anticipation of their supposedly wise predictions proving unpopular. Yet in the pictorial tradition of antiquity, Cassandra is shown more often than not in the proto-pornographic scene when she is raped by Ajax in the temple of Athene.

Of all the depictions which have come down to us, only eight show Cassandra giving prophecies, eight depict the scene with the Wooden Horse, twenty-three portray the confrontation with Paris. Seventeen show Apollo taking away her power to convince others and four represent her being killed by Clytemnestra. But there is a total of 105 showing her being raped by Ajax.[12] The publishers Luchterhand are an example of the fact that not much has changed since then. Although in the popular wisdom of our time Cassandra is known almost exclusively as a voice – everyone knows that a

Plate 2   This scene on a vase from the fourth century BC shows a transitional arrangement of figures. In the centre, Cassandra is clinging for help to an effigy of the goddess Athene, while at the same time Athene appears in person on the left side of the picture. On the right side, Ajax is seizing Cassandra by the hair. A second priestess is fleeing on the far right. (Fitzwilliam Museum, University of Cambridge)

Cassandra is a prophet of doom and gloom, but who knows who Ajax is? – the rape scene was chosen as the cover picture for Christa Wolf's text *Voraussetzungen einer Erzählung: Kassandra*.[13] Furthermore, of the 105 pictures available, it is the most explicit. Juliette Davreux highlights the pornographic function:

> As we know, it is very rare in the art of the sixth or the fifth centuries BC for women to appear unclothed ... Cassandra's nakedness is significant: it indicates that the scene taking place in Athene's temple has all the characteristics of an erotic spectacle.[14]

Plate 3 Here we have the most naked representation of the scene of rape which was chosen by Luchterhand publishers for Christa Wolf's book *Voraussetzungen einer Erzählung. Kassandra*. It is depicted on an Attic bowl from the fifth century BC. (Louvre, Paris)

Since the middle of the nineteenth century, however, women have been claiming Cassandra for themselves. Unlike men, who tend to associate themselves with the exclusive tradition of the prophets or apocryphal truth, women expose the practices of subordination which are linked to the name. In this way, two things are achieved. Women place their own disadvantaged and oppressed situation within the context of a history dating back to early antiquity. At the same time, they bring about this historical revelation by making the silenced mouths and bodies speak again. In so doing they are following the historical dynamics described by Walter Benjamin: 'There is a secret agreement between past generations and the present one. We have been awaited on earth. As with every generation preceding us, we are given a slight Messianic power which the past has a right to.'[15]

In 1852 Florence Nightingale, herself a famous victim of misogynist propaganda ('the angel in the house' or 'the lady with the lamp'), wrote a searing manifesto against the Victorian treatment of women as infantile beings. She ominously entitled it *Cassandra*.[16] She showed it to her friends John Stuart Mill and Benjamin Jowett (the latter then Regius Professor of Greek at Oxford and from 1870 Master of Balliol College), to find out what they thought of it. Both men advised against publication. The manuscript remained unpublished.

Only the revolt of women in the twentieth century against the silence imposed on them for thousands of years, and the accompanying new knowledge which strives to overcome the old androcentric superstitions, are finally throwing light upon the dark continent of female pasts. Benjamin talks of the angel of history.[17] In the face of the historical catastrophe known as progress, which piles ruins upon ruins and throws them down at his feet, the angel would like to stop, wake the dead, and rebuild what has been smashed. It is just this sort of reconstruction that Christa Wolf has undertaken in her ground-breaking novel *Kassandra*. In this twentieth-century poet's restoration of the Bronze Age prophetess's tongue and voice, we have the first successful attempt in the history of the Cassandra myth to gather the fragmented pieces of her body and her speech together and make her whole again.

NOTES

1   Mikhail M. Bakhtin, *The Dialogic Imagination: Four Essays*, ed. Michael Holquist (University of Texas Press, Austin, 1981), p. 294.
2   Ibid.
3   Jean-François Lyotard, *La condition postmoderne: Rapport sur le savoir* (Minuit, Paris, 1979); tr. Geoff Bennington and Brian Massumi, *The Postmodern Condition: A Report on Knowledge* (Manchester University Press, Manchester, 1984), p. 10.

4 J. C. Flügel, 'A note on the phallic significance of the tongue and speech', *International Journal of Psychoanalysis*, 6, 2 (1925), pp. 209–15, esp. p. 210.

5 Ibid., p. 215.

6 See Thomas Pékary, *Das römische Kaiserbildnis in Staat, Kult und Gesellschaft* (Gebr. Mann, Berlin, 1985), esp. ch. 9, 'Damnatio memoriae und spontane Statuenvernichtung'.

7 Flügel, 'Phallic significance of the tongue' p. 215.

8 Longus, *Daphnis and Chloe*, book 3, ch. 23.

9 Mary Ellmann, *Thinking about Women* (Harcourt Brace Jovanovich, New York, 1968), pp. 149–50.

10 Helene Foley, 'Sex and state in ancient Greece', *Diacritics*, 5 (1975), pp. 31–6, esp. p. 36.

11 Phyllis Chesler, *Women and Madness* (Avon Books, New York, 1973), pp. 68–9.

12 Juliette Davreux, *La légende de la prophétesse Cassandre d'après les textes et les monuments* (Droz, Paris, 1942), pt 2: 'La tradition artistique', pp. 102–223.

13 Christa Wolf's work on Cassandra consists of two different books: her novel *Kassandra* and *Voraussetzungen einer Erzählung: Kassandra*, a metanarrative about the details on various levels of experience which informed the production of the novel. Both were published by Luchterhand, Darmstadt and Neuwied, 1983.

14 Davreux, *Cassandre*, pp. 140–1.

15 Walter Benjamin, 'Über den Begriff der Geschichte', in *Gesammelte Schriften*, ed. Rolf Tiedemann and Hermann Schweppenhäuser (Suhrkamp, Frankfurt/M., 1972–89), vol. 1. 2 (1974), pp. 693–4, tr. 'Theses on the philosophy of history', in Walter Benjamin, *Illuminations*, ed. Hannah Arendt (Collins/Fontana Books, London, 1973), pp. 255–66, esp. p. 256.

16 Florence Nightingale, *Cassandra*, in *The Cause*, ed. Ray Strachey (Virago Press, London, 1978), app. I, pp. 395–418. The work had previously appeared in Florence Nightingale's book *Suggestions for Thought in Searchers after Religious Truth*, pt II: 'Practical deductions', privately printed in 1859.

17 Benjamin, 'Über den Begriff der Geschichte', pp. 697–8 'Theses on the philosophy of history', pp. 259–60 (see ch. 1 n. 6 above).

4

Female Reason and Symbolic Violence

When Prince Albert was approving the designs for the new Parliament in 1849, he proposed that the classical sculptor John Gibson make a small but symptomatic alteration. On either side of the throne on which Queen Victoria was to sit, Gibson had placed the 6-foot allegorical statues of Justice and Wisdom. Albert proposed that Wisdom should be replaced by Charity for, as he put it: the sovereign is a lady. The Prince's correction was yet another display of the precarious relationship in Western history between femininity and reason.[1]

We know from our daily practice, of course, that women have no problems with reason in everyday life. If women's actions did not exhibit the same capacity for reason as men's do, coexistence would be impossible. At the same time, this very rationality has come under suspicion for being instrumental, for appearing to legitimize the structures of domination from which Western societies cobble together their patriarchal identity. That is, women's insistence on their share of reason seems to set the seal on social discrimination against them. Women find themselves in a classic double bind. If they lay claim to reason for themselves, they will seem to be promoting their own oppression. If they criticize this notion of reason, the only space left to them is the traditionally female one: the irrational space of madness, intuition, emotionality, the soul, gentleness and charity.

The evaluation of this area of so-called non-reason or anti-reason, which a section of the women's movement employs as a critical space uncolonized by male versions of reason, nevertheless remains bound within a binary scheme. Even the most advanced positions in the field of practical reason which, following the works of Dorothy Dinnerstein, Carol Gilligan and Nancy Chodorow,[2] play off female modes of ethical reason against deficient male modes, finally risk confirming the traditional opposition of cold autonomy versus warm relationality. This is especially apparent in the work of Carol Gilligan, in which women finally rediscover their ethical place in the realm of nurture. In contrast, Seyla Benhabib has built in a safeguard against a vulgarizing reception of her theory of the 'general' and 'concrete' other. Warning against simply reversing values while maintaining the original polarized scheme, she writes:

> The distinction between the 'generalized' and the 'concrete' other . . . is not a *prescriptive* but a *critical* one. My goal is not to prescribe a moral and political theory consonant with the concept of the 'concrete other'. For, indeed, the recognition of the dignity and worthiness of the generalized other is a *necessary*, albeit not *sufficient*, condition to define the moral standpoint in modern societies. In this sense, the concrete other is a critical concept that designates the *ideological* limits of universalistic discourse. It signifies the *unthought*, the *unseen*, the *unheard* in such theories.[3]

The stability of binary oppositions such as this, and their intransigence in the face of all attacks on them, derives from their ideological status. That is, they are forms of language and thought that influence reality in such a way that they are experienced in real life. This real experience serves to maintain the power of binary conceptualization, and this in turn repeatedly feeds back into social experience.

Certainly the vicious ideological circle does not work quite so smoothly as it might appear. Its efficacy needs to be supported with force, and the transparency of such force in moments of crisis testifies to the ideological character of the circle, and hence of its function in the maintenance of political domination. For this reason, criticism of the oppositions should not simply stop at the reversal of their evaluations, which must be deconstructed in the Derridean sense. This can be accomplished in various ways. We might show, for example, that these oppositions are in fact nothing of the kind, but rather artificial polarizations which, once we approach them from a different angle, merge with one another, and merge most strongly at the point where their separation seems most complete. We might also expose the historical and social force necessary for their maintenance, and hence foreground their artificiality. And we might expose the dominant interest inscribed within these mechanisms.

Feminist research has shown how women were excluded from the areas in which reason was produced. Two strategies were prominent in this process, and in the example of the story about Prince Albert they are clearly interrelated.

First: women were physically forbidden access to those places and institutions whose practices were involved to a particularly strong degree with the discourses of reason. In the case of the Queen and her privileged access to the public political arena, an older, aristocratic principle of the blood is operating against the backdrop of parliamentary democracy. The aristocratic model of the representational public sphere can transcend the inequality of the sexes that is inscribed within the model of bourgeois, parliamentary life by its separation from the private arena, which is marked off as female.

The Prince nevertheless managed to separate the body of the Queen from the body of Reason. Instead of the Queen he banished the allegory of Wisdom from the political stage. In everyday life, on the other hand, the doors of the universities, parliaments, theatres, churches and offices remained firmly closed to women. If we consider the history of the opening of these doors, the process took longest where the apprenticeship in reason lasted longest: in science, law, mathematics and philosophy. Thus, in the Middle Ages, for example, girls taught at home were deprived of access to knowledge through the Latin language, which separated the domestic and public domains of education.

Together with institutional coercion the second significant strategy for barring women's entrance into the halls of reason is the use of symbolic force. This too appears in the story about the Prince.

Symbolic force operates by first personifying abstractions and subsequently universalizing them. We can, as a result, speak of *reason* as such, and weave world-historical narratives about the epic of progress or the epic of the decline of the Enlightenment. And we can also encode abstractions like these metaphorically within the male/female framework. This opposition describes not only a biological difference, but crucially a cultural relation of dominance, and can thus, through its metaphorical application, inflate all linguistic differences into a power-laden opposition. In terms of the history of the concept of reason, this means that in all cases where the concepts of mind and matter are constructed within a relationship of domination they are encoded as male or female. As thinking about mind always presupposes mind, and is chiefly practised by men, it is no surprise that the transcendence of body by mind became a *male* principle.

In her book *The Man of Reason*, Geneviève Lloyd follows this pattern through the history of Western philosophy: from Plato and Aristotle, through Augustine, Aquinas, Descartes, Rousseau, Kant and Hegel up to Sartre and Simone de Beauvoir. She reaches the conclusion:

> It is not a question simply of the applicability to women of neutrally specified ideas of rationality, but rather of the genderization of the ideals themselves. An exclusion or transcending of the feminine is built into past ideals of Reason

as the sovereign human character trait and correlatively ... the content of femininity has been partly formed by such processes of exclusion.[4]

Lloyd also criticizes de Beauvoir for the same reason. In Lloyd's view, in order to remain faithful to the Hegelian ideal of transcendence she derived from Sartre, de Beauvoir had to suppress the female body as the thing to be transcended.

> 'Transcendence' in its origins, is a transcendence *of* the feminine. In its Hegelian version, this is a matter of breaking away from the nether world of women. In its Sartrean version, it is associated with a repudiation of what is supposedly signified by the female body, the 'holes' and 'slime' which threaten to engulf free subjecthood. It is as if, in the lack of a Hegelian nether world, all that is left for subjecthood to transcend is the female body itself. In both cases of course, it is only from a male perspective that the feminine can be seen as what must be transcended. But the male perspective has left its marks on the very concepts of 'transcendence' and 'immanence' ... This is what makes the ideal of a feminine attainment of transcendence paradoxical.[5]

But in that case, why is the allegorical figure of Wisdom female? Here we have a kind of bastardized sign. It represents both the once natural superiority of female knowledge and female speech rooted in women's power of reproduction and the violent appropriation of that knowledge by man. The medieval allegory of lady Wisdom is a copy of the Roman Minerva and her antecedent, the Greek Athene. Athene is already the product of the male power of reproduction, the virgin birth from the head of Zeus, the father of the gods. Nevertheless, Athene has a mother, the goddess Metis, literally 'cleverness' or 'good advice'. According to Hesiod's *Theogony*,[6] she is Zeus' first wife, and when she is pregnant with Athene, Zeus swallows her. Lines 886–98 of the *Theogony* say that, by means of this incorporation, Zeus wished to prevent the prophesied birth of a son who would be superior to him, after the birth of his equal, Athene. Line 899 says, on the other hand, that he swallowed Metis so that she would tell him of 'good and evil' things. The two reasons are not exclusive, but complementary in the light of a patriarchal creation of meaning. While the god annexes the power of reproduction and omniscience, he can also prevent the Oedipal threat of a future son, but, by means of Oedipal desire, bind the eternally virgin daughter to the principle of male predominance.

A very similar story is told of the Muses and their mother Mnemosyne. The Muses too are virgins, and after their birth they immediately set off to see their father Zeus. They assume the power of memory from their mother, who disappears from the *Theogony* story immediately after giving birth to them. From then on, however, the daughters place their gift primarily at the service of the glorification of their father Zeus. While Athene and the

Muses thus personify the effectiveness of the *logos*, they site it in the sphere of the male through their paternal descent, their virgin state and the consequently subliminal – through Oedipal desire – sexuality of their inspiration.

So although we know purely from experience and everyday life that women are not less reasonable beings than men, the theorizations of this knowledge and consequently its communication to the collective cultural memory runs into the barriers of institutional and symbolic violence. They are the same barriers that mark the difference between public and private. Nancy Fraser in particular has pointed out that the terms 'public' and 'private' are by no means as neutral as they appear.[7] Rather they reproduce, by their real but unconscious identification with the positions of male and female, the relationship of dominance between men and women. If we consider once more the institutions which were particularly connected with the concepts and procedures of reason, and to which women had access either with difficulty or not at all, we shall see that these are the institutions which constitute the public sphere from the very beginning. So it is not only in the symbolic sphere that the scope of 'reason' is secured by excluding the feminine; in precisely the same way the public sphere comes only about via the institutions of reason and its control of access – through absence of women.

In public institutions another factor becomes apparent which separates women from the practices of reason: the manifestation of the rational as language.

In *Being and Time*, Heidegger defines the ontological connection between reason and speech as follows:

> If we say that the basic signification of *logos* is 'discourse' [*Rede*], then this word-for-word translation will not be validated until we have determined what is meant by 'discourse' itself. The real signification of *logos*, 'discourse', which is obvious enough, gets constantly covered up by the later history of the word *logos*, and especially by the numerous and arbitrary interpretations which subsequent philosophy has provided. *Logos* gets 'translated' (and this means that it is always getting interpreted) as 'reason', 'judgment', 'concept', 'definition', 'ground' or 'relationship'. But how can 'discourse' be so susceptible of modification that *logos* can signify all the things we have listed, and in good scholarly usage? ... *Logos* as 'discourse' means rather the same as *dēloun*: to make manifest what one is 'talking about' in one's discourse ... The *logos* lets something be seen (*dēloun*), namely, what the discourse is about; and it does so either *for* the one who is doing the talking ... or for persons who are talking with one another, as the case may be. Discourse 'lets something be seen' (*apo*) ... that is, it lets us see something from the very thing which the discourse is about. In 'discourse' (*apophansis*), so far as it is genuine, *what* is said is drawn *from* what the talk is about, so that discursive

communication in what it says makes manifest what it is talking about, and thus makes this accessible to the other party. This is the structure of *logos* as *apophansis* . . . When fully concrete, discoursing (letting something be seen) has the character of speaking – vocal proclamation in words. The *logos* is *phonē*, and, indeed *phonē meta phantasis* – an utterance in which something is sighted in each case . . . And because the function of the *logos* lies in merely letting something be seen, in *letting* entitles be *perceived*, can *logos* signify the *reason*.[8]

What is important for our argument in Heidegger's development of the concept of *logos* is the necessary association of knowledge, conceived as the revelation of something to be seen, with speaking as communication. This embryonic model of reason as linguistic intersubjectivity, becomes a fully fledged theory of communicative reason in the work of Habermas.

The connection between speaking and reason has disappeared from the contemporary use of the German word *Rede* ('speech') but still exists in the Dutch term of *rede* ('reason'), in the English *reason* and *to reason* and in the French *raison* and *raisonner*.

We know from Habermas's theory that one of the necessary conditions of successful communication is the absence of pressure or coercion. But this very absence of force, of compulsion and control, is something that women, when they speak, cannot presuppose. This holds for both the public *and* the private spheres. It is not only that the dominance of men is documented and maintained by the public/private opposition: male domination actually disfigures the private sphere in such a way that the energy which sustains that opposition is fuelled by this very act of distortion. The two spheres only differ in the nature of exclusion, not in the fact of exclusion as such. Whereas in the public sphere everyone present is allowed to speak, but not everyone is present, in the private sphere everyone is present, but not everyone is allowed to speak. There has been substantial research into this problem. In 'The Castration of Cassandra' I have suggested that communicative force against women ultimately relies on the threat of physical force.[9]

If we agree with Habermas when he says: 'The individuating effect of the linguistically communicated socialization process derives from the linguistic medium itself',[10] then women are systematically hindered in their individuation, and hence in the training of their reason, by the prohibitions on speech. In order to illuminate how force regulates gender-specific access to the institutions of public reason, symbolic reproduction and the discourses involved in them, I should like to consider two episodes from the social and dramatic history of our cultural identity: the phenomenon of 'shell-shock' in the First World War, and Euripides' tragedy *Medea*.

In *The Female Malady*, Elaine Showalter examines the social causes for the massive manifestation of female hysteria in Victorian England. It is therefore ironic that it was Prince Albert himself who divided the body of

Queen Victoria from the body of Wisdom. For the division of the bodies visibly reflects the separations and disjunctions, the disabling and deprivations inflicted by female socialization in the nineteenth century. In hysteria, the body itself, in its psychosomatic wholeness, becomes a substitute semiotic system, once the individual has been deprived of access to language, reason and action.

From this point of view of gender theory, female mass hysteria in the Victorian age tells the story of the incarceration of woman in a maternally demarcated, relational, symbiotic area of subjectivity; it tells of the amputation of her self and her autonomy. Without the aid of gender theory, hysterical phenomena run the risk of becoming hypostatized. In a patriarchal interpretation they turn into the anthropological constants of the feminine in general, as the etymology of the word 'hysterical' indicates; while a radical feminist interpretation elevates them to the sign of an alternative feminine potential. But this deployment as the critique of a closed male rationality can easily slide into the glorification of real madness.

The reading invited by gender theory, which alone shows the defect to be the result of socializing coercion, is impressively substantiated by Showalter's analysis of male 'shell-shock'. Just as female hysteria is a reaction to the irreconcilable conflict between the desire for autonomy and a socially imposed inarticulacy, so 'shell-shock' is revealed as male hysteria in the face of the absolute impotence of the subject in the trenches of Flanders and France. The helplessness of the soldiers confronted with the threat of death from an overpowering machinery of destruction, symbolized in the exploding grenade suddenly thrown from nowhere, leads to flight into shock.

The syndrome of hysteria is expressed in the breakdown of the masquerades of male narcissism, such as honour, duty, bravery, fame and toughness, all of which result from a grotesque overdevelopment of autonomy at the expense of the capacity for relationship. Showalter comes to this conclusion:

> We can ... see now that shell shock was related to social expectations of the masculine role in war. The Great War was a crisis in masculinity and a trial for the Victorian masculine ideal. In a sense, the long-term repression of signs of fear that led to shell shock in war was only an exaggeration of the male sex-role expectations, the self-control and emotional disguise of civilian life ... Both men and officers had internalized these expectations as thoroughly as any Victorian woman had internalized her lesson about feminine nature. When all signs of physical fear were judged as weakness and where alternatives to combat – pacifism, conscientious objection, desertion, even suicide – were viewed as unmanly, men were silenced and immobilized and forced, like women, to express their conflicts through the body.[11]

The similarity to female hysteria, the documented fragility of the male gender role was something that could be recognized neither officially nor, in most cases, privately by the victims themselves. In political terms, the mass phenomenon of male hysteria would have meant a serious threat to morale on the field. In private it was felt to be emasculating, and many cases of shell-shock were directly connected with impotence. For this reason, the euphemistic term 'shell-shock' evokes the rigorous exactions of war, concealing its real meaning, the threat of feminization.

The authorities' intuitive recognition that shell-shock was a critique of the war, the protest of the unconscious against patriarchal values, provoked the same brutal treatment as English psychiatry had already used in dealing with female hysteria, where the resistance of the women affected to the female role forced upon them had been no less apparent. Methods of healing were, for that reason, more like acts of punishment. What were to be punished were symptoms whose appearance meant that madness and reason could no longer be neatly divided between categories of female and male. 'The Great War was the first and, so far, the last time in the twentieth century that men and the wrongs of men occupied a central position in the history of madness.'[12]

If that which is excluded powerfully emerges in the dead centre of an exclusion zone, then in Freud's language we speak of the 'return of the repressed' or the phenomenon of the uncanny, or, in the language of deconstruction, of the breakdown of binary schemata. Just as the repressed dimension of fear emerges at the core of male rationality under the most extreme conditions, so in *Medea*, Euripides stages the explosion of female speech and female reason right at the heart of male exclusiveness.

Drama is the most public literary genre, and the theatre itself is one of the major institutions of public life. If the dramatic text brings the voices of female characters on to the stage, then women begin to speak precisely where they are excluded. In the Greek drama this intrusion of female speech is at its most radical. Pericles' dictum that the best woman is she who not only does not speak but does not get herself spoken about, or the fact that in legal matters the *polis* could often barely establish whether a particular woman existed at all, make the terror of a figure like Medea entirely comprehensible.

Medea is the story of a woman who escapes social death by making extreme sacrifices. She must violently sever her matrimonial, maternal and family ties in order to recover the independence necessary for her social survival.

Here is a summary of the story: Medea, the daughter of the king of Colchis, falls in love with the Greek Jason, and helps him, against her own father, to bring the Golden Fleece back to Greece. To make her flight possible, she kills her brother. As Jason's hereditary throne has been usurped, they find fit exile with Creon, the king of Corinth. In order to return to political power himself, Jason wants to marry Creon's daughter and rejects Medea. Creon banishes Medea, fearing her revenge. But Medea, after becoming a citizen within the *polis* of Athens, destroys Creon and his daughter and her own sons by Jason. Her action is justified by Jason's violation of an oath. All of Medea's acts of violence can be read as a mirror-image of the force to which she has always been subjected. The degree of force necessary for her liberation is equivalent to the force required for the original oppression.

Not only does Medea speak before an audience made up solely of men, not only does she speak through the mouth of a male actor, but she speaks from the very centre of the patriarchal public arena. The stage and the orchestra, where the chorus and the actors performed in the fifth century BC, lay within the holy grounds of the temple, and right behind the stage itself was the Temple of Dionysus. At the time of Lenea and Eleutheria, when the dramas were performed, the tributes from the Athenian confeder-ates were piled up in the orchestra, while their envoys likewise sat among the spectators. The orchestra was the former holy circle, the place where, when the drama was still performed in the old *agora*, the trials and parliaments were also held. In this respect the orchestra is the incarnation of the public sphere. It is the stage of religion, of politics, of law, commerce and art. It is precisely here that Medea's speech annihilates the constraining binary structure of *oikos* and *polis*. The identity of the *polis* is marked off from the outside world of the barbarians and the internal realm of the female-occupied *oikos*. Through Medea, the woman and barbarian from Colchis, the forces of exclusion *in* the text destroy the *polis* of Corinth and, as a speech act beyond the text, invade the *polis* of Athens.

Medea speaks in a way that is neither mad nor barbaric. In the *agon*, the skilful dispute in thesis and counter-thesis of the protagonists, she reveals the most advanced techniques of dialectic and rhetoric. Her argument is so logical that her *agon* with Jason attains the performative power of a legal dispute. Like Antigone against Creon or the Erinnyes against Apollo and Orestes, Medea also founds her case in a specific way. But unlike her dramatic precursors she emerges victorious from her verbal duels. Her dialogical reasoning, her heroic temperament and her bloody acts of vengeance, to which her own children fall victim, are finally justified in a utopian, fairy-tale manner by the Euripidean convention of the *deus ex machina*.

Medea's power of reason is confirmed in two ways. She is the epitome of a rational being by the very fact that she engages in dialogue. Beyond this she is the representative of a particular form of practical reason, an ethics which proves superior in her *agon* with Jason. The impact of different models of practical reason always presupposes the unity of a pre-existing communicative reason. Communicative reason, on the other hand, develops only in the debate through the possibility of dissent by negation and consequently, in the end, by the destruction of symbiosis.

Medea shows that drama, as a textual genre and a performing practice, is a direct attack on the prohibition of reason and speech for women. Here women are permitted to speak in a way that is, in reality, only permitted to men. The dramatic text revolves round a conflict verbally expressed in dispute, in argument, in polemic. In the tragedy this conflict is insoluble within the framework of conditions which the tragedy reveals as the cause of its catastrophic events. One party in the dispute loses. But the dispute itself is an *agon*, that is, a dispute with a winner. The character with the better arguments is the victor. The same communicative structure lies at the heart of the legal dispute. Indeed, the theatrical *agon* is often an actual legal dispute culminating in a judgement, with the spectator numbered among the judges along with the characters in the drama. The relation between the judging viewer and the judging protagonist is most clearly expressed in the figure of the Greek chorus, which reflects the society of the *polis*, and in the fact that the performance itself took place at the site of real legal disputes in the life of the *polis*.

The coincidence of personal conflict and public legal case can be demon-strated most impressively where, by the rules of decorum, the noble charac-ters – kings and queens, heroes and gods – appear. Every private dispute becomes a legal precedent by virtue of the public sphere embodied in the antagonists themselves. This is the case not only with Greek drama where the *deus ex machina* is almost always a judging deity but also in classical French and German drama, as well as many of Shakespeare's tragedies (*Oresteia, Antigone, Oedipus, Phèdre, Le Cid, Iphigenie, King Lear, Mac-beth, The Merchant of Venice, The Winter's Tale, Egmont, Don Carlos*, etc.). In bourgeois drama, with the loss of the hero's power to represent the public sphere, the conflict is often displaced into an actual, potential or previous legal case (as for example in *The Doll's House, The Dance of Death, The Broken Jug, The Wild Duck, John Gabriel Borkmann, The Rats, The Caucasian Chalk Circle, Prinz Friedrich von Homburg, Woyzeck, Danton's Death*, etc.).

In drama the female voice is given the power to say 'no', to contradict, to argue, to fight, to judge and to pass sentence. Ironically, the female protagonists achieve autonomy and power at the very point in history where women themselves are banished from the stage. It is as if the fact of male actors ruling the stage extended the definition of femininity in the text. This comes to light not only in the work of the Greeks, but also in Shakespeare and particularly in his comedies. By the reversal of gender roles made possible by the use of boy actors, and exploited in countless plots involving the exchanging of clothing, the female characters acquire hitherto undreamt bravado of verbal wit and dynamic power. At the same time the dissolution of rigid gender roles injects the male performers with a healthy dose of femininity.

For this reason, conservative cultural philosophers have always attempted to neutralize the subversive potential of dramatic practice. Plato himself realizes that on the stage, through the sound of real voices and the presence of living bodies, the borderlines between reality and fiction are blurred. For this reason he makes a clear distinction between lyric and epic poetry on the one hand and dramatic poetry on the other. The latter is the more dangerous, for it can influence both the players themselves through the playing of roles (an argument which Brecht will later employ positively) and the spectators through a representation by presence in which the signifiers are bodies. In the third book of the *Republic*, concerning education, the guardians of the *polis* should not embody unworthy roles, 'for we soon reap the fruits of imitation in life, and imitation, if continued without interruption from childhood onwards, leaves its mark, affecting the body, the voice and the mind'. They should therefore represent neither slaves nor labourers nor elements of nature but, most important of all, not women.

> Since then we care for the moral welfare of our guardians, we will not allow them to take the parts of women, young or old (for they are men), nor to represent them abusing their husbands or presumptuously quarrelling with heaven, when they imagine themselves happy, or crying and complaining in misfortune. Far less can we permit representation of women in sickness or love or child-birth.[13]

This was the argument subsequently used by the Puritans against the representation of female roles by boy actors, which they feared might promote male homosexuality.[14] But it was above all Rousseau, in his *Letter to d'Alembert on the Theatre*, who singled out for attack the powers of the drama, which he saw as destructive for an established social order.

> Love is the realm of women ... A natural effect of plays of this kind is therefore to extend the empire of the female sex, to make women and girls the tutors of the public, and to give them the same power over the public that they have over their lovers. Do you think, Sir, that this order is free of disadvantages, and that in so carefully increasing the influence of women men will be better governed? There may exist in the world some women worthy of being listened to by an honest man; but should he, generally speaking, take advice from them, and is there no means of honouring their sex without debasing our own?[15]

Thus even the Greek heroes lament their dependence on women, not of course because of love, but because of their reproductive power. On the other hand Rousseau again refers positively to the subservient role of women in the *polis*. 'The motto in those days was that the country with the purest morals was the one where women were least spoken of; and that the most honest woman was the one spoken of least.' He then proceeds to criticize women's ability to speak in his own time, and therefore, with reference to female reason and female speech, makes a devastating critique of dramatic practice:

> On the stage it is even worse. They basically know nothing in the world, although they judge everything; but in the theatre they are skilled in the sciences of men, philosophers, thanks to the authors, they put our sex in the shade with their own talents ... Go through most modern plays: it is always a woman who knows everything, who teaches men everything ... The nurse is on the stage and the children are in the stalls.[16]

It is symptomatic that Rousseau feels obliged, in a little footnote, to exempt Greek tragedy from this accusation. He sees the parallels very clearly, but must, in the case of his idealized Greeks, excuse them for the dominance of their stage heroines by referring to the rules of decorum:

> If [the Greeks] treated them differently in the tragedies [i.e. allowing women to speak], it was because, following the political system of their theatre, they were not angry if it was thought that characters of high rank have no need of modesty, and are always exempt from the rules of morality.[17]

It has been pointed out by feminist historians that political movements towards democracy throughout Western history have not necessarily improved the situation of women. This may be because such crises of class-specific identity formation must be compensated for by the rigidification of gender identities, as the most casual stroll through the history of philosophy attests. But the differential character of language undermines these fixed positions even where women themselves are not permitted to speak. The stage, with its representation through presence, unsettles the performative character of dramatic speech acts, blurring the distinctions between reality and fiction. Plato, the English Protestants and Rousseau were keenly aware of this. In his debate with Searle, Derrida theoretically underpinned the impossibility of a clean separation between reality and fiction. When Searle insists that fictional speech is an exception, Derrida claims that social speech acts are the exceptions among all possible speech acts. Only the non-seriousness of speech acts guarantees the repeatability, and only because of that repeatability are there speech acts with performative power. It is no coincidence that in this debate speech on the stage assumes a vital role. Derrida comes to the conclusion that:

> The logic of parasitism is not a logic of distinction or opposition . . . A parasite is neither the same as nor different from that which it parasites . . . the so-called "standard-cases" are reproduced, mimed, simulated, parasited, etc. *as* being in themselves reproducible, already *parasiticable*, as already impure.[18]

On the other hand speech acts on the stage by virtue of the 'reality' of actual bodies are always to be taken seriously.

As in the discourse of nineteenth-century psychiatry, so in the agonistic drama the clean gender divisions built into classical philosophy break down. Where philosophy suppresses the voices of female reason and argument, they reappear in other discourses. Greek drama is an example of this. In this sense George Steiner, too, argues in his admirable study of the reception of the figure of Antigone:

> It may well have been the case that Greek tragedy, at least so far as we know it, was the particular medium in which female agents (though impersonated by masked men) could deploy their unrestricted enthousiasmos and humanity. It may well have been that those elemental rights of femininity, even of feminine primacy in certain capabilities and situations, which were denied to women in everyday life, in law, in Platonic politics and the Aristotelian classification of organic beings were one of the impulses behind, and extraterritorial licences of, Greek drama. If this supposition is right, it would tie in closely with the ultimate origins of drama in the dialectic of man and woman as I have inferred it. The tragedies of Aeschylus, Sophocles and Euripides retain their archaic force, their intimacy with the primordial, because in them the encounters between men and women reach back to the roots of dramatic form.[19]

This may be the reason why the reception of Greek drama, as a privileged scene of female speech and female reason, has continued uninterruptedly until the present. For only in the *agon*, in radical dialogue, in unintimidated counter-debate, sharp polemic (does Büchner not compare his Woyzeck to a knife?), in the power to say 'no', in the heterogeneity of irresolvable contradictions, are autonomy and intersubjectivity immediately apparent. The radicalism of female reason such as this is expressed in the 'outrageousness' of the protagonist's words and the 'monstrousness' of her deeds, whether she is called Antigone, Clytemnestra, Cassandra, Hecuba, Iphigenia, Andromache, Phaedra, the Bacchae or Medea. Irreconcilability and the pleasurable fear that it produces are the historical signs of a female reason exiled from history.

NOTES

1   T. Matthews, *The Life of John Gibson* (London 1911), p. 175, quoted in Marina Warner, *Monuments and Maidens: The Allegory of the Female Form* (Pan Books, London, 1987), p. 209.

2   Dorothy Dinnerstein, *The Mermaid and the Minotaur: Sexual Arrangements and the Human Malaise* (Harper and Row, New York/London, 1978); Carol Gilligan, *In a Different Voice* (Harvard University Press, Cambridge, Mass., 1982); Nancy Chodorow, *The Reproduction of Mothering. Psychoanalysis and the Sociology of Gender* (University of California Press, Berkeley/Los Angeles/London, 1978).

3   Seyla Benhabib, 'The generalized and the concrete other', in Seyla Benhabib and Drucilla Cornell (eds), *Feminism as Critique: Essays on the Politics of Gender in Late-Capitalist Societies* (Polity Press, Cambridge, 1987), p. 92.

4   Geneviève Lloyd, *The Man of Reason: 'Male' and 'Female' in Western Philosophy* (Methuen, London 1984), p. 37.

5   Ibid., p. 101.

6   Hesiodus, *Theogonia*, ed. F. Jakoby (1930).

7   Nancy Fraser, 'What's critical about Critical Theory?', in Benhabib and Cornell, *Feminism as Critique*.

8   Martin Heidegger, *Being and Time*, tr. John Macquarrie, ed. Edward Robinson (Blackwell, Oxford, 1962), pp. 56–7.

9   Helga Geyer-Ryan, 'The castration of Cassandra', ch. 3 in this volume.

10 Jürgen Habermas, *Nachmetaphysisches Denken: Philosophische Aufsätze* (Suhrkamp, Frankfurt/M., 1988), p. 19.

11 Elaine Showalter, *The Female Malady: Women, Madness and English Culture, 1830–1980* Virago Press, London, 1987), p. 171.

12 Ibid., p. 194.

13 Plato, *The Republic* tr. Desmond Lee, 2nd rev. edn, (Penguin, Harmondsworth, 1977), p. 154 (book III, 195e).

14 William Robertson Davies, *Shakespeare's Boy Actors* (New York, 1939); Elbert N. S. Thompson, *The Controversy between the Puritans and the Stage* (Russell & Russell, New York 1966).

15 Jean-Jacques Rousseau, *Lettre à d'Alembert sur les spectacles*, in *Oeuvres Complètes*, vol. 1 (Librairie Hachette, Paris 1870), pp. 178–271, p. 209 (author's translation).

16 Ibid.

17 Ibid.

18 Jacques Derrida, 'Limited inc. abc . . .', *Glyph*, 2 (1977), pp. 162–254, esp. pp. 231–2.

19 George Steiner, *Antigones: The Antigone Myth in Western Literature, Art and Thought* (Oxford University Press, Oxford 1984), p. 237.

5

Adultery as Critique

A few years ago the Austrian author Elfriede Jelinek wrote a radio play entitled 'What happened after Nora left her husband?'[1] The question will have occurred to many of those who have seen Ibsen's play about Nora Helmer leaving her doll's house. What did a woman do in 1878 if she had no profession but was no longer able or willing to live with her husband?

In Elfriede Jelinek's version, after a series of humiliating experiences Nora returns with resignation to her doll's house.

I mention the play for two reasons. First of all it shows how modern literature of times past can be for us. Literature and culture are not museum-pieces, but analyses of problems that have preoccupied people throughout the ages, albeit in different historical forms. Nora's fate has lost nothing of its acuteness even in our own time. For what do women do today if they want to leave their marriage but have no opportunities on the job market? Secondly, it answers – particularly in its ending – an additional question: is adultery the only way out of marriage? Could not unhappy women simply have got divorced? Divorce was a legal possibility. But even in the language of the nineteenth century, which was quite capable of dealing with personal matters, it would have been impossible to represent in a courtroom the experiences that drove women out of their marriages. In order to give verbal expression to these new experiences a complete novelistic narrative, of which these adulterous women are the heroines, is required. We latter-day readers have the judge's role. And our textual interpretation is the analysis of the case.

But there is an additional argument against divorce as a solution. Divorce was prohibited to the women in question because it would have involved a catastrophic loss of social status. Physically, too, they would hardly have been in a position to earn a living. In *Effi Briest* this situation becomes very clear.[2] Effi's fate, the social consequence of female sexuality outside marriage, is reflected in female characters from the most diverse social classes. Although all of these women endure terrible hardships, they can still keep themselves alive through their own work, humble though it may be. Only Effi dies. She dies because her identity – her body, mind and psyche – is socially formed in such a way that none of the paths to survival is open to her. All adulteresses, not only Effi, have internalized the world through the process of their socialization; they are a part of that world, which they then reject in the act of adultery.

This inability to survive, brought about through physio-psychological formation, is comparable to the physical deformation of Chinese women. However much they might have wanted to walk out of their marriages and into the world, their feet, bound from childhood, would have made it impossible for them to do so. In their acts of adultery Emma Bovary, Effi Briest, Anna Karenina and Kate Chopin's Edna Pontellier are all rebelling, whether consciously or unconsciously, against the patriarchal system that imprisons them in their marriages. But a part of their individuality, their personalities, their identities, has itself been colonized by patriarchal thinking. The medium is their membership of a social class. So adultery is always a twofold sign, combining rebellion and its concealment: marriage is annulled as a patriarchal relationship of power and sexuality, yet simultaneously maintained as a locus of class privileges.

Elfriede Jelinek's Nora returns to her husband because she can no longer bear her life as an unskilled factory worker. All the women workers in this play want nothing but marriage. Dehumanization on the production line is greater, for them, than dehumanization in bed.

Nevertheless, in what follows, I should like to stress the importance of rebellion. In the long run only rebellious texts can maintain their place in the cultural tradition.

In this essay I should like to deal in detail with three novels in particular: *Madame Bovary* by Gustave Flaubert, *Effi Briest* by Theodor Fontane and *The Awakening* by Kate Chopin.[3]

Madame Bovary was published in 1857 and is set amongst the French provincial middle classes. Fontane wrote *Effi Briest* in 1894–5, and its setting is in the milieu of the Prussian nobility, state officials and the officer caste. It too is first set in the provinces, and later in Berlin. Kate Chopin was the first woman writer to make an adulteress a heroine. Edna Pontellier belongs to the circle of rich Creoles of the commercial class in 1898 New Orleans. There are other celebrated novels about adultery: Tolstoy's *Anna Karenina*, Nathaniel Hawthorne's *The Scarlet Letter*, and the famous novel of a surreal adultery which ushered in the subject of the century in 1807: Goethe's *Elective Affinities*.[4]

All of these novels have one important thing in common. They are not concerned with adultery as such, but specifically with the wife's adultery.[5] For this reason we must ask ourselves two questions: Why is a husband's adultery never thematized, but only that of the wife? Indeed, why do adultery and the wife's adultery seem to be almost synonymous? And why was it in the nineteenth century that this subject became so current in the most advanced literature?

I think there is a single answer to both questions. The nineteenth century saw the collapse, both ideologically and in real terms, of the political façade, the result of the democratic demands of a progressive bourgeoisie in the eighteenth century in its response to a corrupt feudalism. The bourgeois marriage functioned as a moral legitimation of the political and social struggle. Theoretically, it was based on the demand for sexual fidelity on the part of both spouses. This idea – counter to the tradition of Roman and Germanic law – was fought for by Christianity. But it could never have been effective within a patriarchal system. As late as 1884, French law punished adulteresses with prison, adulterers with fines that were generally dropped. In patriarchy filiation, succession, passes through the name of the father. In a purely biological sense a man can never be sure that he is the father of the child. For this reason there are paternity suits, while maternity suits would be an absurdity. In order to ascertain paternity, the natural, biologically observable line of reproduction via the mother is replaced by the abstract, cultural line of the father. Paternity is culturally ensured by the wife's obligation to monogamy.[6]

Thus adultery on the wife's part is a direct affront to patriarchal law and the patriarchal state, whose foundation is, after all, marriage. If the husband commits adultery these foundations are not affected. Male adultery is not a social fact, but a purely private one. It is located on the level of morality, of ideology, where its functions are at best legitimizing. It does not exist at all on the level of power. For this reason a film about Japan, a country which does not historically share the European tradition of the rhetoric of enlightenment and demands for equality, was able to state in lapidary fashion: if the Japanese husband betrays his wife, she has one possibility alone – she must come to terms with it.

In *Effi Briest* the legal, state-enforced insistence on the wife's fidelity is made very clear. Effi's husband, Instetten, discovers his wife's adultery after seven years, purely by chance. The affair is long over and forgotten. Instetten would like to forgive Effi, because he loves her and his happiness depends on her presence. But that is the private side. As a high state official, and as a husband, he must reject Effi and shoot his rival in a duel. He is honour-bound to do so. In the concept of male honour the legal claims and empowerments of the patriarchal state are conveyed through the private person of the individual man.

Christianity and, even more strongly, the Enlightenment, called for the according of equal status to men and women within marriage, but left the husband's legal privileges of power untouched. Legal authority within the family is the husband's exclusive property. But as a democratic, enlightened citizen he should not exploit these privileges in despotic fashion, but rather deploy them responsibly, treating his family in a just manner. Given these conditions, husband and wife, despite the husband's actual hegemony, are bound together in an equal cooperation. Political integrity in the face of a corrupt nobility and in favour of the underprivileged masses, and private integrity with regard to family and wife are mutually validating. As long as this legitimation continues to function, the wife's fidelity can be constructed as objectively progressive. For this reason nothing piques his emotions more intensely than sexual onslaughts by the nobility on his wife and daughters. Thus the great bourgeois novels of the eighteenth century deal with the triumphs of the modesty of bourgeois women. Such are *Pamela, Clarissa, La nouvelle Héloïse, The Sorrows of Young Werther.*[7]

Amongst the nineteenth-century bourgeoisie there was little trace of the former ideals of the French Revolution and the Enlightenment. They were engaging in power-politics so as to defend their new privileges against the encroaching lower classes. There was little trace of *égalité, fraternité, liberté*. The successive revolutions of 1830, 1848 and 1870–1 in Paris made that more than clear. But while the husband's private authority had been endorsed by his political integrity, as the one grew enfeebled so did the other. There were no objective reasons for male supremacy. So women broke their marriage contracts. In parallel with socialist theories and political movements, the first political women's movements came into being from the mid-nineteenth century onwards. They were fighting for the public and legal equality of women, and above all for the right to vote.

At the same time literature made it quite clear that the private is political. As the bourgeoisie grew reactionary, marriage had turned from a zone of protection into a prison. The Enlightenment and the Romantic movement had fought for human rights, autonomy and the fulfilment of personal happiness. Women recognized that in patriarchy it was marriage that stood between them and personal happiness, their autonomous existence. This did not occur only in the novel of adultery. Ibsen and Strindberg analyse the torture chambers of unhappy marriages, while in Chekhov happy marriages no longer exist. The great women writers of the nineteenth century did not marry: Emily Dickinson, Annette von Droste-Hülshoff, Karoline von Günderode, Emily Brontë, Anne Brontë, Jane Austen, George Eliot, George Sand. (Charlotte Brontë got married in 1854, a year before her death and stopped writing at the wish of her husband.)

But the novel of adultery most clearly reveals the medium through which women's oppression is fundamentally and subtly manifested: sexuality, which is problematized in the nineteenth-century novel for the first time in literature. The issue is no longer love, which can lead to marriage, and in which sexuality is implied in some metaphorical or veiled sense. In *Effi Briest, Madame Bovary* and *The Awakening* we are presented with such marriages. Their volatile mixture disintegrates before our eyes, breaking down into the ingredients that had been artificially compounded in the Christian bourgeois marriage: procreation, sexuality, love and a legal contract. From this point onwards, and into the literary future of the twentieth century, these warring elements can no longer be united. We might even say that the literature of the twentieth century emerges from this very heterogeneity.

In the nineteenth century women became more aware of their sexual needs for the first time. This is one of the reasons why Kate Chopin called her novel *The Awakening*. But in the nineteenth century this was still a fatal experience. The rebels were still being punished. They were punished by the society that played one of the leading roles in their stories, and they were punished by their authors, however much sympathy they might have had with them. Emma Bovary poisons herself. Effi Briest dies of consumption. Anna Karenina throws herself in front of a train. Edna Pontellier drowns herself. These modes of death reveal one thing above all else. In patriarchy women who leave a place assigned to them by men have nowhere to live. Christa Wolf aptly calls a novel about a nineteenth-century woman poet who committed suicide: *Kein Ort. Nirgends* (No Place. Nowhere).[8] Between the parental home, the marital home and the brothel there was nowhere for women to go. This is chiefly apparent in their economic immaturity. In this, women are no different from their children. Effi Briest returns to live on her parents' financial contributions after she leaves her husband. But she cannot return to the parental home, as her parents fear social stigmatization. First of all she lives in a boarding-house for single women, then in a little rented flat. She has nothing to do, no job. This lack of location reveals the loss of her social identity. Above all, her death symbolizes her social death.

The same is true of Emma Bovary. She poisons herself not, as we might assume, because she is unhappy in love, but because she can find no way of paying her debts, the result of massive overspending on a luxury lifestyle. This parasitically and symbolically occupies the space where Emma, given her intelligence and energy, should be socially active. She attempts to manage her husband, a doctor, in such a way as to win a social position for herself as well. Only when this project comes to nothing through her husband's inadequacy does her hypertrophy begin, the megalomaniac cult of her own personality, precisely what a male discourse would dismissively refer to as female narcissism.

At the same time the deaths of these female protagonists are also a punishment bestowed by their male authors. Tolstoy, Fontane and even Flaubert are far from granting unconditional support to female adultery. They do give these women a voice, but it is to some extent a male voice. This is apparent in the fact that marriage itself is not condemned as an institution. A bad marriage is branded, we might say, as a pathological deviation from an otherwise tolerable norm.

In the dullness, boredom and deceit of the Bovary marriage Flaubert sees a reflection of the superannuated, degenerate middle class within which it operates. Emma is just as hollow as her husband. Her individuality is likewise patched together out of the now meaningless, functionless fragments of the bourgeois image of the world, composed of Classical and Romantic elements. Emma draws her culture from magazines and the love stories of a decayed Romanticism. Charles Bovary, the doctor, knows nothing, for he could pay little for his training.

Effi Briest's marriage is precarious from the outset because there is an age difference of some twenty years between herself and Instetten, and because the marriage is arranged. The clearest indication of its pathological state is that Instetten had already been the suitor of Effi's mother. Fontane, who based his story on a real case, adds these traits. Both authors also make it plain that the women commit adultery out of boredom. Boredom because they live in little provincial towns and have nothing to do. Thus, the more reasons given for the breakdown of these marriages, the more strongly marriage *per se* is defended. Yet it becomes clear that the wives in each of these marriages have a heavier cross to bear, and the theme foregrounded by Kate Chopin is very much in abeyance in the other novels: marriage is problematic because it is defined by both sexual desire and fidelity. But Chopin shows from the start that every marriage is primarily a more or less subtle relationship of power and suppression. Prisons, asylums, armies and factories have one thing in common above all: they are relatively excluded from normal society because public judgement cannot penetrate them. These spaces are free arenas for the exercise of power because within them power hierarchies emerge in their true colours, and those in possession of power are to a large extent exempt from legal controls. They are islands of a pre-bourgeois age, because power relations are controlled and balanced much less by the internal regulation of conscience than they are in external, historical, bourgeois society. Marriage is another of these blind spots, as the widespread modern discussion of violence and rape in marriage has shown. This becomes apparent in Chopin's work, but not in Flaubert and Fontane.

The difference between the male and female perspectives could be summed up as follows: Flaubert and Fontane show marriage as a means of communication between private and public. This public sphere is, in line with historical conditions, occupied by classes that have grown to be anachronistic and consequently corrupt. In Flaubert, this means the middle classes, in Fontane the characteristically German *fin-de-siècle* alliance of the nobility, the military and the upper middle classes. The social and patho-logical aspects of these classes also corrupt their marriages in the form of class concerns and money matters.

In Chopin, on the other hand, the failure of the marriage is the consequ-ence of the power relation in which the sexes are organized. The temper-amental despotism of the stronger partner is given free rein. In Chopin these are extremely delicate observations, subtle signs of control and power, because the social class in which the novel takes place is an extremely cultivated one.

But another important factor links these three novels. It constitutes their additional innovative dimension, which directly connects them with the literature of our own century and also with contemporary debates in feminism. This factor is the de-centring of the Romantic concept of love, which has linguistically organized Western sexual relations since the elev-enth century. This throws up the question: is our semantics of love, the code of intersubjective intimacy, perhaps in the final analysis a male discourse?[9]

In her novel *L'amant*,[10] Marguerite Duras has her female central charac-ter say to the man who loves her: 'I had rather you didn't love me. But even if you love me, I would like you to do to me what you normally do to women.' The issue here is the woman's sexual pleasure, and the suspicion that the man's emotional intensity might act as a hindrance upon it. In his essay 'On the Universal Tendency to Debasement in the Sphere of Love', Freud explains the mental mechanism of this mutual exclusion. Love and pleasure, Mary and Eve, do not appear on the same stage.

The novels we are examining are concerned with marriage contracts and sexuality. Sexuality is always initially connected with the state of being in love, but this quickly wanes. The problematization of the concept of love becomes apparent in the absence of this emotion. But in the process marriage loses its emotional protective layer. For it is love that unites the long-term marriage contract with short-lived sexual attraction. Without this buffer marriage is exposed to the explosive power of sensual desire.

Love and the fidelity that goes with it are achievements of internal control. They are acts of solidarity on the part of the conscience, presuppos-ing a high level of autonomy of the ego. But neither Emma nor Effi has this. Flaubert is concerned with revealing the damage that an impoverished upbringing can inflict on so-called femininity.

And Effi's relationship with Instetten is not internally powered by affec-tion; rather it is externally determined by social convention. But these authors go one step further. Their heroines are unable to forge stronger internal bonds even with their extramarital partners.

Flaubert's men are either merely façades or emotional ruins. The only one among them who is capable of love is the obviously limited Charles. Fontane does not directly describe inner life or sexuality. In his work these dimensions are apparent only in a veiled form, in metaphors and little subsidiary stories.

Chopin's Edna is more aware. She realizes that men, emotionally armoured by the practice of power, are barely receptive to the needs of women. Love, which might only be possible between true equals, could therefore exist only as an illusion or ideology designed to conceal power relations.

She sees something else, too: even love is not protected against the disturbances of sexuality. Sexuality is the basis of love. But this does not mean that the perpetual motion from one man to the next can be brought to an end. According to Freud and Lacan, a more fundamental unease is inscribed within sexual unease. It is an unspecific, unconscious desire, in which one seeks an object capable of recreating the totality of the former symbiosis of mother and child. This void, this fundamental lack is occupied by sexuality first and foremost, but only ever for a certain space of time. In practical terms anything can occupy that space, in order to satisfy the urge: love, marriage, children, work, art, science, sport. But nineteenth-century women were still to a large extent excluded from both social, professional activities and cultural and creative work. The restless urge found no outward expression. It was forced back into the private sphere of the emotions, of sexual desire, but a desire which was unrealizable. We are familiar with the images of women handed down to us from the nineteenth century. The bedridden women, the nervous, the hysterics, the depressives. One solution to this state of affairs is psychoanalysis. But, in its classical form, it is not enough. It does not go to the root of the problem, but seeks to make it easier for women to adapt to it. In some respects psychoanalysis too is yet another male discourse.

Kate Chopin's Edna swims away from all this into the sea, and she doesn't come back. Nor does she return in the twentieth century. Neither she nor Emma nor Effi. In the novels their authors surround them with a pointed sequence of water metaphors. This connects them with the mythology of female water-beings, the sirens, the little mermaid, Melusine and Undine. They are creatures who cannot live on dry land, men's land, who find no place for themselves there. And there is no secure place for them in the twentieth century, either. In Virginia Woolf, the journey to the lighthouse, where water and land meet, does not take place. Ingeborg Bachmann wrote a story called *Undine Walks Out* and a fragmentary novel-cycle about women in a men's world, which she aptly entitled 'Modes of Death'.[12]

The women die because they have left the space traditionally reserved for the so-called 'feminine'. One cognate sense of the English word 'adultery' is 'adulteration' – contamination, pollution. The common root is the Latin *adulterare*, which also has a double meaning. If dirt is defined as 'matter in the wrong place', adultery is 'a wife (or husband) in the wrong place'. In our case a wife in the wrong bed. Adulteresses, that is, confuse the categories, polluting the clean 'demarcations' with which men have divided up reality amongst themselves.

The fact that twentieth-century men are still the accomplices of their nineteenth-century antecedents can be read in the voices of our contemporary literary critics. They pronounce the death sentence yet again. Their accusation: that Emma, Effi and Edna didn't want to be female, they wanted too much, they wanted the 'male' share as well.

But nature does not tell us what is female: men define it. Masculinity and femininity are social constructs in which dominant interests are always inscribed as long as they appear in such an oppositional form. On this point the nineteenth-century authors were much more avant-garde than their later critics who wish to defuse the explosive power of these novels.

Fontane, Flaubert and Chopin draw their heroines with the delicate lines of androgyny. They wear men's clothes, dream of adventurous professions, rave about other women and their beauty, are sexually dominant, and often wild and unpredictable in their behaviour. Like adultery, these traits blur the contours of sexual identity, so clearly outlined by patriarchy. The authors too were condemned to minor forms of social death. Flaubert was hauled up before the courts by the censors. Kate Chopin was socially ostracized throughout her life.

What happened to the polluting women *in* the text in the nineteenth century happens in the twentieth century to the women who pollute the text itself. The famous women authors of our own time, the true modernists and avant-gardists of the text, commit suicide: Virginia Woolf, Sylvia Plath, Unica Zürn, Anne Sexton, Ingeborg Bachmann. In their writing they shift the conventional contours of the literary text, the limitations of the place assigned to them, the dubious certainties of their own sexual identity. And they pay for it. In her novel *Malina* Ingeborg Bachmann wrote: 'All men are sick. But it is women who die of that sickness.' The great nineteenth-century novels of adultery recount the case history.

NOTES

1   Elfriede Jelinek, 'Was geschah, nachdem Nora ihren Mann verlassen hatte?' (What happened after Nora left her husband?), in *Was geschah, nachdem Nora ihren Mann verlassen hatte? Acht Hörspiele, von Elfriede Jelinek et al.*, ed. Helga Geyer-Ryan (Deutscher Taschenbuch Verlag, Munich, 1982).

2 Theodor Fontane, *Effi Briest* (1894–5).

3 Gustave Flaubert, *Madame Bovary* (1857); Kate Chopin, *The Awakening* (1899).

4 Leo Tolstoy, *Anna Karenina* (1875–7); Nathaniel Hawthorne, *The Scarlet Letter* (1850); Johann Wolfgang von Goethe, *Die Wahlverwandtschaften (Elective Affinities)* (1807).

5 The most recent study on adultery in literature is Tony Tanner's book *Adultery in the Novel* (Johns Hopkins University Press, Baltimore/London, 1979). Though Tanner's study is extremely stimulating and full of new insights, it is clearly written from an all-male perspective. Adultery is seen merely as an attack on a bourgeois institution, whereas its critique of marriage as a patriarchal structure could produce more penetrating insights. The fact that Tanner does not problematize adultery in the nineteenth-century novel as exclusively committed by the wife can alone explain statements like the following: 'By analogy we may say that if the marriage bond is rendered undesirable – and that is the ultimate implication of adultery – then by extension nothing in society is truly "bonded", and the state of chaos envisaged here in graphic terms by Vico may recommence at the very centre of the most civilized society. As though by some reverse mythical all-at-onceness, society at its heart returns to that "infamous promiscuity of things and women" from which man, by means above all of the idea of marriage, first emerged into true social humanity' (p. 66).

6 'The Name-of-the-Father is the fact of the attribution of paternity by law, by language. Paternity cannot be perceived, proven, known with certainty; it must be instituted by judgement of the mother's word ... What guarantees the mother's word, the mother's fidelity to her word, in short, what guarantees the mother's fidelity? Any suspicion of the mother's infidelity betrays the Name-of-the-Father as the arbitrary imposition it is.' Jane Gallop, *Feminism and Psychoanalysis: The Daughter's Seduction* (Macmillan, London, 1982), pp. 47–8.

7 Samuel Richardson, *Pamela, or Virtue Rewarded* (1744); *Clarissa, or the History of a Young Lady* (1748); Jean-Jacques Rousseau, *La nouvelle Héloïse* (1764); Johann Wolfgang von Goethe, *Die Leiden des jungen Werthers* (*The Sorrows of Young Werther*) (1774).

8 Christa Wolf, *Kein Ort. Nirgends* (Luchterhand, Darmstadt/Neuwied, 1979).

9 Cf. Niklas Luhmann, *Liebe als Passion. Zur Codierung von Intimität* (Suhrkamp, Frankfurt/M., 1982); tr. Jeremy Gaines and Doris L. Jones, *Love as Passion: The Codification of Intimacy* (Polity Press, Cambridge, 1986).

10 Marguérite Duras, *L'amant* (Editions de Minuit, Paris, 1984).

11 Cf. Anna Maria Stuby, 'Sirenen und ihre Gesänge. Variationen über das Motiv des Textraubs', *Gulliver*, 18 (1985), pp. 69–87.

12 Ingeborg Bachmann, *Undine geht*, in *Werke*, ed. Christine Koschel, Inge von Weidenbaum and Clemens Münster (Piper, Munich, 1978), vol. 2, pp. 253–63. The cycle consists of the novel *Malina* (1971) and the two unfinished novels *Der Fall Franza* and *Requiem für Fanny Goldman*, in *Werke*, vol. 3.

6

Abjection in the Texts of Walter Benjamin

After many years experience I have recently become *conscious* of how much more peculiar, particularly how very much different, nature looks after sunset. Beautiful and strange.

Letter to Herbert Belmore, 18 July 1911

Unless a defect in the lighting suddenly produced that strange twilight when colour faded from the landscape. Then it lay secluded under an ashen sky; it was as though I should have been able to hear the wind and bells had I merely paid more attention.

'Imperial panorama', in *Berliner Kindheit um Neunzehnhundert*

The Mothers

In the fields of theory and language, Walter Benjamin sets out to salvage images. In his *Passagen-Werk* he writes: 'The original interest in allegory is not linguistic but optical. "Les images, ma grande, ma primitive passion."'[1] In this quotation from Baudelaire, images are associated with passion, a passion which, in this case, is both grand and primitive. As far as its source is concerned, passion is always archaic. Benjamin often quotes Faust, who descends to the Mothers in order to retrieve the original image of Helen.[2] The Goethe reference to the Mothers has a double significance for our understanding of Benjamin's writing. Firstly, the woman's body is salvaged in the form of an image, in memory, by Faust's descent. At another point, it becomes apparent that this image can only be obtained at the price of a possible loss of identity. Faust must immerse himself in the pre-symbolic realm of the imaginary in the space of the pre-Oedipal mother with its menacing destruction of the 'I'. The horror of this space is due to its emptiness, which is beyond all experience and consequently all identification:

MEPHISTOPHELES: Goddesses sit enthroned in reverend loneliness
                Space is as naught about them, time is less;
                The very mention of them is distress
                They are – the Mothers.
FAUST: Mothers!
MEPHISTOPHELES: Are you awed?
FAUST: The Mothers! Why, it strikes a singular chord.
MEPHISTOPHELES: And so it ought. Goddesses undivined
                By mortals, names with shrinking by our kind.
                Go delve the downmost for their habitat;
                Blame but yourself that it has come to that.
FAUST: Where is the road?
MEPHISTOPHELES: No road! Into, the unacceded,
                The inaccessible; toward the never-pleaded,
                The never-pleadable. How is your mood?
                There are no locks to probe, no bolts to shift;
                By desolations harrowed you will drift.
                Can you conceive of wastes of solitude?

When Faust, pointing to his experiences in society, answers in the affirmative, Mephistopheles says:

> And had you even swum the trackless ocean,
> Lost in its utter boundlessness,
> You still saw wave on wave in constant motion,
> Though for your life in terror and distress.
> Still there were sights. You would have seen a shift
> Of dolphins cleave the emerald calm the drift
> Of clouds, sun moon and stars revolve in harness;
> There you see Nothing – vacant gaping farness,
> Mark not your own step as you stride,
> Nor point of rest where you abide.

Faust replies:

> Let me explore that scope,
> Within your Naught to find the All, I hope ...
> Yet not in torpor would I comfort find;
> Awe is the finest portion of mankind;
> However scarce the world may make this sense –
> In awe one feels profoundly the immense.[3]

Faust turns full circle from the abject into the sublime.

The Abject

The void which opens up in the realm of the Mothers is the emptiness of the abject. Kristeva describes it as that position in the psychography of the individual in which neither subject nor object exist but rather the pure movement of splitting, the very creation of positionality itself.[4] At this point, this moment, there are not yet any of the semiotic traces which will later go on to produce the perception of the body ('no road'). Still less is there any mirror-image in which the subject and object are fully differentiated from each other in the imaginary space. ('No road! Into the unacceded, / The inaccessible; toward the never-pleaded / The never-pleadable'.) The emptiness is the fundamental deficiency in the first separation. It is the existential void, and all definitions of later subjectivity must ultimately help to conceal it.

This emptiness is the zero point of subject and object, the very end of all regression, but also the starting-point of differentiation. The splitting towards difference is brought about through the child's identification with the father of his 'personal prehistory,' a Third Party towards which the interest of the mother is diverted, away from the child.

By turning away from its mother, the child rejects her and she becomes abject. In this first detachment of mother and child, a position is created for the later formation of the subject–object relationship, but the traumatic and fundamental loss of the first object is also introduced. The ambivalent nature of the archaic relationship with the mother again becomes apparent as an ambiguity, in the response of revulsion. Revulsion is a mixture of fear of losing one's identity and a fascination with this loss, where the pleasure of fusion, the pleasure derived from the abandonment of identity in the undifferentiated, becomes discoverable.

The Abject and the Sublime

The pleasure and fear (*Angstlust*) of revulsion, the memory of the space of pre-Oedipal emptiness in the imaginary, resurfaces in the post-Oedipal, symbolic space as the aesthetic experience of the sublime. The experience (*Er-fahrung*) of the sublime, the experience of 'sublimated' revulsion, finds its sign in the trope of allegory.

Lyotard analyses the Jewish religion of image-banishment and of non-remembered patricide as a foreclosure of castration.[5] It is accompanied by the foreclosure of the figure of the feminine and the mother. Since the word, and ultimately writing, are privileged over the body and the image, the power of the father and the repression of the mother prevail. By retrieving images, not in opposition to language, but rather *into* language, and above all the language of epistemology, as well as by means of figurative speech, the maternal sphere (the imaginary) turns up as an effect in the paternal sphere (the symbolic order). This effect is the presence of the body in the realm of signs. Resurrecting the body into the machinery of the sign can take various forms. It can occur as the return of the repressed under the sign of negation. This is found in the work of Paul de Man. Or it can appear as transgression with a revival of the abject position. This is the project of Walter Benjamin.

The figure of allegory is reflexive, a display of all productions of meaning through arbitrary signs. Its revolting wound shamelessly proclaims that there is a gap within the sign which cannot be concealed by a supposedly 'organic' rhetoric. And yet, due to precisely this breach between body and meaning, the body appears all the more naked.

Transgression

In everyday life the psychic position of the abject is fused with a social value system of purity and filth.

Under ultimately contingent circumstances, objects normally categorized as rubbish can be elevated into positivity, and are thus 'sublimated' into a collector's item, for example, or any other value of distinction.[6] The zero-position of garbage within the realm of real and symbolic objects is analogous to the position of the abject in the psychic domain. To this extent transgression is both a reactivation of psychic *Angstlust*, and a breach in the symbolic order of a culture.[7]

In *Berliner Kindheit um Neunzehnhundert*, Benjamin describes a key transgression of his adolescence:

In one of those streets which I strolled through at night, on endless wander-ings, I was surprised, when the time came, by the arousal of sexual desire in me under the most peculiar of circumstances. It was on Jewish New Year's Day, and my parents had made preparations to put me in some or other religious ceremony. It was probably to do with the reform church to which my mother showed some sympathy for reasons to do with family tradition, *whilst my father was naturally more used to the orthodox ritual. He neverthe-less had to give way.* [The words italicized are missing from the final hand-written draft.[8]] For the occasion of this feast day, I had been commended to a more distant relative whom I was supposed to fetch. However, whether it was because I had forgotten the address, or because I couldn't find my way, it grew later and later, and my wandering around became increasingly pointless. To venture into the synagogue on my own would have been completely out of the question since my protector had the entrance tickets. My aversion to the virtual stranger on whom I was dependent, as well as my suspicion of the religious ceremonies which promised nothing other than embarrassment, were mainly to blame for my misfortune. Then, all at once, in the midst of my hopelessness, I was overcome by a hot wave of fear – 'too late, you've missed the synagogue' – but before it had subsided, indeed at precisely the same moment, I was overcome by a second wave – 'whatever happens, let it – it doesn't concern me.' And both waves crashed inexorably together in the first great feeling of desire in which the violation of the holy day mixed with the bawdy nature of the street which first made me sense the services it was supposed to provide for awakening desires.[9]

The 'violation' of the symbolic order – into which, in this case, the feminine has already entered through the maternal reform church[10] – and the 'violation' of the mother in the permitted image of the prostitute are merged together in the simultaneity of *Angst* and *Lust*.[11] Benjamin's description is strikingly similar to Freud's account of his wanderings through the streets of a small Italian town.[12] If we further recall Baudelaire's relationship to the streets of Paris, or Breton's in *Nadja*, the connection between the maternal-feminine dimension, the category of space, and the practice of writing, can be seen through the sexual cathexis of the urban body ('house of pleasure', 'street walker') in the male imaginary world of these authors. In the chapter entitled 'Walking in the City' in his book *The Practice of Everyday Life*, Michel Certeau identified

> three distinct (but connected) functions of the relations between spatial and signifying practices . . . the *believable*, the *memorable*, and the *primitive*. They designate what 'authorizes' (or makes possible or credible) spatial appropriations, what is repeated in them (or is recalled in them) from a silent and withdrawn memory, and what is structured in them and continues to be signed by an infantile (*in-fans*) origin.[13]

Benjamin's *Berliner Kindheit um Neunzehnhundert* testifies to the specific formation of the imaginary where the impression of space, the nature of objects, and the mother's body form the original scene for the later development of theory.

As early as 1913, in his letters to Herbert Belmore, Benjamin voiced his ideas on prostitution. Contrary to all popular moralizing, he sees in the prostitute a cipher to the human condition in a society characterized by power and the market.

> 'For you're still asking too timidly: "Either all women are prostitutes, or none are?" No: "Either all people are prostitutes, or none are?" Well, answer as you like. But I say: all of us are. Or are supposed to be. We are supposed to be things and objects before culture . . . The hooker *represents* [my emphasis] the perfect culture industry.'[14]

The prostitute is made into the allegory of a culture structured by venality. 'It drives nature from its last shrine – sexuality.'[15]

He goes on to develop this idea more fully in his analysis of *Elective Affinities*. For Benjamin, enlightened nature in Goethe's novel reverts to the condition of demonic nature. This is a nature in which the transcending light of successful enlightenment is extinguished by a dark mixture of passions and the corrupting laws of social privileges.

Nevertheless, the allegorization of the prostitute into a cipher for the commodity, which in Baudelaire and Benjamin is made into the key to modernity as a whole, is not as innocent as it appears. All people are ultimately commodities on the market, but for women this is doubly so: they are commodities on the labour market and on the sexual market. The very existence of a pictorial space in which the female body is made the object of commodity allegorization is itself a sign of patriarchal power.

Necrophilia?

As a sexualized image, woman is always killed off, since the patriarchal gaze turns the woman's body into an object, rendering it silent. Memory is associated with representations of the body and objects, and hence with images. Resurrecting the maternal body from the pre-Oedipal space would then have always been the presentation of a corpse lying concealed beneath outward appearance. Helen, the 'beautiful' Helen, can only ever be an image, and as such she is turned automatically into the deathly image of the prostitute. Ironically, in his jealousy at Helen's dalliance with Paris during the classical Walpurgis Night – anticipated in complacent comments made by viewers of the imaginary spectacle – Faust becomes the victim of his own patriarchal constructions of femininity as prostituted femininity. In words which perhaps contain more truth than Faust had foreseen, Mephisto says: 'Let the phantom do what it may! ... You're doing it yourself, this grotesque phantom-play.'[16]

Nevertheless, it is only through this dual aspect of the image – a necessary illusion which is the legacy of the mirror stage, the Oedipal projection of the woman as whore – that the body of the (phallic) mother can be reached. Thus, within the image, the whore, the allegory, the mother's body is present and absent at the same time: 'l'écriture allégorique est écriture du figurale et destruction de tout figuratif au sens stricte'[17]; 'le réalisme de la déformation détruit tout idealisme de la transfiguration.'[18]

These quotations point towards a dual mortification. There is, on the one hand, the reification of the image into an object by the gaze which is already premissed in the term 'figural'. And on the other hand, the pictorial is destroyed when its existential emptiness is pointed up: the deformation or destruction of the figural which reveals the reinstatement of the image – 'l'idéalisme de la transfiguration' – as an illusion.

If we project this dual destruction of the image on to the temporal axis of psychography, then regression leads us back through the deathly Oedipal interpretation of the image and the as yet non-sexualized mirror-image, into the emptiness of positionality, which is discoverable only in the act of abjection. Here, where room is first made for the later 'I', the mother is mortified into the abject mother. It is this dual pattern of murder which is expressed in the allegory. In *The Origin of German Tragic Drama*, it is no coincidence that Benjamin refers to 'the "Egyptians"' [who had] 'buried corpses in wooden images'.[19]

The Violence of Semiosis

Nevertheless, the living body of the mother has not completely disappeared. It is present in the act of violence – '*déformation*' and '*destruction*' as process, not result – which all signifying practices must repeat afresh if they intend to produce meaning. Semiosis is the 'acting out' of murder and castration within the sign. The more the signifier and the signified are torn apart to form hermetic constellations and hard edges, the deeper the essential abyss opens up between them which is only bridged by conventions. In this abyss, violence reveals itself as a strain on meaning. Through its violent, unmediated construction, allegory in the form of figurative speech or emblem is the allegory of each semiotic and hermeneutic act. For in Benjamin, an unmistakable semantics of violence plays around the figure of allegory. He quotes Breitinger, who calls the allegory a *prison* of the concept. It is a question of the *membra disjecta*, both of allegorized bodies on the baroque stage, and of language which is in the *sadistic* hands of the allegorist.[20] Allegory *enslaves*,[21] it *exploits*; meaning is *torn apart* in it, and the language of the baroque is severely *convulsed* by *rebellion* on the part of the elements which make it up.[22] In particular, allegory is the scene in which the body – especially the female body – is dismembered. (Probably any body which makes itself available as an object of the actions of eyes and hands is automatically designated female, regardless of whether the actual body of a woman or a man is involved.) Regression behind the mirror-images leads into the depths of the *corps morcelé* which is stretched between the aggressive force field of the pre-Oedipal mother and the attraction of the – non-phallic – father of personal prehistory.

The archaic pull of the abject, the simultaneous revulsion and fascination of fusion, appear in Benjamin's work as an irreconcilable juxtaposition of *Lust* ('pleasure') and melancholy in the face of the destruction of the subject and its inwardness. The reduction of the individual to a creature, a doll, an automaton, a machine, a dismembered body, the disembowelment of inner space – all are deeply enjoyed and just as deeply mourned. This explains Benjamin's fascination with the victim. In this point he concurs with Brecht and Bataille on the most 'murderous' level.

However, the victim does not only describe the exchange between nature and culture, individuation and fusion in terms of desire. Rather the victim guarantees the connection between desire and sign. The 'maternal-murderous' incision, the theoretical breach, as Kristeva terms it, which excises meaning from the semiotic body of the infant and hence its entry into the symbolic order, has an analogy on the societal level in the ritual of sacrifice. The dead body is a sign of the full differentiation of the social order from chaos and the individuation of its members through a social allocation of places.

Benjamin's reading of *Elective Affinities* as the history of a demonic restoration of 'fallen' society to the natural order culminates in the analysis of the character of Ottilie as a victim. This interpretation was written at the same time as *The Origin of German Tragic Drama*, with its culmination in the development of the concept of allegory. Both texts reveal the pleasure Benjamin derived from transgression. It is manifested as a fascination with the destruction of inwardness and autonomy as illusions, *and* as a mourning for their loss. Mourning determines the interpretation of melancholy, the lament for the loss of the aura, of narration, of *mémoire involontaire*. These mimetic phenomena no longer manifest themselves (*(er)-scheinen*) because the celestial stars have ceased to shine as guarantors of transcendence and significance. 'Passing away is the primeval phenomenon of fading illusion' ('Das brechende Auge ist das Urphänomen des verlöschenden Scheins').[23]

The god that went into hiding in the seventeenth century, and died in the eighteenth, was the transcendent guarantor of meaning. His death inevit-ably brings in its wake the erosion of the moral subject and the evacuation of the worldly shell. The baroque tragic drama prefigures this state of existential evacuation:

The great German dramatists of the baroque were Lutherans. The rigorous morality of its teaching in respect of civic conduct stood in sharp contrast to its renunciation of 'good works'. By denying the latter any special miraculous spiritual effect, making the soul dependent on grace through faith, and making the secular-political sphere a testing ground for a life which was only indirectly religious, being intended for the demonstration of civic virtues, it did, it is true, instil into the people a strict sense of obedience to duty, but in its great men it produced melancholy. Something new arose: an empty world.[24]

Sexual Pleasure and the Destruction of the Subject

The crisis of the transcendent certainty of salvation is followed by the decay of the body. After all, even the body is only a body in the light of transcendent significance. Without it, the body is nature, any sort of matter, an object, a corpse, even when the body is still alive. The allegorical *furor* can thus swirl together bodies, objects, and parts of the body indiscriminately. Hence Benjamin talks about the 'creature', a concept that replaces the member of a community legitimated by its certainty of salvation. The creature's emptiness is repeated in baroque tragedy as if under a repetition-compulsion. The protagonists appear as puppets, playing-card kings, marionettes and miniatures.[25] Just as meaning drains out of the bodies of words under the gaze of the allegorist, and is crushed and dismembered into syllables and letters, so blood pours from crushed and dismembered human bodies.

The energy associated with maintaining difference is liberated in the pleasure derived from the destruction of the body and meaning. The free outflow of this energy is expressed in orgasm or laughter. 'Rarely, if ever, has speculative aesthetics considered the affinity between the strict joke and cruelty. Who has not seen children laugh where adults are shocked?'[26] Benjamin suggests that this childlikeness which laughs, and this adulthood which is horrified, alternates in the sadist. Even laughter is violence. For 'Laughter is shattered articulation.'[27] Benjamin repeatedly outlines the connection between allegorization, sadism, fetishism and abjection. In this context, we can again see affinities with the anthropology of Bataille and Brecht.

Not only do the subjects of his theoretical investigation – baroque tragedy, Baudelaire, Surrealism, Paris, commodities – contain a potential for violence cathected by desire; Benjamin's own figurative speech is also a rhetoric of violence. His metaphors, comparisons and allegories evoke objects and bodies in an extremely vivid way, but also their brutal destruction. The allegory is bloody: ' "l'appareil sanglant de la Destruction" is the court of allegory.'[28] It dominates and rapes: 'All kinds of intimacy with objects is alien to the allegorical intention. To touch it means, for allegory, to rape it. To recognize it means to see through it.'[29] In his allegorical perception of allegory, Benjamin associates the body of the sign with the feminine, the meaning of the sign (the allegorical intention, the 'allegory' *tout court*) with the masculine. The scene of allegorization thus becomes a scenario of sexual violence. It takes the form of polygamy, sadism and voyeurism:

> the allegorist ... by no means avoids that arbitrary rule which is the most drastic manifestation of the power of knowledge. The wealth of ciphers,

which the allegorist discovered in the world of the creature stamped profoundly by history, justifies Cohen's complaint of 'extravagance'. It may not accord with the authority of nature; but the voluptuousness with which significance rules, like a stern sultan in the harem of objects, is without equal in giving expression to it. It is indeed characteristic of the sadist that he humiliates his object and then – or thereby – satisfies it. And that is what the allegorist does in this age drunk with acts of cruelty both lived and imagined ... The 'opening of the eyes', which baroque painting makes into 'a schema' ... betrays and devalues things in an inexpressible manner. The function of baroque iconography is not so much to unveil material objects as to strip them naked ... As writing, as a caption, which in emblem-books forms an intimate part of what is depicted he drags the essence of the depicted before the image.[30]

In the images used by Benjamin, aggression is directed in the final instance at the body of the mother which is to be violated and made to bleed and die. The essence of all allegorical images is, therefore, the most abject, the corpse. On the last forty pages of *The Origin of German Tragic Drama* the chapter headings appear in the following order: 'Allegorical Dismemberment', 'Dismemberment of Language', 'The Corpse as Emblem'. The revolting essence of the corpse results from the undifferentiated fusion of the most basic opposition in the social order – that between life and death – to an amorphous, organic-inorganic mass. It is not that the corpse is a direct metaphor for the body of the mother. But in the deep abjection which befalls a person in the face of dead life, the primeval *Angst/Lust* of separation from the 'maternal' body is most intensely experienced.

Describing Baudelaire's poems 99 and 100, Benjamin sketches a primordial landscape of abject experience. Aggression has disappeared from it, but the specific scenario and its moods of emptiness are preserved: the archaics of the scene as expressed in the words of Mephistopheles, the pictures of de Chirico or Dali, or in Eliot's *The Waste Land*; the phallic mother (since the Oedipal father is missing); the father of 'personal prehistory'; incorporation/ identification; the deathly atmosphere of absence and emptiness and of castration; but also the death of the subject in fusion ('deathly idyllic'); the fascination and abjection of the mother on Baudelaire as a screen ('offensive').

In Baudelaire's work the 99th and 100th poems of the fleurs du mal stand *apart* and *separated* like the *great idols of the Easter Islands*. It is known that they are among the *oldest* pieces in the book; to crown it all, Baudelaire has indicated to his *mother* that she is referred to in these very poems which he has *not given a title* because publicizing this secret connection would be *offensive* to him. What distinguishes these poems is a *deathly idyllic mood*. Both, and especially the first, breathe a *peace* which is hardly ever encountered in Baudelaire. Both posit the image of the *fatherless* family; but the son, *far removed from assuming the father's place*, leaves it *vacant*. The distant, setting sun in the first poem is a symbol of *the father whose gaze* – grand oeil ouvert dans le ciel curieux – *lingers with remote interest and no jealousy* on the *meal* that *mother and son* share with each other. The second poem conjures up the image of the *fatherless family* gathered not around a table but rather a *grave*. *The sultriness of life, pregnant with begetting, has here given way completely to the cool night air of death*.[31]

Out of the deathly silence looms the *facies hippocratica* of the allegorical landscape. *Rigor mortis* is not only the other side of divisive forces, but is also loneliness in the absence of the maternal body, which is exchanged for identification with the father of personal prehistory. Catatonia and mania are closely related in psychosis.

Heterogeneity and Salvation

The journey to the Mothers on which Benjamin embarks as a theorist and philosopher has been made before him by writers, especially modernist writers. The way back into the pre-Oedipal semiotic is gruesome and dangerous because in it the negativity and heterogeneity of desires are reactivated. However, without them there is no renewal and no creativity. Wherever the new is meant to come forth, the old must be changed. Heterogeneity is the archaic legacy of the broken symbiosis with the mother. It is the death drive which leaves no attained position intact, and leaves no agreed significance, no collective meaning, no institution or subject as they were. Heterogeneity – the alternation of stasis and change – also beats time in tragic drama: 'The *Trauerspiel* is ... characterized ... by the irregular rhythm of the constant pause, the sudden change of direction, and consolidation into new rigidity.'[32]

By tearing apart all unities in the allegorical gesture, combining them afresh, and shaking them up again, heterogenesis dances around the abyss, unveiling it to the shuddering gaze. In the face of it, meaning falls away from things and words. Words become objects. Words and objects become refuse. Benjamin says: 'In the anagrams, the onomatopoetic phrases, and many other examples of linguistic virtuosity, word, syllable, and sound are emancipated from any context of traditional meaning and are flaunted as objects.'[33] Kristeva sees precisely this occur at the periphery, as she terms it, of primal repression where the 'I', in the process of becoming separated from the mother, begins to form whilst experiencing feelings of 'repugnance disgust, abjection. There is an effervescence of object and sign – not of desire but of intolerable significance; they tumble over into non-sense or the impossible real, but they appear even so in spite of "my self" (which is not) as abjection.'[34]

We have said that pleasure in abjection, the destruction of all transcendent and transcendental guarantees, is only one side of this position. The other is mourning and melancholy. Pleasure in destruction must be paid for by abandoning the narcissistic autonomy which is introduced through separation from the mother. 'Abjection is therefore a kind of narcissistic crisis, it is witness to the ephemeral aspect of the state called "narcissism" ... abjection gives narcissism its classification as "seeming".'[35] But, says Kristeva, 'abjection is a resurrection that has gone through death (of the ego). It is an alchemy that transforms death drive into a start of life, of new significance.'[36]

There is no way back to the mother since 'the abject is violence of mourning for an "object" that has always already been lost.'[37] Neither is there any going back to an unhistorical 'natural' nature. Where the light of significance is turned off, no darkness reigns, no brightness, but rather a pale half-light. This is what Benjamin means by 'demonic.' Equally, after it has been smashed into pieces, language does not revert to a *tabula rasa* of pure semantic freedom. 'Even in their isolation, the words reveal themselves as fateful. Indeed, one is tempted to say that the very fact that they still have a meaning in their isolation lends a threatening quality to this remnant of meaning they have kept.'[38]

Fear is the glimpse into the abyss when meaning flows out of phenomena. The allegory and the sublime both group around the experience of vertiginous depth or emptiness. Of course, in Kant's conception of the dynamic sublime, the subject seems to be overwhelmed by too much nature – lightning and thunder, water, wild animals, ravines. For Burke, on the other hand, it is precisely a lack of nature that horrifies the human being: a 'universe of death', as he calls the horror of emptiness. This horror is arrived at through the withdrawal of nature, 'privation of light: terror of darkness; privation of others: terror of solitude; privation of language: terror of silence; privation of objects: terror of emptiness; privation of life: terror of death'.[39] This is the horror of abject emptiness.

Allegory and the sublime are both extremes of a semiotic practice in which the arbitrariness of the sign disappears behind the illusion of the natural, the organic, brought about by convention or rhetorical devices. The fact that every symbol is a well concealed allegory, and all beauty a stabilized sublime, is only shown by extremes of figurative speech. This, says Benjamin, is because the extreme 'example of a form or genre' is 'the Idea ... and as such does not enter into the history of literature'.[40]

However, just as, in experiencing the sublime, the (narcissistic) subject saves itself from being destroyed in a-morphous nature through a new impulse of reason, so the allegorist 'wakes up' in 'God's world'.

What for Kant constitutes reason is redemption for the baroque. In both cases, the abject is sublimated.

> For it is precisely visions of the frenzy of destruction, in which all earthly things collapse into a heap of ruins which reveal not so much the ideal quality of allegorical contemplation, but rather its limit ... In the death-signs of the baroque, allegorical reflection finally veers round, in a backward movement of redemption ... The spell of utter fragmentation, death and dispersion is broken ... After all, this is the essence of melancholy immersion: that its ultimate objects, in which it believes it can most fully secure for itself *that which is abject*, turn into allegories, and that these allegories fill out and deny the void in which they are represented, just as, ultimately, the intention does not faithfully rest in the contemplation of bones, but leaps forward into resurrection.[41]

Benjamin adopts this gesture of the melancholic in its entirety. The cipher of the Messiah must redeem the abject imaginative space of history with its products of putrefaction, catastrophic heaps of rubble, the rags, the rubbish, the obsolescence of old fashions and unsaleable goods, the ruinous constructions, empty wrappers and étuis of the bourgeois subject. In Benjamin's philosophy of history, the Messiah becomes the body of the signifier 'redemption', whereas the meaning of the signifier 'redemption' – whose body is the Messiah – is the 'Marxist Sublime'[42] of the imaginative space of politics.

The experience of the sublime is linked to the experience of the abject. 'Sublimation', says Kristeva,

> is nothing else than the possibility of naming the pre-nominal, the pre-objectal, which are in fact only a trans-nominal, a trans-objectal. In the symptom, the abject permeates me, I become abject. Through sublimation, I keep it under control. The abject is edged with the sublime. It is not the same moment on the journey, but the same subject and speech bring them into being.[43]

Creativity and Abjection

The texts which Benjamin examines, as well as his own texts, are abject. They are stretched between, on the one hand, language as the 'rubbish heap of literature, as a fund of creativity', and on the other 'the corpse of language'.[44]

Benjamin's texts arouse 'aversion' because they do not obey the doxa of discourses. They do not allow themselves to be unequivocally assigned to the dominant theories. Are they Marxist? If they are, which Marxism do they follow? Or are they mystical? Metaphysical? Religious? Jewish? Are they modernist? Postmodern? Avant-gardist? Are they a matter of theory? Philosophy? Sociology? Anthropology? Literature? Are they fragmentary? Montages? Or secretly totalizing? Are they dialectical? Is the order of the *Passagen-Werk* intentional, or is it a disorder attributable to circumstances? Is it temporary or finished? Is it supposed to be a collection of quotations, or did Benjamin never manage to write the metatext?

'"Abjection", according to Bataille, "is the inability to assume with sufficient strength the imperative act of excluding abject things," an act that "establishes the foundations of collective existence". Waste is what a culture casts away in order to determine what is not itself, and thus to establish its own limits.'[45] We could say that the trajectory of Benjamin's life and death was a road paved with continuous expulsions from various collectives. Its end was the circumstance of his death. He killed himself in distress. His grave is unknown. He was himself treated like refuse. What began with his texts was finished on his body.

As Benjamin refused to define the limits of his textual bodies sharply enough, allowing 'impure' elements of the pictorial and the figurative, the narrative and avant-gardist, into his theoretical texts, and permitting 'bleak' mixtures, his writings have been subjected to even more inflexible rituals of sacrifice and bowdlerization by the academic community. Benjamin suspected this, and consequently prefaced his analyses of *Elective Affinities* and *The Origin of German Tragic Drama* with detailed instructions on how to read his texts. The motif of proper reading runs throughout his whole work. However, his efforts were in vain.

His expulsion began early on with the rejection of his *Habilitation*, an 'amalgam' of literary analysis, philosophy of language, cultural theory and sociology of religion. In its agoraphobia, the academic community was bound to find it revolting. It ended with Adorno's far-reaching critique of the *Passagen-Werk*, and the rejection of the first version of the 'Baudelaire'. Schooled in the Hegelian dialectic, and thinking in terms of highly subtle mediations and a totality of negativity, Adorno sensed that movement is not provided by a dialectic in the form of 'dialectic images' or 'dialectics at a standstill', but rather by the rough edges of heterogeneous constructions.

The Writing of Love

Let us return to the beginning. Benjamin's fundamental violation of taboos consists of reintroducing images, both as object-representation and as tropes into the very territory of the logos: the written language. It is the infusion of what has been added to the masculine, with the feminine. 'The *Vernichtung* of the figurative is also a *Verneinung* of the maternal,' says

Lyotard. Benjamin's texts introduce the sensuousness of language into the abstraction of the concept, a sensuousness which was banished from theory and religion under the domination of Greek and Jewish thought.

Looking, as a non-dominating and mimetic act of seeing and beholding – 'grand œil ouvert dans le ciel curieux' – and the tonal body of language originate in the realm of the imaginary, the maternal. The gaze, the image, the body of language, and language itself, are central to Benjamin's thinking. This is why the dominance of (pre-Oedipal) space over (Oedipal) time is emphasized in his work.

It is the maternal voice which gives the child its first identification with the earliest third party – the father of personal prehistory.

> The loving mother, different from the caring or clinging mother, is someone who has an object of desire, beyond that she has an other with relation to whom the child will serve as a go-between. She will love her child with respect to that other, and it is through a discourse aimed at that Third Party that the child will be set up as 'loved' for the mother. 'Isn't he beautiful' or 'I am proud of you' and so forth, are statements of maternal love because they involve a Third Party; it is in the eyes of a Third Party that the baby the mother speaks to becomes a he, it is with respect to others that 'I am proud of you' ... Without a Third Party, the bodily exchange [is not maternal fondness but] abjection or devouring.[46]

We shall have to consider whether the banishment of the physis from theories of signification, the binary, critical opposition of spoken and written language in deconstruction, are similar techniques for repressing the pre-Oedipal space. Benjamin quotes Schiebel who '[attributes] the reception of words, as it were, to the sense of taste.'[47] This literal incorporation of words has nothing to do with the hypostatization of an identical subject rooted in the complementary dimensions of inside/outside. Here language, including written language, is actually seen as a *part* of the body, not as its other. Benjamin interprets the bombast of the baroque as a sign of a linguistic natural longing for nature whose tone of language must nevertheless burden itself with cultural significance.

> Language which, on the one hand, seeks, in the fullness of sound, to assert its creaturely rights, is, on the other hand, in the pattern of the alexandrine, unremittingly bound to a forced logicality ... The gesture, which thereby seeks to *incorporate* meaning, is of a piece with the violent distortion of history. In language, as in life, to adopt only the typical movements of the creature and yet to express the whole of the cultural world from antiquity to Christian Europe – such is the remarkable mental attitude which is never renounced even in the *Trauerspiel*.[48]

On the subject of the 'passion for the organic' which has for a long time been attributed to the figurative baroque, Benjamin says explicitly that 'such words refer not so much to the external form of the organic as to its mysterious interiors.'[49]

Benjamin's theory of language proceeds neither from a nostalgic hypostatization of some primeval state of Adamic language, nor from the melancholic 'allegorical intention' which only reveals castration in every act of speech. Both parties are necessarily present in the speech act, moulded together – indeed, fused together. Benjamin quotes Ritter: 'do we ever have a thought or an idea without its hieroglyph, its letter, its writing? . . . Their original, and absolute, simultaneity was rooted in the fact that the organ of speech itself writes in order to speak. The letter alone speaks, or rather: word and writing are, at source, one, and neither is possible without the other.' And not only that. Even written language, in which the pleasure of the sound turns into the sadness of meaning, has a tendency to run on into the figurative, forming the 'space' of what is read. 'In the context of allegory the image is only a signature, only the monogram of essence, not the essence itself in a mask. Yet there is nothing subordinate in writing; it is not cast away in reading, like dross. It is absorbed along with what is read, as its "shape".'[50]

In the innermost part of written language, within difference as a producer of meaning, Benjamin discovers the image which enters into reading and lends volume and three-dimensionality to a purely chronological progression, moulding itself, as it were, into the reader; similarly, he sees the same dynamics manifesting themselves whenever people deal with objects in the spatial. Adorno refers to Benjamin's admission that 'I am not interested in people. I am only interested in things.' And Adorno remarks: 'The power of negation that radiates from it is one with its productive power.'[51] But what kind of negativity is it? Certainly not an ascetic fading-out of the individual as a criticism of its distortion made against ideological assurances of wholeness. It is instead a search for the moulds of objects which have shaped people in the same way that a baking tin forms cakes. The only negative aspect is the etching of the medium from which positive forms of the subject-body and his imaginary are modelled; the étui person, the stroller in the crowd, the physiognomy of Baudelaire, his strange voice. This is no remembrance (Er-'innerung') of things, but rather remembrance ('Erinnerung') through things. The inner space, this dimension between soma and phantasma, is firstly created by objects in the same way as the sense of space in a room is first evoked by its furniture. Adorno insists on the mediation of differences in the exclusively conceptual medium (the 'paternal'). Benjamin, however, in *Berliner Kindheit um Neunzehnhundert*, shows how the subject is formed in the construction of an imaginary cosmos by dealing with objects, spaces and sounds. This formation cannot be conceived either by an economic base-superstructure theory, nor by a critical theory of conceptual argumentation. Benjamin states explicitly that his cultural theories are resumptions of his childhood experiences.[52] They have been entered not only by the legacy of pre-Oedipal abjection, but also by the legacy of the mirror-stage – it is here that the child as a unified body is situated for the first time in a space continuum, under the reassuring gaze of the mother.

Benjamin avoids the 'prison house of language' without abandoning language. As for him, language is inseparable from the figurative, right into the very positionality of difference; so, conversely, images and objects only come into existence in language. The *Passagen-Werk* is precisely not a picture-book, but a montage of quotation and commentary. The double helix of writing and figure is given its most pregnant expression in Benjamin's concept of *configuration*. The omission of metalanguage in the *Passagen-Werk*, which applies Benjamin's semiotics most radically, is not the asceticism of an unmediated materialism of objects; nor is it positivism or magic, as Adorno suggests. It is the phenomenology of the dispersion of a thought pattern, regarded by many commentators as a disorder. 'As the salvation of phenomena takes place by means of ideas, so too does the presentation of ideas through the medium of empirical means. For ideas are not represented in themselves, but solely and exclusively by adjoining concrete elements to the concept: as the configuration of these elements.'[53]

Benjamin compares the relationship between idea and objects to the relationship between a constellation and the stars. Then he resurrects the mother from the dead, towards the sky: he posits the idea in relation to the mother.

> Ideas – or, to use Goethe's term, ideals – are the Faustian 'Mothers'. They remain obscure so long as phenomena do not declare their faith to them and gather round them like the children. It is the function of concepts to group phenomena together, and the differentiation which is brought about within them thanks to the critical power of the intellect is all the more significant in that it brings about two things at a single stroke: the salvation of phenomena and the representation of ideas.[54]

Out of the darkness of abjection (mothers without children), Benjamin, in an about-turn to the sublime, and with the aid of the ('paternal') critical concepts of rationality, has placed the Mothers in the sky. From there, the starlight of reason illuminates the phenomena with redemptive meaning.

> Where in Ovid is it said that the human face
> is created in order to reflect the light
> of the stars?
>
> *Passagen-Werk*, vol. 5.1, 336.

NOTES

1 Walter Benjamin, *Das Passagen-Werk*, in *Gesammelte Schriften*, ed. Rolf Tiedemann and Hermann Schweppenhäuser (Suhrkamp, Frankfurt/M., 1972/89), vol. 5, ed. Rolf Tiedemann (1982), esp. pt 1, p. 422.

2 Walter Benjamin, *The Origin of German Tragic Drama*, tr. John Osborne (Verso, London, 1985), p. 35; *Gesammelte Schriften*, vol. 3, ed. Hella Tiedemann-Bartels (1972), p. 194; *Das Passagen-Werk*, vol. 5.1, p. 139.

3 Johann Wolfgang von Goethe, *Faust: A Tragedy*, tr. Walter Arndt, ed. Cyrus Hamlin (W.W. Norton, New York, 1967), pp. 156–7.

4 Julia Kristeva, *Powers of Horror. An Essay on Abjection*, tr. Leon S. Roudiez (Columbia University Press, New York, 1982).

5 Jean-François Lyotard, 'Figure foreclosed', in *The Lyotard Reader*, ed. Andrew Benjamin (Blackwell, Oxford, 1989), pp. 69–110.

6 See Michael Thompson, *Rubbish Theory: The Creation and Destruction of Value* (Oxford University Press, Oxford, 1979).

7 Transgression and the revaluation of rubbish are always strategies of a revolt from above. Value-systems around the pole of pure/impure are systems of order which safeguard hierarchies of power and privileges. (Using the examples of the Stevengraphs, Thompson describes how these first enter the rubric of antiques from the rubbish-category of the kitschy and worthless, when they switch from women's possession to men's.) Sexual transgressions are often combined with a downward social transgression.

8 Benjamin, *Gesammelte Schriften*, vol. 7 (ed. Rolf Tiedemann and Hermann Schweppenhäuser (1989), pt. 431, pp. 2. 431–2. In the 'complete handbook copy' which Benjamin intended for publication, the 'Erwachen des Sexus' (Awakening of the Sexus) no longer appears in the main body of the text but rather in Appendix S, vol. 7. 2, p. 692.

9 Walter Benjamin, *Berliner Kindheit um Neunzehnhundert*, in *Gesammelte Schriften*, vol. 4.1, ed. Tillmann Rexroth (1971), p. 251.

10 Lyotard also sees a connection between the maternal and particular forms of religion. Referring to Freud's tearing up of certain pages in a picture-book which his father had jettisoned, he says: 'The illustrations deal with Persia, which like Egypt is the land of a mediating religion ... Tearing out the plates breaks the mediation of the mother.' *The Lyotard Reader*, p. 105.

11 Sigmund Freud, 'On the universal tendency to debasement in the sphere of love', in *The Complete Psychological Works* (Hogarth Press, London, 1981), vol. 11.

12 Sigmund Freud, 'The uncanny', in *The Complete Psychological Works*, vol. 17, p. 237.

13 Michel de Certeau, *The Practice of Everyday Life* (University of California Press, Berkeley, 1988), p. 105, quoted in Victor Burgin, 'Chance encounters', *New Formations*, 11 (1990), p. 80.

14 Letter to Herbert Belmore of 23 June 1913, in Walter Benjamin, *Briefe*, ed. Gershom Scholem and Theodor W. Adorno (Suhrkamp, Frankfurt/M., 1978), p. 67.

15   Ibid.
16   Johann Wolfgang von Goethe, *Faust: A Tragedy*, p. 165.
17   Christine Buci-Glucksmann, 'Féminité et modernité: Walter Benjamin et l'utopie du féminin', in *Walter Benjamin et Paris. Colloque international 27–29 juin 1983*, ed. Heinz Wisman (Les Editions du Cerf, Paris, 1986), p. 418.
18   Ibid., quoting Gilles Deleuze, *Francis Bacon. Logique de la sensation* (Editions de la Différence, Paris, 1981).
19   Benjamin, *Origin of German Tragic Drama*, p. 222.
20   Ibid., p. 200.
21   Ibid., p. 202.
22   Ibid., p. 207.
23   Benjamin, *Das Passagen-Werk*, vol. 5. 1, p. 402.
24   Benjamin, *Origin of German Tragic Drama*, pp. 138–9.
25   Ibid., pp. 124–5.
26   Ibid., p. 126.
27   Benjamin, *Das Passagen-Werk*, vol. 5. 1, p. 410.
28   Ibid., p. 435.
29   Ibid., p. 423.
30   Walter Benjamin, *Ursprung des deutschen Trauerspiels*, in *Gesammelte Schriften*, vol. 1. 1, pp. 360–1 (author's translation).
31   Benjamin, *Das Passagen-Werk*, vol. 5. 1, p. 449; emphasis added.
32   Benjamin, *Origin of German Tragic Drama*, p. 197.
33   Ibid., p. 207.
34   Kristeva, *Powers of Horror*, p. 11.
35   Ibid., p. 14.
36   Ibid., p. 15.
37   Ibid.
38   Walter Benjamin, *The Origin of German Tragic Drama*, p. 208.
39   Jean-François Lyotard, 'The sublime and the avant-garde', in *The Lyotard Reader*, p. 205.
40   Walter Benjamin, *The Origin of German Tragic Drama*, p. 38.
41   Walter Benjamin, *Ursprung des deutschen Trauerspiels*, p. 406 (author's translation; emphasis added).
42   Jean-François Lyotard: 'What is the sublime in Marx? Very precisely it is to be found at the point he calls labour force . . . This is a metaphysical notion. And within metaphysics, it is a notion which designates what is not determinate. What is not present and supports presence . . . The whole theory of exploitation rests on this idea which is sublime', in *Postmodernism: ICA Documents* 4, ed. Lisa Appignanesi (London, 1984), quoted in Terry Eagleton, *The Ideology of the Aesthetic* (Blackwell, Oxford, 1990), p. 231.
43   Kristeva, *Powers of Horror*, p. 11.
44   Maud Ellmann, 'Eliot's abjection', in *Abjection, Melancholia and Love*, ed. John Fletcher and Andrew Benjamin (Routledge, London, 1990), p. 180.
45   Ibid, p. 81.
46   Kristeva, *Powers of Horror*, p. 34.
47   Walter Benjamin, *The Origin of German Tragic Drama*, p. 209.
48   Ibid., p. 210 (emphasis added).

49   Walter Benjamin, *Ursprung des deutschen Trauerspiels*, p. 384 (author's translation).
50   Ibid., p. 388.
51   Theodor W. Adorno, 'Vorrede II', in Benjamin, *Briefe*, p. 17.
52   Susan Buck-Morss, *The Dialectics of Seeing: Walter Benjamin and the Arcades Project* (MIT Press, Cambridge, Mass./London, 1989), pp. 278–9.
53   Benjamin, *Origin of German Tragic Drama*, p. 34.
54   Ibid., p. 35.

Part III

Sexual Politics and National Identity

7

Prefigurative Racism in Goethe's *Iphigenie auf Tauris*

Recently, I saw a video of the film *Eagle's Wing* directed by Anthony Harvey, and I was struck by the at first unlikely, but in the end fundamental correspondences it displayed with Goethe's *Iphigenia on Tauris*. At the climax of the film the action is concentrated upon an archetypal constellation of Western culture. Not surprisingly it is a triangle. The noble Red Indian White Bull, in the course of robbing a stage-coach, has abducted a beautiful virginal girl, dressed in white, whom he keeps as his prisoner. They are pursued by a young white Westerner who is after the Indian's famous white horse, Eagle's Wing, which had once belonged to the white man.

Through a network of parallels the girl and the horse are both used to signify a state of crisis: whiteness in the wrong place, that is, in the hands of another race. In the course of the chase, sexual tension grows between the brave and his prisoner, while at the same time the white appearance of the girl and horse become increasingly soiled. The progress of passion is presented as a process of defilement. So a spectator who knows the appropriate cultural code can be pretty sure that the ending will not turn out to be a happy one.

After a showdown, the Red Indian rides away on his horse and the others are left stranded apart and helpless in the desert. Thus, however heroic and proud White Bull has been allowed to appear through the script and the photography, the central taboo has been preserved, even by a film which has openly tried to advocate more liberal tendencies than the normal Western would do. There was no chance of bringing together a white woman and a coloured man. In fact, the film sorts everything out quite traditionally: on one side we find the Red Indian, on the other the two whites. Despite the superficial reversal – victorious native, defeated intruders – the terms of the triangular grouping remain exactly the same. That they do so is a testimony to the power and prevalence of the mastercode which not only dictates the plot of this modern film, but which is already to be found informing a German play written two hundred years earlier in an otherwise quite different culture. In both the modern film and the classical drama, it is the position of the white woman which is forcefully inscribed into the imaginary scenario. Furthermore, in *Eagle's Wing* she is severely punished for having abandoned her subjection to the white patriarchal law which can only be defined by the subjection of the woman. This law tells us what a woman is in relation to men and in relation to race.

Goethe wrote a first prose version of *Iphigenie* in 1779 and, after a long stay in Italy, rewrote it in iambic pentameters. With this play, orthodox literary history informs us, he had matured from his rebellious *Sturm und Drang* youth into an attitude of serene renunciation. Nevertheless, his reconciliation with reality, expressed through the play's final, all-embracing harmony (slightly tinged with resignation), is continually in conflict with what has to be repressed in order to achieve this harmonious ending. In a famous essay Theodor W. Adorno showed how this classical humanism (as the process of individuation through renunciation is normally described) is only a frail bridge over the abyss of unappeasable passions generated by the exertion of different structures of power and control.[1]

Before we go into the details of Goethe's version and consider its reception in Germany, we should briefly look at the European tradition of the Iphigenia plot. In the seventeenth and eighteenth centuries there emerges a plethora of Iphigenia adaptations in France, Italy and Germany, the most famous being the drama by Guimond de la Touche, *Iphigénie en Tauride* (1757), and especially the opera by Gluck and Goethe's play, both of which were first performed in 1779. All these adaptations go back, of course, to the original Greek play by Euripides. Its success in its own time and with later generations is due to the success with which Euripides humanizes the original myth. This myth only tells us the story of *Iphigenia in Aulis*. The army of Agamemnon is unable to set sail for Troy because Artemis has becalmed the seas, in order to punish Agamemnon for having killed a sacred hind. He can only atone for this by sacrificing his daughter Iphigenia. In writing a second part to the story, *Iphigenia in Tauris*, Euripides departs from the myth. Here the sacrifice is not demanded by the goddess, but is the result of an error on the part of the old seer, Calchas. Just as Iphigenia is about to be killed, Artemis sets a sheep in her place and brings Iphigenia in a cloud to Tauris in Asia Minor, where Artemis is worshipped by the barbaric Scythians. Iphigenia becomes her priestess and has to sacrifice to her every stranger who is found on the shores of the country.

One day Orestes and his friend Pylades arrive in Tauris. Orestes is being pursued by the Furies for having killed his mother Clytemnestra, who in turn had slaughtered the returning Agamemnon in revenge for the supposed death of her daughter Iphigenia. Apollo has promised Orestes expiation if he brings the effigy of Artemis back from Tauris to Delphi. The two strangers are captured by the men of the Scythian king Thoas, and Iphigenia is unknowingly about to sacrifice her own brother, thus continuing the bloody curse laid by the gods on the house of the Tantalides. After the central scene of recognition, they conspire to steal the effigy of the goddess and flee from the island in a concealed boat. A plan to kill Thoas first is firmly rejected by Iphigenia, although he is only a barbarian, because he has been her host and protector. Orestes gets rid of the Furies on Tauris, but their plot is discovered. As the winds force the boat back on shore, they are rescued by the *dea ex machina* Athene, who sends a wind and assuages Thoas, who is left behind with nothing. Euripides' humanizing recasting of the myth is evident both in the treatment of Thoas and in the reconciliation between the gods and the Tantalides.

The subsequent reception of the play, especially in the era of the Enlightenment, places increasing emphasis on the freeing of Orestes and Iphigenia from the determination of their fates by the gods, whereas the barbarians are largely neglected. In fact in Gluck's opera the Scythians are shown as bloodthirsty characters without any human feelings; and in Guimond de la Touche's play Thoas is even killed in a battle. We can say that, up until Goethe, there is a deep chasm between the Greeks and the barbarians, and that basically they are presented as having nothing in common apart from their involvement in the merely external action of fighting and plotting.

Goethe's play introduces vital changes. What can be and has been interpreted as a decisive humanistic advance on his predecessors is the total internalization of the conflict and its solution within the psychology of the characters. As the external action becomes transformed into a complex of moral problems, the barbarian king has to be invested with an inner dimension which makes him an equal partner in the ethical debate. In Goethe's play Thoas thus becomes a *noble* barbarian king, and the story as a whole is correspondingly transfigured.

In her total purity Goethe's Iphigenia has changed the cult of human sacrifice in Tauris into one based on animal sacrifice. Nevertheless the drama begins with her complaint about being far from her Greek homeland, isolated in her role as priestess, and it ends with a general attack on the fate of women as subdued – especially as wives – to the moods and whims of men. It turns out that Thoas wants her as his wife. If she refuses he will introduce anew the old custom of human sacrifice. Iphigenia feels a strong aversion to his proposal. Orestes and Pylades arrive and the scene of recognition follows. Under the influence of his pure sister, Orestes falls into a deep coma, during which he beholds the murderous members of the

Tantalides family reunited only after death. After that he is cured of his insanity, the internalized manifestation of the Furies.

Thoas' men discover the strangers and, as Iphigenia is still hesitating over a positive answer to his demand, he orders them to be the first victims of the revived cult. Iphigenia despairs of her belief in the goodness of the gods, and recalls the defeat and repression of the Titans by the new order of gods governed by Zeus. She plots together with Orestes and Pylades, though reluctantly, because she does not want to deceive her fatherly benefactor Thoas. The Scythians have meanwhile discovered the theft of Artemis' effigy, and Thoas, suspicious of the priestess's part in the plot, confronts her in the decisive scene. Iphigenia, disillusioned with her treacherous role, which goes against her dedication to chaste purity, reveals everything to the king, thus placing their fate in his hands, and appealing to his humanity and his earlier promise to let her go if her brother can prove his identity and provide the means for her return to Greece. Moreover, it transpires that they do not need to steal the effigy of the goddess, because Orestes can interpret Apollo's ambivalent order 'Bring the sister home to Delphi' (V. vi) as a reference to his own sister Iphigenia.

Thoas agrees reluctantly, saying simply: 'Go then' (V. vi). In response to Iphigenia's plea that he should be more friendly and thus provide a basis for mutual visits in the future, he ends the drama with the words 'Fare well' (V. vi).

If we compare Goethe's version with those which preceded it, the decisive change lies in the sexual interest which Thoas takes in Iphigenia. Although he himself speaks of his desire to dispel the loneliness of his house after the sudden death of his son (I. iii), Iphigenia's monologue takes a more disillusioned view of his intentions: 'Does he want to drag me into his bed?' (I. ii). And here, I think, we have the crucial tableau which structures our perception of the play: a white, pure, virginal sister-figure standing between her brother, who wants to bring her home into their father's house, and the sombre half-savage who holds military and sexual power and who wants to take that absolute purity away from her.

In his book *Male Fantasies (Männerphantasien)* Klaus Theweleit has analysed the novels and autobiographies of officers in the pre-Fascist paramilitary formations (the *Freikorps*), which were operational against the victorious Communists in Germany and the Baltic after the revolution in 1919.[2] In all these texts he discovers a distinctive strategy in the presentation of women: they are transformed into white, asexual mother- and sister-figures. Sexuality is projected as something degrading on to the so-called 'red' women of the working classes and the Russian women who fought in the Red Armies. At one fell swoop, the political enemy is bound up with sexuality, and progressive politics are 'debased' by these connotations of a menacing, castrating female sexuality. The ideal of a woman in a patriarchal society becomes ultimately that of the dead woman, woman mortified into something white and bloodless, and this white mother/sister ideal is the guarantee and basis of a patriarchal identity. As such, the white de-sexualized woman provides the cultural basis of the status quo. How this image is used to support forms of male domination, such as the institution of the army or the state or the family, has been worked out by the anthropologist Sherry B. Ortner.

In her essay entitled 'Is female to male as nature is to culture?' she comes to this conclusion about the ambiguous symbolic value women have in a patriarchal culture:

> We can begin to understand then how a single system of cultural thought can often assign to women completely polarized and apparently contradictory meanings, since extremes, as we say, meet. That she often represents life and death is only the simplest example one could mention. For another perspective on the same point, it will be recalled that the psychic mode associated with women seems to stand at both the bottom and the top of the scale of human modes of relating. The tendency in that mode is to get involved more directly with people as individuals and not as representatives of one social category or another; this mode can be seen as either 'ignoring' (and thus subverting) or 'transcending' (and thus achieving a higher synthesis of) these social categories, depending on the cultural view for any given purpose. Thus we can account easily for both the subversive feminine symbols (witches, evil eye, menstrual pollution, castrating mothers) and the feminine symbols of trans-cendence (mother goddesses, merciful dispensers of salvation, female symbols of justice, and the strong feminine symbolism in the realm of art, religious ritual and law). If women's (culturally viewed) intermediacy between culture and nature has this implication of generalized ambiguity of meaning charac-teristic of marginal phenomena, then we are also in a better position to account for those cultural and historic inversions in which women are in some way or other symbolically aligned with culture and men with nature.[3]

Among the other examples which Ortner gives is 'Nazi Germany, in which women were said to be the guardians of culture and morals', and 'European courtly love, in which man considered himself the beast and woman the pristine exalted object'. One can recognize without difficulty in the above feminine symbol of transcendence the white sister/mother figure in Theweleit's male fantasies. Ortner's point about their function in the symbolic discourse being to achieve a higher synthesis of the social categor-ies, of which that culture is an expression, enables us to understand the libidinal idiosyncrasy which hovers around that image.

If the repression of sexuality in the image of women is constitutive of a man's cultural identity, then it must be concluded that a threat to that identity, or what is subjectively felt as such, must, in order to be effective, be mediated by a reinvocation of repressed female sexuality. Inseparably, this means that a *racist* discourse in patriarchal society necessarily always includes a discourse on the sexuality – or rather the non-sexuality – of that society's representative woman. This is perfectly illustrated by the observations made in a somewhat journalistic study called *Sex and Racism in America*. The author observes that: 'Sexually the southern white man has mixed (and is mixing) almost at will with Negro women. What he has proclaimed is that Negro men and white women shall not mix. By and large, this has been (and is) the white man's sexual proclamation for the entire nation.'[4] When the author states that 'the race problem is inextricably connected with sex' and that 'the sexualization of the race problem is a reality', it would in fact be more accurate to say that the race problem as such only exists *as* a sexual problem.

If we return now to Goethe, we can see that the power of his play, in comparison with the other versions, lies exactly in its presentation of the basic male fantasy of the Western white world. We have the white, pure sister in both senses. She is a sister to a brother and she is a healer, a dispenser of salvation, a symbol of justice. As priestess she is the performer of the central cult of the society. This cult is dedicated to a goddess, who herself embodies the main ideological positions assigned to women in a male society: the virgin and the woman who gives birth.

From this perspective what seems to be the humanist advance of the German text could also be read as a much more subtle discourse of social and racial control. Whereas in the earlier versions the abyss between the Greeks and the Scythians is practically unbridged (with the Greek cult even being assimilated by the barbarians, for example, and the effigy of Artemis being carried back to Delphi at the end), one could say that in Goethe's text the desire for the imperial Greek culture is already deeply implanted in the psychology and culture of the Scythians. Thoas longs for the socially elevated woman and always will, because he cannot attain her, and the cult central to the national identity stays back in Tauris with the effigy of Artemis. Goethe's play inscribes into our perception two main images. First, the white woman is sexually threatened by the barbarian or savage; and second, the barbarians are really yearning for all that is Greek. That this is the dominant effect is evident in Adorno's interpretation. He complains that the humanism of the text is only a thin veneer, especially because it is achieved purely at the expense of the barbarians. Thoas himself is left behind with empty hands, observes Adorno, a circumstance which tacitly assumes the Scythian desire for the Greek.[5]

Only in the light of such an analysis can we explain the text's cultural power in the German literary tradition and education. Considered in terms of drama or spectacle the play has repeatedly been described as lifeless, undramatic, abstract, cold, colourless, boring. The play's survival and pre-eminence in the theatre over the last two centuries, despite this kind of judgement, can only be accounted for if we seek the rationale of its appeal at a level deeper than the merely theatrical.

What I would suggest is that its function and importance derive from its capacity to shape and mould the subject into a specific patriarchal and ethnic identity. As Germany, even in the eighteenth century, had not yet become a nation-state, whose identity could be constituted through its confrontation with, and control of, other ethnic groups, it can construct the requisite subjectivity only in more generalized and vague terms. It thus employs a notion of a sort of European identity, the outlines of which are not to be found in the social or political domain, but in the cultural sphere. The imaginary body of that European culture is the classical heritage.

Edward Saïd has traced the discourse of orientalism back to the texts of Homer, Aeschylus and Euripides. Referring to *The Bacchae* and *The Persians* he concludes: 'The two aspects of the orient that set it off from the West in this pair of plays will remain essential motifs of European imaginative geography. A line is drawn between two continents. Europe is powerful and articulate; Asia is defeated and distant.'[6] The difference in political power then gets translated into the discourse of cultural achievement. Europe enters the stage as the bringer of culture into the land of the barbarians. In this respect the deep affinities between the Greek and the German treasure-house of images (another central text in the Austrian classical tradition being Grillparzer's adaptation of Euripides' *Medea*) spring from the fact that both nations are situated right on the borderline between Europe and Asia. The explicit imperialist actualization of this implicit constellation in literature and mythology was more likely to occur here than in other European nations. The history of the Germanic empire has always been determined by its relation to Asia. It begins with the colonization of the former eastern part of Germany in the Middle Ages, and its traumas are rooted in the threats posed by the Huns and the Turks. It is thus not surprising that the culture-versus-barbarism topos played and still plays an essential role in the ethical rationalization of colonial interest. If one looks at where Tauris is situated, it is in fact in today's Crimea, in the very heart of that Russia which was the chief target of German imperialism.

In his study *Der deutsche Drang nach Osten (The German Drive towards the East)*, Wolfgang Wippermann analyses the connection between German imperialist politics and the historical discourse of the nineteenth century.[7] There is only one conclusion to be drawn from his extensive material: that the moral justification for colonial politics is exclusively drawn from the subject-position of cultural superiority. The Germans had brought culture to the Slavs, a population which, according to Hegel, had no history of its own. So strong was the topos that by the end of the century a sort of quasi-natural law of the East surrendering to the West had come into existence in the historians' imagination. Hitler had no trouble building his aggressive imperialism of *Lebensraum im Osten* on the foundation provided by traditional German historical and imaginative discourse. The political impact of Goethe's play is mediated through the cultural formation of Germany's intelligentsia in the nineteenth and twentieth centuries.

If we consider the history of the reception of *Iphigenie auf Tauris*, it is quite clear that it is a text for the educated elite. It is based on knowledge of antiquity, and it is the epitome of an anti-popular literary tradition. Saïd points out that 'the closeness between politics and Orientalism, or to put it more circumspectly, the great likelihood that ideas about the Orient drawn from Orientalism can be put to political use, is an important yet extremely sensitive truth.'[8] Analogously we might say the same about the relation between the imaginative body of a culture and its more discursive disciplines. The tableau, the staging, the image which the pictorial mind constructs in reading (or in the direct reception of a theatrical production) organizes the narrative pattern which structures the discourse of historiography. But historiography is again in turn produced by a cultural elite.

So the direct reception of *Iphigenie* in literary criticism and in the educational institutions is confined to the most elite social strata from which the specialists in other academic disciplines are recruited. During the Third Reich, with its chronic petit-bourgeois, pseudo-proletarian distrust of the humanistic tradition and its representatives (one need only recall Goering's infamous remark, 'When I hear the word culture I reach for my gun'), *Iphigenie* disappears into the background, immured in academic Goethean philology and the curricula of the secondary schools. But it had fulfilled its function. The pre-racialist topos of culture-versus-barbarism has been translated by German Fascism into racism pure and simple. Jews and Slavs, both from the East, have become a subhuman race. Both have been endowed with an aura of abnormal sexual appetite. Although this image of the Jew has disappeared from the German ideological tradition along with the Jews themselves from German territory, the image of the sexually vile Russian has remained powerfully present in the national 'memory' of the Russian soldiers raping German women on their way to victory in 1945. I am not suggesting, of course, that the Russians did not rape during the war. What is significant is that in the national memory the rapes committed by the Americans, Canadians, English, Moroccans and French are not remembered at all, whereas the Russians are recalled as having done nothing but rape.

German anti-socialism is, in my opinion, deeply rooted in racism. As a result any rational discussion in purely political terms stands little chance of penetrating to those deeper recesses where the ethnic and the patriarchal identity of the German male merge into one.

Goethe succeeded in giving precise expression to this crucial formation. He could do so because he had an inherited body of writing at his disposal which, in the imaginative power of its patriarchal and imperial values, corresponded to Goethe's own position. That it happened at this time, that is, shortly before the French Revolution, is scarcely a coincidence. According to the studies of Ruth Benedict and Hannah Arendt,[9] racist discourse had first been used by the French aristocracy against the supposed equality of all men after the French Revolution. Goethe writes his play as a close confidant and civil servant of Duke Karl-August of Sachsen-Weimar, a tiny German replica of French absolutism. He has a love-relationship with the lady-in-waiting Frau von Stein, who is said to have been always dressed completely in white. It is generally agreed that she was the model for Iphigenia. Goethe himself, while writing his play, is simultaneously engaged in conscripting the sons of the local peasantry as Weimar's contribution to the Prussian army. In a letter to his lover, Frau von Stein, Geothe writes: 'I can hardly proceed with my play. King Thoas is being made to speak as if no weaver in Apolda is about to starve.'[10] The connection between the barbarian king and the deprived working-class population shows clearly that Goethe's own class-consciousness – or rather his unconscious class-consciousness – has fuelled his play with the ideological fire which feeds an internal as much as the external colonialism. The opposition of culture and barbarism organizes the perception in both cases.

That it continues to do so is evident from the blurb on the cover of the video of the film *Eagle's Wing*, with which I began. It promises a gripping adventure in which a white man finds himself by fighting his way through 'the barbaric country of the red indians'.

NOTES

1 Theodor W. Adorno, 'Zum Klassizismus von Goethes Iphigenie', in *Noten zur Literatur* (Suhrkamp, Frankfurt/M., 1981), pp. 7–33.
2 Klaus Theweleit, *Männerphantasien* (2 vols, Verlag Roter Stern, Frankfurt/M., 1977, 1978); see ch. 8 n. 14 for English tr.
3 Sherry B. Ortner, 'Is female to male as nature is to culture?', in *Woman, Culture and Society*, ed. Michelle Zimbalist Rosaldo and Louise Lamphere (Stanford University Press, Stanford, Calif., 1974), pp. 85–6.
4 Calvin C. Hernton, *Sex and Racism in America* (Grove Press, New York, 1965).
5 Adorno, 'Zum Klassizismus', pp. 507–9.
6 Edward W. Saïd, *Orientalism* (Routledge & Kegan Paul, London, 1978), p. 57.
7 Wolfgang Wippermann, *Der 'Deutsche Drang nach Osten'. Ideologie und Wirklichkeit eines politischen Schlagworts* (Wissenschaftliche Buchgemeinschaft, Darmstadt, 1981).
8 Saïd, *Orientalism*, p. 96.

9   Ruth Benedict, *Race and Racism* (Routledge & Kegan Paul, London, 1983), pp. 111–27: 'Racism and class conflict'; Hannah Arendt, 'Race-thinking before racism', *Review of Politics*, 6 (1944), pp. 36–73.
10   *Goethes Briefe an Frau von Stein. Auswahl in fünf Büchern*, ed. with intro. Hermann Camillo Kellner (Reclam, Leipzig, n.d.), pp. 114–15 (letter of 14 May 1778).

8

Sexuality in Robert Musil's *Young Törless*

Robert Musil's novel *Young Törless* extends a compelling invitation to study the entanglement of constructions of sexual difference with the politics of fantasy and the reproduction of politics.[1]

The novel is based on the author's experiences as a pupil at two military boarding-schools of the Habsburg Empire at the end of the nineteenth century. Musil's tracing of the connection between the unconscious of upper-class male adolescents and the symbolic order into which they are educated has led many critics to read this text as an anticipation of the fascist horrors to come. But *Young Törless* does more than this. Beyond the analogy between the text's representation of sadism and the atrocities of fascism it deciphers the realities of masculine psychology and men's conditioning, of which fascism is but one consequence.

In the figure of young Törless Musil shows us the formation of a character who will end up as a sterile intellectual and aesthete who will tolerate anything, as long as he can pursue the traditional paths of social discourse and the refinement of his narcissistic sensibility. The other possible outcome of the transgressive onset of adolescent sexuality Musil was able to save for himself. By diverting the danger of aestheticism and intellectualism from his own personality through the act of writing, he emerged as the other of the aesthete, namely the productive artist, who could channel and sublimate those destructive drives into the creative power of art.

If we compare Musil's case with that of Joyce, we might suggest that while Joyce, owing to his more marginal position in the Anglo-Irish symbolic order, was able to fulfil himself as an artist, not only in his own life but also in the narrative of *A Portrait of the Artist as a Young Man*, Musil could only do so in his life, but not in his writing. In his fiction he was forced to confront the barren double of the artist, the barren double of himself as acquiescent in the Habsburg status quo.

The novel is set at a military public school for upper-class boys in Bohemia-Moravia, on the margins of the Austrian Empire. There, after a melancholy farewell to his parents and especially his mother, Törless's life becomes involved with five characters: the prostitute Bozena, who initiates him into sexuality; the young prince, the sublime object of Törless's admiration and devotion; Beineberg and Reiting, the sadistic class tyrants with whom Törless forms an uneasy alliance; and finally Basini, the effeminate victim of the boys' blackmail for theft and sadistic sexual practices. The book ends with the school's investigation into the scandalous affair after Basini gives himself up in order to save his life. He is expelled, Beineberg and Reiting stay, and Törless, after a subtle apologetic speech, leaves and returns to the parental home.

Traditional criticism has consistently sidelined the novel's flagrantly central preoccupation with sexuality. *Törless* is concerned, we are told, with much more sublime matters such as epistemology, the philosophy of the subject, and linguistic scepticism. Sexuality is marginal, as are its so-called 'aberrant' and 'deviant' forms.

Musil has lent his own powerful voice to this choir, and interpreters and critics have eagerly allowed themselves to be diverted into mystical emotionality. Most curiously, Musil wrote in a letter dated 21 December 1906:

> But one thing is of supreme importance to me. I do not wish to make pederasty comprehensible. Of all abnormalities it is perhaps the furthest from me. At least in its contemporary form. It is mere chance that I chose it, it was due to the plot that I happened to have in my memory. Basini's place could be taken by a woman, and the place of bisexuality by sadism, masochism, fetishism.[2]

We cannot believe what the letter-writer says here if we are to take the novelist seriously. For *Törless* is precisely about homosexuality and bisexuality, sadism, masochism and fetishism. For this reason no woman could take Basini's place, because Basini is *like* a woman. The so-called *succès de scandale* of *Törless* among the general public in 1906 is more revealing than the critical pieties of the academic fraternity. This higher obfuscation springs from the very mentality whose genesis, structure and social function Musil's novel opens to question. Because male sexuality is so radically explored throughout the novel, it seems deviant and confused to the so-called normal eye. Where human existence is organized through structures of power and exploitation, there can be no sexuality in whose dynamic these structures are not inscribed. Just as the cadets' boarding-school, the 'seedbed of the nation' (*Pflanzschule der Nation*) as it used to be termed, is implanted in the heart of an impoverished, colonized minority, so the internal hothouse of the school itself breeds the rituals designed to discipline the instincts into conformity with the system. Epistemological discourses in the novel, parodies of sublime spiritualization, become the means of masking and elevating a sordid reality. In revealing this interpenetration of politics, sexuality and textuality, Musil's novel goes even beyond Freud's theory, holding up to it the mirror of its own origins.

In the pictures that Musil develops for us in the dark-room of *Young Törless* there are no women to be seen: group portraits without ladies. The absence of women is not gratuitous, as Musil will later tell us,[3] but significant and necessary. In this primal scene of a militaristic patriarchy, woman functions not as a reality, but as a sign. She marks the boundaries of the symbolic universe of this male society. As the maternal, she marks the supreme social imaginary leading to sanctity; as a threatening, alien and phallic sexuality, she represents the borderline with chaos. This scheme of binary femininity not only signifies the dualism of nature and culture, but also shapes the structures of male desire in many cultures.[4]

In 1912, in his essay 'On the universal tendency to debasement in the sphere of love', Freud describes the reasons for men's physical and psychological impotence. He sees them as rooted in the repression of sexual desire for the mother in the little boy, and consequently the separation of the affectionate and sensual currents in the man as they affect his relationships with women. Whereas in the case of physical impotence the man's whole sexuality remains bound to unconscious incestuous fantasies, the psychological form is revealed in a limited object-choice.

> The whole sphere of love in such people remains divided in the two directions personified in art as sacred and profane (or animal) love. Where they love they do not desire and where they desire they cannot love. They seek objects which they do not need to love, in order to keep their sensuality away from the objects they love ... The main protective measure which men have recourse to in this split in their love consists in a psychical debasement of the sexual object ... As soon as the condition of debasement is fulfilled, sensuality can be freely expressed.

Freud reaches the conclusion: 'We can now understand the motives behind the boy's phantasies ... which degrade the mother to the level of a prostitute. They are efforts to bridge the gulf between the two currents in love, at any rate in phantasy, and by debasing the mother to acquire her as an object of sensuality.'[5]

In the present context a further observation of Freud's is important, according to which a 'sphere of love' thus divided into the high and the low will contain perverse sexual aims such as coprophilia and sadism, based on 'the need on the part of men to debase their sexual object'.[6]

In *Törless* it becomes apparent that Musil is exposing, in a particular historical and political context, the process by which the Manichaean instinctual structure described by Freud becomes fixed in the male individual. For this reason I do not believe that Claudio Magris, for example, is right when he says he sees *Törless* as disclosing the emergence of the 'racial and mystifying irrationalisms' of fascism,[7] or that he can read Beineberg and Reiting as representatives of fascistic sadism. Musil goes much further. He shows us instinctual dispositions which function within a political system of colonial, social and sexual domination. Fascism can be securely erected on these *fin-de-siècle* structures of the collapsing Habsburg Empire. Magris believes that the events in *Törless* are 'a crushing blow to the idealistic optimism and solid rationalism' of the nineteenth century,[8] and that the 'harmony and magnanimous idealistic image of the *Grand Siècle* with its belief in a unified and classical view of the world end up in the degradation of the young cadets' filthy perversions'.[9] In this he shows himself to be trapped in the very dualisms and male fantasies that are staged and problematized in the novel. Rationalism and barbarism, idealism and perversion are not diachronic alternatives or historical stages, but rather the preconditions of each other. This is the path of knowledge pursued by young Törless.

Musil's text offers an analytic dramatization of how Törless's predicament is connected to wider structures of attitude and behaviour, as though the whole framework 'is exposed to your gaze like the worm-holes you see when a piece of timber splits open'. Both the railroad to Russia at the start of the novel, and the road homewards with which the narrative concludes, lead directly to this novel's 'heart of darkness', the black and blood-red attic room of a sexuality drenched in power. In this respect it is no coincidence that Musil wrote a novel of adolescence, despite his own assumption to the contrary. For during adolescence we see a sundering of the components of what we are used to calling the subject or identity, before they appear to condense into a harder and more opaque mask of selfhood.[10]

Bozena

Under the pressures of puberty, the figures of his mother and the part-time prostitute Bozena begin to merge for Törless. The fear, confusion and fascination that this unleashes in him reveal the original division of the two instinctual currents, exactly as described by Freud. But in Bozena we can also see how the unconscious of the little rich boy is a political unconscious in a quite specific way, one in which sexuality is socially coded.

For as a contrast to and a precondition of sublimation into the elevated, refined, light-filled world of his parents, a quite different archive comes to light. Condemned as dirty, low and dark, it consists of the heterogeneous parts discarded during the formation of Törless's character. It is what makes him a member of his class, since it must vanish from his body and his consciousness. This dark zone is ambivalent.

> Repugnance and fascination are the twin poles of the process in which a *political* imperative to reject and eliminate the debasing 'low' conflicts power-fully and unpredictably merge with a desire for this Other ... The result is a mobile, conflictual fusion of power, fear and desire in the construction of subjectivity: a psychological dependence upon precisely those Others which are being rigorously opposed and excluded at the social level.[11]

The primary fact of a sensuality repressed on the grounds that it is dirty brings all other repressions to the surface, but now in a thoroughly sexual-ized form. Thus the figure of Bozena condenses, for Törless, the forbidden elements of the other, repressed into the lower regions. She is a member of the Slavic population. In her figure racial heterogeneity, the result of ethnic discrimination within the framework of imperial power-politics, is intensi-fied by the lowliness of her peasant background, and, in her particular case, the inferiority of the serving-wench and chambermaid.

Bozena's extraordinary sexual fascination goes beyond racial and social prohibitions. Her body too inhabits the realm of perversion, in which Törless's world is turned upside down. Bozena's body occupies the same place as the grotesque body in the inverted world of the carnival, a return of the repressed organized and sanctioned by society as a whole. This body is the opposite of the classical sublime ideal of beauty, and of the consequent differentiated aesthetic of the body.

> She had not yet become actually ugly, but her face was strikingly lacking in any kind of charm, and she evidently went to some trouble to emphasise this by her general air and behaviour ... For 'the young gentlemen from the college'. . . she deliberately displayed her crudest and most repellent qualities, because ... in spite of that they still came creeping along to her just the same. (p. 35)

Musil stresses this aspect by adding, in the face of the facts: 'Had Bozena been pure [!] and beautiful ... he would perhaps have sunk his teeth in her flesh, so heightening their lust to the point of pain' (p. 37).

The bodies of serving-girls, at work and thus in violent motion, have often exerted an extraordinary sexual attraction on upper-class men, as Bozena points out. Törless is no exception:

> Outside the doors ... the women-folk were standing, in their wide skirts and coarse shifts, their broad feet caked with dust, their arms bare and brown ...

Almost naked children tumbled about in the mud of the yards; here and there as some woman bent over her work her skirt swung high, revealing the hollows at the back of her knees, or the bulge of a heavy breast showed as the linen tightened over it. It was as though all this were going on in some quite different, animal, oppressive atmosphere, and the cottages exuded a heavy, sluggish air, which Törless eagerly breathed in. (pp. 15–16)

The children in the mud, the women's bodies revealed and fleshed out as they work, are the exact, 'animal', opposite of the physically disciplined, the erect, observing man and the fine lady. It is here, in Bozena's world, that Törless recalls the aesthetics and fine manners of his parental home, where bodies are stylized into incorporeality. He remembers the 'bright rooms', the 'well cared-for, immaculate, unapproachable faces', the 'cultivated, cool hands', the 'perfected manners of that society, which never for an instant allowed itself any slip from its own style' (p. 40).

The fascination exerted by the working women and Bozena derives not only from the taboo of their social baseness, but also from their secret power. These are women who do have power, who deal in a concrete fashion with the world and its matter. In Bozena this aspect is intensified by a certain worldliness and an independent pride. It is, in the last analysis, male fantasies of submission to the matriarch that seek satisfaction in these images of womanhood. And back comes everything that had to be repressed in these men, whose upbringing has been geared to hardness and dominance: the original impulses of empathy, affection and fusion. Because of the need to exclude them during the education of the little boy, on the grounds that they are unmanly, patriarchy categorizes and proscribes these impulses as 'base' and 'female'. In such a context 'subjectivity can only ever be the oppression and objectivication of the other person. This mode of being a subject is based on supremacy, never intersubjectivity.'[12]

If Törless is also fascinated by forms of self-effacement, mystical unions and fusions, these can never escape their masochistic dimension and are, for this very reason, finally doomed to failure. Törless's desire, in his encounter with Bozena, is for a self-staged submission and erasure of the ego rather than the return to a kind of natural, undistorted or authentic sexuality beyond all class deformations, as certain critics have argued.[13]

Even in his experiences of nature-mysticism, Törless is always an object in a sphere influenced by *other* forces. Thus the sky draws his gaze into infinity without leading him to any goal, and the wall into which he melts fills his passive ears with sounds, and looks at *him* rather than the other way round. He feels as if inanimate objects are 'attacking him with a hundred eyes', and in his first attic experience with Basini his orgasm is produced not only by what he sees but also by what he hears. Above all he constantly feels himself under the gaze of the circle of light around the lamp, which he perceives as an eye. This gaze enslaves him to such an extent that he feels the need 'to wallow in the pool of it – to crawl right into that dusty corner on all fours, as if that were the way to guess it'. (p. 102).

But already with Bozena he had been seized by the desire for the collapse of his erect little 'lordly ego', his body-armour, as Klaus Theweleit would say.[14]

> 'There would be nothing for it but . . . to let himself be protected by Bozena. The thought went shuddering through him. But that was it! That was just it! Nothing else! This fear, this self-abandonment, was what seduced him anew every time. This stepping out of his privileged position and going among common people – among them? no, lower than them! . . . Bozena appeared to him as a creature of monstrous degradation, and his relationship to her, with the sensations it evoked in him, was like a cruel rite of self-sacrifice. (p. 36)

So not only the boundaries between the socially high and the socially low, between incestuous and ethnic inner and outer zones are blurred in Bozena; in the desire for submission, which Musil characterizes as female, the differences between the sexes become confused in Törless too.[15]

In Törless's fantasies, his fellow-pupil Beineberg is transformed downwards, back into the writhing, jerking, grotesque body of sexual transgression. Of Beineberg's looks we learn:

> it was not the ugly, it was precisely the more attractive features that made him so peculiarly uneasy . . . If he thought the clothes away from the body, it became quite impossible to hold on to the notion of calm slenderness; what happened then, instantly, was that in his mind's eye he saw restless, writhing movements, a twisting of limbs and a bending of the spine such as are to be found in all pictures of martyrs' deaths, or in the grotesque performances of acrobats and 'rubber men' at fairs. And the hands, too, which he could certainly just as well have pictured in some beautifully expressive gesture, he could not imagine otherwise than in motion, with flickering fingers. And it was precisely on these hands, which were really Beineberg's most attractive feature, that his greatest repugnance was concentrated. There was something prurient [*unzüchtiges*] about them . . . And there was for him something prurient, too, about the body, which he could not help associating with dislocated movements. But it was in the hands that this seemed to accumulate, and it seemed to radiate from them like a hint of some touch that was yet to come, sending a thrill of disgust coursing over Törless's skin. (pp. 21–2)

This fear connected with the pleasurable collapse and destruction of Törless's subjectivity is conjured up by the forest and darkness which accompany the scenes of masochistic submission. Not only is Basini's torture-chamber dark, not only is Bozena's house in the gloomy, strange forest, but in the scene with Beineberg a dark leaf blowing against the dark window of the cake shop draws Törless's imagination outside into sombre reminiscences of submission.

The struggle of the subject to ward off its disintegration is revealed in the anxieties summoned by darkness. If we assume that all cultural achievements draw their nourishment from the same instinctual reservoir as sexuality, it can come as no surprise that for Törless cultural discourses also begin to erode from within as a result of their contamination by debased sexuality. Mathematics and religion run through the novel as leitmotifs, from an early mention of homework to the speeches of the teachers of those subjects following Törless's self-portrayal. Just as the pure mother is pulled down, in the figure of Bozena, to her secret, dirty physical centre, so the most sublime social discourses, of holiness and logic, reveal their secret, impure core. In the midst of solid mathematics lies everything that has been severed from it, the swamp-like imaginary; and likewise in religion, in the sacred, there is revealed the erotic body that has been repressed from it, the grotesque body of the flagellated, tortured man, the sacrificial victim.

This body, which will later become thoroughly material to Törless in the form of Basini, at first exists only in similes, images and dreams. Törless's 'voluptuous pride' in 'egoistic suffering' is compared with a chapel 'where, surrounded by hundreds of flickering candles and hundreds of eyes [those eyes again!] gazing down from sacred images, incense was wafted among the writhing flagellants' (p. 4). In the prince's company he feels 'rather as though he were in some little chapel far off the main road ... as though with his finger-tips he were tracing the lines of an arabesque, not thinking about it, merely sensing the beautiful pattern of it, which twined according to some weird laws beyond his ken' (p. 7).

Beineberg's behaviour is compared with that of a 'lecherous priest who had taken leave of his senses and was weaving equivocal words into the solemn formulae of a prayer' (p. 42). In a metonymic textual progression the grotesque body is revealed as a knot of ideas in which the cadet lies writhing, and in the droop of a perverse curtain-cord: 'The cord must have got stuck at the top, or it had slipped off the roller, and now it hung down, hideously twisted, and its shadow crept like a worm across the bright rectangle on the floor. It was all grotesquely, frighteningly hideous.'

Mathematics is similarly sexualized. If it had at first been Törless's hope 'to cast a glance, as it were, past the master and into his man's daily cohabitation [*Konkubinat* – !] with mathematics' (p. 109), in a dream he sees the teacher repeatedly stroking Kant's cheek, while speaking in a voice that seems to be 'unravelling [*abfingern*] the long skein of some theorem in a mathematics lesson' (p. 127). Beineberg's sexualized hands had already been described as being 'in motion, with flickering fingers [*in fingernder Beweglichkeit*]'.

Zögling, pupil, is etymologically derived from *Züchtung, Aufzüchtung* – growing, cultivation. *Zögling* Törless is obsessed by everything that is *unzüchtig* – prurient, obscene. Obscenity (*Un-zucht*) is the animal in the divine, the fantastic in the logical, the female in the male, ugliness in beauty, the object in the subject. Obscenity is the breakdown of binary categories, dualisms, polarized and hierarchized differences, but in such a way that the negative and trivial are injected into the positive and the elevated. In this way Törless's fascination with filth, mud, earth and dust becomes easier to understand.

Starting out from William James's 'Dirt is matter in the wrong place', Mary Douglas, in her study *Purity and Danger*, shows that the fear of dirt is the fear of disorder. 'Dirt then is never a unique, isolated event. Where there is dirt there is system. Dirt is the by-product of a systematic ordering and classification of matter, in so far as ordering involves rejecting inappropriate elements.'[16] This threat to order always comes from below:

> Seen from the ego's position the system of ... purity is structured upwards. Those above him are more pure. All the positions below him, be they ever so intricately distinguished in relation to one another, are to him polluting. Thus for any ego within the system the threatening non-structure against which barriers must be erected lies below.[17]

Törless breaks down these barriers. He breaks them down along the demarcation lines of a symbolic system inscribed within him and his social class as a structure of identity.

Basini

The observations I have made so far culminate in the figure of Basini. In the structure of the novel his position is analogous to that of Bozena. This is apparent in the almost identical sequences of consonants in their names. If Bozena represented the Slavic race in the desires of Habsburg imperialism, Basini represents the Italian race. Both embody the colonial other into which repressed sexuality is projected, to be reflected back with an even greater fascination.

What distinguishes Basini from Bozena in the novel is his centrality. After his expulsion from the school 'it [*es*] all seemed dead. Almost as if that boy, in whom all those relationships had intertwined, had broken the circuit with his departure (p. 215). With Basini the Id [*das Es*], the knot of desire, the whole instinctual machinery has disappeared. Törless, who is never shown in the novel as a creative, productive writer, finally returns to the bosom of his class and family. Although removed from direct economic and political power, nevertheless, as a consumptive, sterile aesthete, he retires to the site of the accumulation of symbolic capital. We are familiar with such lives from the work of Thomas Mann, Hugo von Hofmannsthal, Huysmans and Wilde.

Basini is the centre, because he embodies within him the fluidity of categories. He slides downwards from the same elevated position that all the pupils hold at the beginning. Only after the fall of this angel, which reduces him to the level of Bozena, do we recognize in the figure of the young prince the elevated equivalent of the figure of the mother. The aura of aristocracy and religion grant him the same aesthetic consecration as the formal perfection and sublime tenderness of the mother. But Törless is also a double of Basini: the mixing of high and low that occurs in the space of his imagination is materialized in Basini's body.

Basini and Bozena are not only equated in terms of their ethnic otherness. They are also both socially soiled because, according to the ideology of a society based on property, their money is in the wrong place. Bozena's 'baseness' is the consequence of her capacity to dispel the sentimental illusions shoring up the institution of the family. The fact that the sordid little secret of financial dealings lies at the centre of the family is reflected in the despised figure of the paid woman: 'she represents the danger of a juxtaposition of the whore and the wife, the governess and the mother, the "servant girl" and the "noble lady" which reveals the true structural relation of the women in the family ... Such juxtaposition, such identification, must not take place.'[18] Similarly, small-scale theft such as that practised by Basini, were it not proscribed, would reflect theft on a larger social scale, which divides people into rich and poor.

But Bozena too is basically a thief. She takes money for something that does not actually need to be paid for in a patriarchy. The peasant who, instead of paying Bozena, threatens her with a stone, has instinctively understood this state of affairs. (Hence the logic of the pimp. Only the presence of this man behind the woman can guarantee that the business relation that the client is so keen to turn back into the illusion of a sexual relation remains simply a business relation.)

Just as Basini and Bozena are both thieves, they are also both prostitutes. Even before Basini lapses into theft, his fall is introduced on the much more basic level of his feminization. While the reader, with reference to Bozena, could still succumb to the illusion that it was only a feature of the feminine, its sexual aspect, that indicated 'baseness' in Basini it is revealed to be femininity as such. After having seen the precariousness of the elevated position of motherhood in Törless's fantasies, since it can at any time be reduced to whoredom, it becomes clear that woman, simply by virtue of her sex, is always a whore in a patriarchal society. For, according to Bataille, the powerless must put themselves at the disposal of others.[19] It is quite logical, at the end of a long series of female similes, that Basini's movements should be compared to those of a 'clumsy girl'.

The signification of Basini's baseness by femininity is the primary one. The signification by theft is a logical construction based upon it. Rather than examining the countless connotations of and comparisons with the feminine, I shall merely quote the central sexual transformation of Basini which culminates in his metaphorical sentencing to death:

> He was a little taller than Törless, but very slight in build, with slack, indolent movements and effeminate features. He was not very intelligent, but he had a pleasing manner, a rather coquettish way of making himself agreeable ... Occasionally, too, he lied – out of vanity ... The moral inferiority that was apparent in him and his stupidity both had a single origin. He had no power of resisting anything that occurred to him and was always surprised by the consequences. In this he resembled the kind of woman, with pretty little curls on her forehead, who introduces doses of poison into her huband's food at every meal and then is amazed and horror-struck at the strange, harsh words of the public prosecutor and the death-sentence pronounced on her. (pp. 68–9)

Basini's castration is also implied in this process of feminization. 'His visits to Bozena had begun only because he wanted to play the man. Backward as he was in his development, it was scarcely to be supposed that he was impelled by any real craving.' The problematic aspect of this passage is revealed linguistically in the narrator's slip, 'it was scarcely to be supposed', since there is no narrative ground for the doubt thus created. Who is speaking here? These are the words of the narrator, and an omniscient narrator at that. But an omniscient narrator knows his characters inside out. What we have here is a kind of reversed *style indirect libre*, in which the narrator's perspectives are not insinuated into his protagonists, but rather the partial vision of a character relativizes the omnipotence of the author.

Of what is this hiatus in the narrative perspective symptomatic? Is the narrator even more brutal and sadistic towards Basini than the pupils are? Or is he unconsciously resisting the reduction of a fundamentally masculine character to the status of eunuch? The impossibility of an unambiguous answer relates to the ambivalence of Basini's sex as well as to the unreliability of the narrator – and of Törless – in their responses to this character.[20]

The feminization of Basini, as carried out by the narrator, sanctions his further degradation to animal status (he is called an 'insect', a 'filthy beast', a 'pig'), and thence to an object. Basini says of Reiting: ' "He says, if he didn't beat me, he wouldn't be able to help thinking I was a man, and then he couldn't let himself be so soft and affectionate to me. But like that, he says, I'm his chattel, and so then he doesn't mind."' Foucault observes in the course of discussing homosexuality among the ancient Greeks that 'when one played the role of subordinate partner in the game of pleasure relations, one could not be truly dominant in the game of civic and political activity.'[21] This point is lent added weight in the rational, militarized modern age by the fact that even intersubjective feelings of affection, adaptation and devotion corrupt the subject as a dominant one, and must be discriminated against in the discourse of power as passivity and weakness.

In the communal torture of Basini the pupils preserve their subject-status in accordance with the codes of domination but also within the field of domination's diametrical opposite, love. If the discourse of subject and object is a method of domination in the philosophical sphere (think of the figure of Kant in *Törless*), the same is true of torture and sadism in the realm of eroticism.

> Sadism . . . wants the non-reciprocity of sexual relations, it enjoys being a free appropriating power confronting a freedom captured by flesh. That is why the sadist wants to make the flesh present to the other's consciousness *differently*; . . . he makes it present in pain. In pain facticity invades consciousness, and ultimately the reflective consciousness [of the torturer] is fascinated by the facticity of the unreflective consciousness (of the victim).[22]

The sexual sadism of the pupils corresponds to their fantasies of omnipotence in philosophy and politics. While Beineberg goes so far as to wish to defy the laws of gravity as a kind of demiurge, Reiting hopes to achieve political power as a master manipulator, and Törless sees himself as an author. All these fantasies are tried out on Basini's body, and provide concrete evidence for the idea that all cultural achievements are also testaments to barbarism.

But Törless's relationship with Basini is more highly differentiated. For him, Basini is living proof that his transgressive, masochistic fantasies are capable of realization. 'And this profound humiliation, this self-abandonment, this state of being covered with the heavy, pale, poisonous leaves of infamy, this state that had moved through his dreams like a bodiless, far-off reflection of himself, all this had now suddenly *happened* to Basini' (p. 60).

For this reason Törless wishes to know whether his imagination concurs with Basini's own inner experience. But he is forced to realize that his and Basini's perspectives do not converge.

Törless enjoys the conscious transgression of the law in the imaginary sphere. It is a consciousness that simultaneously sets his own destruction in motion.[23] That is why he is always associated with the terms *self-*

debasement, *self*-sacrifice and *self*-renunciation. He himself is sovereign in the destruction of his sovereignty. That is the self-division he vainly hopes to discover in Basini.

Basini cannot provide this experience, because Törless's fantasies neglect one thing: in the *real* enforcement of the transgression scenario the roles of the participants are unequally distributed. There are perpetrators and there are victims. Their perspectives are divorced: the division within a single person, which Törless feels, is absent. Basini is not a thief because he infringed a prohibition for the pleasure of doing so (and this is precisely what Törless wishes to hear when he forces this confession out of Basini – with the result that it is not a *self*-confession); he is a thief because he needs money.

Nor does he allow himself to be tortured because he enjoys the disappearance of his consciousness into the body of pain – rather he is a forced object, a victim. When Törless asks:

'What happens inside you? Does something burst in you? Tell me! Does it smash like a glass that suddenly flies into thousands of splinters before there's even been a little crack in it? Doesn't the picture you've made of yourself go out like a candle? Doesn't something else leap into its place, the way the pictures in the magic-lantern leap out of the darkness?' (pp. 156–7)

Basini can never experience transgression with its dualistic feeling of consciousness/body, subject/object, but only with the image of the subject that recognizes itself as raped and suffering. He does not even give Törless and those in power the comforting concession that he desires his humiliation.

Just as the whore, by being paid, embodies the fact that all sexual relationships in societies with unequally divided power are prostitution and never mutuality – that power always produces prostitution, never love – in Basini it becomes apparent that all physical relationships are based on force. Törless understands in the end what Basini means and has to admit: 'my feeling about myself would be exactly as simple and free of ambiguity as his feeling about himself' (p. 157). He recognizes 'this incomprehensible relationship that *according to our shifts of standpoint* [my italics H.G.] gives happenings and objects sudden values that are quite incommensurable with each other, strange to each other' (p. 216). Törless only understands this because, at moments, he himself has perceived the threat that Beineberg and Reiting represent for him, too, and because on these occasions he has sensed the position of those lower down in the power hierarchy, not in fantasies but in reality.

Only after this demystification of slavery as an intensification of pleasure do we have a brief glimpse into a love relationship as it might occur between equals. Its stimulus is physical beauty. It is symptomatic that for this relationship to take place all the other pupils must be absent on holiday at home, so that the school for a moment becomes a classless idyll. It consequently collapses with the return of the pupils, who, as a collective super-ego, immediately reintroduce the previous inequality between Törless and Basini. In the return of Törless's shame, his former social ego is re-enthroned. The idyll is closed. From now on Törless returns to enjoying the solipsistic fantasy of debasement, which sexuality with Basini becomes for him from this point onwards. But whereas he had previously enjoyed, in a kind of escape from the heights of his own world, its obverse in dirtiness, he is now aroused by knowledge of his own refinement compared with those beneath him. With the stylization of pleasure from the forbidden other into a new experience of his own sensibility in the form of nausea, he has returned to the bosom of his class.

'Sublimation may be detected not only in the rejection of social practices stigmatized as "vulgar", it may be seen subtly at work in the upward transcoding of such practices.'[24] Törless has once more escaped being declassed. Musil writes:

> Yet he felt like one who had awakened from the throes of some long agony – like one who had been brushed by the silent and mysterious finger-tips of dissolution ... Then he knew that he *would* debase himself, but he supplied it all with a new meaning. The uglier and unworthier everything was that Basini had to offer him, the greater was the contrast with that awareness of suffering sensibility which would afterwards set in. (p. 168)

The future Törless is described as the aesthetic intellectual who, in excess, orgies, every enjoyment of the repressed and forbidden other, is not actually concerned with these so much as with the refinement of his soul, his inner life. Sublimation is bound up with dominance. Strategies of taste, tact and sensibility are strategies of downward delimitation: 'the sensitive soul marks out its own spiritual superiority, not by despising the [vulgar] ... but by discovering a special transcendental quality to [it] ... and through it an intuition of the divine where others find but coarse pleasure.'[25] Unlike his contemporary, Stephen Dedalus, who abandons all family, religious and national bonds, Törless returns to the (maternal) bosom of his family, conforming and adapting. 'He now knew how to distinguish between day and night' (p. 216). His mother is struck by his 'cool composure', and the chaotic nature inhabited by Bozena has withered into biological concepts. From the wood, its spell broken, his own mental landscape gazes back at him: 'It looked utterly insignificant and harmless, merely a dusty thicket of willow and alder' (p. 217).

NOTES

1 Robert Musil, *Die Verwirrungen des Zöglings Törless* (Rowohlt, Hamburg, 1906). The page references in parentheses are to the Picador edition of the English translation *Young Törless*, tr. Eithne Wilkins and Ernst Kaiser (Secker & Warburg, London, 1955).

2 Letter draft on a loose sheet in diary vol. 30: to W. (1906), quoted in Robert Musil, *Prosa, Dramen, Späte Briefe*, ed. Adolf Frisé (Rowohlt, Hamburg, 1957), pp. 723–4.

3 Ibid.

4 Sherry B. Ortner, 'Is female to male as nature is to culture?', in *Woman, Culture and Society*, ed. Michelle Zimbalist Rosaldo and Louise Lamphere (Stanford University Press, Stanford, Calif., 1974).

5 Sigmund Freud, 'On the universal tendency to debasement in the sphere of love' (1912), in *On Sexuality*, Pelican Freud Library, vol. 7, tr. Angela Richards (Harmondsworth, 1953), p. 252.

6 Ibid., p. 255.

7 Claudio Magris, *Der habsburgische Mythos in der österreichischen Literatur* (Otto Müller, Salzburg, 1966), p. 181.

8 Ibid., p. 182.

9 Ibid.

10 Julia Kristeva, 'The adolescent novel', in *Abjection, Melancholia and Love: The Work of Julia Kristeva*, ed. John Fletcher and Andrew Benjamin (Routledge & Kegan Paul, London/New York, 1990), pp. 8–23.

11 Peter Stalleybrass and Allon White, *The Politics and Poetics of Transgression* (Methuen, London, 1986), pp. 4–5.

12 Susanne Kappeler, *The Pornography of Representation* (Polity Press, Cambridge, 1986), p. 154.

13 See for example Hans-Georg Pott, *Robert Musil* (Wilhelm Fink Verlag, Munich, 1984), pp. 18 and 180 n. 24.

14 Cf. Klaus Theweleit, *Männerphantasien* (2 vols, Verlag Roter Stern, Frankfurt/M., 1977, 1978); tr. Erica Carter, Chris Turner and Stephen Conway *Male Fantasies*, vol. 1: *Women, Floods, Bodies, History*; vol. 2: *Male Bodies: Psychoanalysing the White Terror* (Polity Press, Cambridge 1987, 1989), pp. 3 and 17.

15 Thus Törless remembers that as a child he always wanted to be a girl (p. 28); the mathematics master calls him a hysteric (p. 213); and towards the end of the book: 'But his inability to find words for it . . . was in itself delightful, like the certainty of a teeming body' (p. 217).

16 Mary Douglas, *Purity and Danger: An Analysis of Concepts of Pollution and Taboo* (Routledge & Kegan Paul, London, 1966), p. 35.

17 Ibid., p. 123.

18 Kappeler, *Pornography of Representation*, p. 204.

19 Cf. Georges Bataille, *L'Erotisme* (Editions de la Différence, Paris, 1981); tr. Mary Dalwood, *Eroticism* (Calder & Calder, London, 1962), p. 132.

20   Or is Musil resisting the description of a homosexual relationship that does not follow the usual male–female, active–passive parameters? Is this effeminization the censorship which alone allows homosexuality to come into the open?

21   Michel Foucault, *Histoire de la sexualité* (3 vols, Gallimard, Paris, 1984); tr. Robert Hurley, *The History of Sexuality*, vol. 2: *The Use of Pleasure* (Penguin, Harmondsworth, 1987), p. 220.

22   Jean Paul Sartre, *L'Etre et le néant. Essai d'ontologie phénoménologique* (Bibliothèque des idées, Paris, 1947); tr. Hazel E. Barnes, *Being and Nothingness: An Essay on Phenomenological Ontology* (Methuen, London, 1958), p. 399.

23   Bataille, *Eroticism*, p. 132: '[The experience of sin] leads to the completed transgression, the successful transgression which, in maintaining the prohibition, maintains it in order to benefit by it. The inner dimension of eroticism demands from the subject a sensitiveness to the anguish of the heart of the taboo no less great than the desire which leads him to infringe it . . . Man achieves this inner experience at the instant when . . . he feels that he is tearing himself, not tearing something outside that resists him. He goes beyond the objective awareness . . . linked with the turning topsy-turvy of his original mode of being.'

24   Stallybrass and White, *The Politics and Poetics of Transgression*, p. 197.

25   Ibid., p. 198.

9

Space, Gender and National Identity

In his seminal study *Orientalism*, Edward Saïd analyses the effects on the image of the self caused by a mental set he calls 'imaginary geography'. According to Saïd, 'imaginary geography' plays a crucial part in the construction of the so-called 'Orient' as the historical and cultural other of Western identity. The East–West divide is a truly symbolic borderline because there is no fixed geographic point from which it could operate. Instead, it is a spatial metaphor for the relationship between the self and the other, which can be actualized at any point of identified interest in the First World.

> It can be argued that Islam (in the shape of the Muslim populations of North Africa, Turkey and the Indian subcontinent) is now the primary form in which the Third World presents itself to Europe, and that the North–South divide, in the European context, has been largely inscribed onto a pre-existing Christian–Muslim division.[1]

The East–West borderline has its roots in the first texts of our cultural heritage, starting with Homer and the Greek dramatists. On to the opposition between ancient Greece and Asia, the later conflict between Christianity and Islam had been grafted, and it was reinforced by the traumatic experiences with the Crusades, the invasions of the Huns and Turks. The political East–West tensions after the Second World War have dramatically deepened the symbolic trench, a territorial splitting which still today, right in the heart of Europe, is corrupting even national politics: witness the aversion of West Germans face to face with their new East German compatriots.

Saïd's enterprise is to reconstruct historically the various cultural discourses which give narrative body to the politics of imaginary geography in the Western symbolic order. In isolating a spatial formation at the heart of cultural narrations of historical identity, Saïd ventures in an important and innovative direction. But he does not investigate the foundations of space as an imaginary formation.

Why is it that underneath the communicative capacities of discourses, knowledge, symbolic exchange and differentiation – beneath, in other words, the structures of time – there seems to persist the bedrock of space and vision (*geo*graphy, *imagi*nation), registers which are, if not independent of time, at least resistant to its sway? But let me turn first to another cultural discourse, where vision also plays a central part: that of art history. What would generally be regarded as the most important representation in the history of Western art? Important because of its widespread dissemination and reproduction, cherished for its symbolic function and its affective value? The portrayal I have in mind is so central to our civilization that we no longer perceive it: the image of Mary holding in her arms the baby Christ.

Consider the composition and spatial arrangement of this pivotal scenario. Apart from being the semantic cornerstone of our Christian heritage, the signifier, the formal execution of the mother–child relationship exerts a powerful influence on our unconscious perception. It is an exact reproduction of the mirror-stage as described by Lacan. We see a baby aged between 6 and 18 months on his mother's arm. He looks straight at the viewer, who stands in the position of the mirror. The mother's look is directed either towards the baby or straight into the 'mirror'. In both cases her look confirms the mirror's function of providing the baby with a premature image of his own corporeal unity and autonomy. In most pictures the baby is gesticulating, the logic of which becomes clear when we read his gesture as the delighted recognition of his own reflection and the kinetic exploration of the space between mother, child and mirror-image. It is the moment when the child for the first time takes the place of a subject opposite an object.

The mirror-stage, providing the baby with the illusion of fullness and presence by imaging the self as a unified body, still belongs to the pre-Oedipal phase. It is the transitory condition for the entry into the Oedipal phase and the symbolic order which are integral to the laws of patriarchy. The narratives of the symbolic order, always structured in time and therefore tilted towards difference and death, offer the child sexual, cultural, historical and political identifications. These narratives will eventually be anchored more or less rigidly in positions of identity, propelled by the unifying impact of the mirror-image.

But this ideal ego, pretending to be autonomous and coherent in the

Plate 4   Charles Henneghien, photograph, 'Emilia looking at Titian'. (reproduced by kind permission of Charles and Paulette Henneghien)

pseudo-security of its space and under the gaze of maternal love, is beset with difficulties.‖Identity, being constructed by way of a mirror-image, always coexists with its alienation from that image of the self as other‖The basic unreliability of identity crops up as emotional ambiguity towards any other, a constant oscillation between affirmative identification and hostile repulsion.

The passage through the mirror-stage and the ensuing Oedipal phase which stabilizes the infant in what Winnicott calls 'a true self', is not only dependent on the interpretive ordering of experiences in the symbolic order, but also on the more archaic mother–child relationship of the pre-Oedipal phase. It is shot through with aggressive introjection and repulsion, only mollified by the indirect influence of the father-of-pre-history as an instance of divergence between mother and child. The so-called true self is not more accomplished than the false self (according to Klein we are all cured psychotics). But it has access to a more flexible identity because of less traumatic experiences with the pre-Oedipal mother, a more successful internalization of the good object, and the softening of mirror-stage effects like rigidity or loss of self as a result of immersion in the diversity of the symbolic order. What light can the mirror-stage – the centrality of which in our culture is captured in the tableau of the Virgin and Child – throw on the question of space as an imaginary formation?

As a result of the massive migrations in our contemporary world the symbolic orders, incorporating the social and sexual contracts which distribute positions of identity, are thrown into crisis. The victims are not only those who are forced into exile and emigration, though they bear the cruellest burden, but those who are confronted with immigration and experience the arbitrariness and relativity of the symbolic order through their encounter with the other.

There is a difference in the case of tourism and communicative technologies where through the exchange of money and goods the symbolic orders of both cultures are preserved. Because there is no hierarchy through power and domination, there is no loss, only seduction.

However, in the case of emigration and immigration, the shock of the other can produce regressions into structures of the mirror-stage or even further back into psychotic dispositions. Thus, after the collapse of the communist symbolic order, extreme cases of xenophobia have emerged in Germany; while in other European countries the rhetoric of racism has accompanied the new nationalisms, which are implicitly anti-feminist as well. The same phenomena erupted in France, when it was suddenly faced with massive immigrations from North African countries.

The call for national purity reflects the re-emergence of an archaic stage in the psycho-biography of the subject, a stage even prior to the mirror-stage. A semantics of purity indicates the virulence of the abject, an effect of the utter fragility of the subject-position. The abject signals the rejection of the overpowering body of the mother at a time when the baby is not yet able to form an object.

In xenophobia, the phobic object stands in for the fear of the re-emergence of an existential void which had been camouflaged by the security of the mirror-image and the laws of the symbolic order.

The anxieties of absence, loss and castration which lie at the root of xenophobia are triggered by the collapse of the fantasy of the whole, unified, undamaged body in a space which is conceived of, metaphorically and metonymically, as the body's extension or double. The importance of this spatial doubling of the body as its own support can be grasped in Gaston Bachelard's *The Poetics of Space*. Bachelard attributes the affective value lining the use-value of a house to the unconscious memory of the mother's womb and body and the bodily imaginations of the infant. He even sees the body as a field of engravings resulting from the subject's tactile and kinetic experiences with the house.

> Beyond memories, our first home is physically inscribed into ourselves. It consists of a cluster of organic habits ... We are the engrams of the functions

of habitation in that first house and all the other houses are only variations of one basic theme. The word 'habit' is very often used in order to signify that passionate relationship between our body which doesn't forget and that unforgettable house.[2]

In 'The city and the imaginary' Donatella Mazzoleni analyses more explicitly than Bachelard both the house and the city as the body's doubles. Against the cultural preference for temporal structures such as narrative or *différance*, she insists on the priority of space in shaping the perception of our bodies.

But the lived experience of non-verbal, pre-logical space is only partly translatable into language or narratable in a story. In it we find the spatialization of primary pulsations – Eros and Thanatos – that cannot be contained by the web of any structure or story. The articulation of these impulses are always twofold: there is a need to return to a space which is a container of life, which can metabolize death itself (living) – then there is the need to symbolize, to deflect outwards the death instinct (constructing). We could perhaps say that constructing, in so far as it is a symbolizing activity, arises from the dwelling of the instincts because of that 'primary paranoia' which attempts to redeem the overwhelming relationship with one's own overshadowing mother figure ... Semiology is not sufficient for our interpretation. What is needed is a 'geotica' and an 'anthropanalysis' of the psychic structures deeply rooted in our cultures: thus an architypology of the imaginary.[3]

Likewise a nation, perceived not so much as a historical, but rather as a geographical unit, in other words as a space, a body with clearly marked contours on a map, a quasi-organic compound of geopolitical details, seems to be imbued with the same imaginary power Bachelard or Mazzoleni detect in the house or the city. Thus in the following quote the term 'city' might readily be replaced by the term 'nation':

the city is also the body's double. Like the house, it is also, in some way, a lived space, anthropomorphic. We can speak of a city as long as the totality of those who produce and live a collective construction constitute a collective anthropoid body, which maintains in some way an identity as a 'subject'. The city is therefore a site of *identification* ... Thus the city has a somatic individuality and a membrane, which may be palpable (in the case for example of city walls), or impalpable, and which both surround and *limit* its somatic individuality.[4]

One thinks immediately of the Great Wall of China or of the Berlin Wall, which was national as well, and we remember that the first refugees in our written tradition (women, by the way) asked for shelter not in another nation, but in another city, the ancient *polis*.

If we conclude that, after the house and the city, the nation might be the body-ego's third double, then we can recognize the pre-logical, pre-linguistic conditions of xenophobia. The influx of strangers is experienced as an assault on and a violent penetration of that unified, but always fragile and precarious body-self, a process that gives rise to the fragmentation and collapse of the imaginary autonomous ego.

Only with reference to such a primeval need for space can the outstanding success of Edgar Reitz's film *Heimat* in Germany be understood. *Heimat* provided the post-war German imagination with an extensive topology of the house, the town and the county, thereby marginalizing the compromised nation as an infected double of the body politic.

The film does not endorse xenophobia in the form of anti-Americanism as much as some critics have argued; rather it equates the United States with the metropolis, a formation whose rank growth can no longer be contained within the perceptual apparatus designed by the unifying and demarcating mirror-stage.

Against such a theoretical background, the logic of the ghetto or the restriction of foreign travellers in ancient Greek cities to the harbour area can be seen as the means of locating, isolating and visualizing an otherwise amorphous enemy – amorphous because, outside the delusions of the imaginary, there is no enemy distinguishable from one's own body.

The legacy of the mirror-stage threatens the subject with two extremes, which will influence every relationship between subject and other: the vanishing of the subject as a consequence of the subject's identification with the other or the aggressive rigidity of the subject as a resistance to the overpowering other. The prerequisite for a stable subject-position after the mirror-stage and the Oedipal phase is a prior positive loving relationship between a baby and a non-possessive mother. Such a relationship alone can provide the balance, the flexibility of identity necessary to avoid the prison of a mortifying body-armour at one extreme and the loss of self in psychotic disintegration at the other. Equally important in this respect is the subject's access to symbolization, where anxieties can be externalized and new identities internalized. If the psycho-biographies of girls and boys show differences, produced in the pre-Oedipal phase by a more intense, symbiotic attitude of the mother towards the little girl, but a more distancing, objectifying attitude towards the little boy, then it may be sexual difference which gives rise to the different reactions of men and women in their encounter with strangers. Of course, according to the law of the *folie à deux* a man and a woman could react with exactly the same paranoid aggression as described by Victor Burgin in his essay on 'Paranoiac Space'.[5] But aggression – murderous aggression against the supposed invader of the pure body politic – is first and foremost a male reaction.

The rivalry of the Oedipal phase and the so-called heroic virtues of the male in the symbolic order enhance the aggressive position of the pre-Oedipal phase and the fortifying effect of the mirror-stage to the point of rigidity. Furthermore, the stronger repression of the incest wish in the male and the consequently more strenuous denial of his own body, both of which are necessary for the preservation of the patriarchal order, make a man's access to his unconscious far more difficult. Yet without an admission of this fundamentally alien sphere of the self there can be no acknowledgement of the stranger as a member of one's kind.

Julia Kristeva reminds us, in her study *Etrangers à nous-mêmes*,[6] that from the very beginning of our subjectivity and individuality, which is based on our splitting into unconscious and consciousness, we are always already strangers to ourselves. Only the life-long, cathartic experience and reliving of that division through art or other imaginative practices can prevent or mitigate the petrifaction of the imaginary self. In spatial terms, this means developing a capacity for mobility, transitory states, nomadism and voyaging; the occupation of places in different narratives, or the renaming of old places and spaces would likewise be involved in rituals of mobility.

But for women all this might look quite different, and neither Kristeva, nor Mazzoleni, nor Burgin, nor Bachelard deals with the possible consequences of sexual difference. For in a patriarchal society, women are in fact doubly strangers: first in their relation to their own unconscious, but second in their function as the margin, the other, the body, the unconscious, the fetish of men. Not only are women's bodies literally less unified and fortified than men's under the permanent threat of male physical violence, of forced intrusion and penetration, but they are also more prone to loss of ego in processes of fusion or identification in amatory states or when the unconscious surfaces. Such a disposition should make it easier for women to confront the stranger without immediate hostility. But, unless her ego is buttressed, she could be in danger of losing her sense of her body's limits, and the reappearance of the existential void could throw into relief anorexic disturbances, depression, melancholia or suicidal attacks.

So, what women might need in order to encounter strangers in a non-traumatic way might be not so much rituals of mobility as conditions to stabilize their bodies in their environment, taking up a place beyond men's spatial and interpretive control. Marguerite Duras has written compellingly of the fascination the *xenos* holds for women, but she also shows the high price which has to be paid in mental stability (*Hiroshima mon amour*, *L'amant*, *Le ravissement de Lol V. Stein*.[7]

Similar observations can be made of the relationships between women and cities in the event of mental crises. A number of celebrated male writers have described their experiences of being marooned in a strange city. These experiences can be compared metaphorically with the crisis of the body and the reappearance of the unconscious in the effect of the uncanny.

Walter Benjamin, in his account of a first stroll in an unknown city,[8] Freud in his wanderings in unfamiliar Naples[9] and Breton in his de-familiarization of Paris under the psychic influence of Nadja[10] – all three undergo an imaginary estrangement of space which they describe in terms of seduction, depersonalization and feelings of the uncanny. However, in their cases, the assault of the 'other scene' is finally pacified by the reintegrating forces of the ego and the rationality of the street map. Only Nadja goes on living an imaginary, magic relationship with Paris, which infuses Breton's rationality with liberating flashes of the unconscious. But when she is left by Breton, who retreats safely into the 'pure' love of another woman, it is Nadja who ends up in a madhouse.

In Sylvia Plath's *The Bell Jar*,[11] the mental crisis of Esther Greenwood makes itself felt for the first time in the bizarre alienation of New York, which is transformed into an environment of abomination.

Likewise, Christa Wolf registers her loss of historical identity, the result of her having discovered that she was being observed by the secret service, as a disintegration of her symbiotic attitude to Berlin. Her home becomes literally *unheimlich*.[12]

Only on condition that the differences between the sexes are taken into account can women be told that really '*Heimat* is a mirage, a delusion'. Reitz says: '*Heimat* is such that if one would go closer and closer to it, one would discover that at the moment of arrival it has gone, it has dissolved into nothingness.'[13]

Heimat might be a delusion; it might even become a dangerous one. Yet, as I hope my argument has shown, it is a necessary delusion. It is as necessary as our inheritance of imaginary unity is unavoidable. But we must be aware of it. And it must not be too rigid. Bachelard sees the dangers of immobility symbolized in what he calls the 'final house'. This would be the house of death, he says, symmetrical with our birthplace or the house of our parents. Instead he praises the dream house, the eternal house of the future, a place, but a place always in the making. It is the openness of the other place, which takes into account the otherness of ourselves. When the good mother is internalized along with the house, the city, the nation, Europe and all the other places of identity, so that they can be left behind in reality, only then can the bliss of otherness – its life-enhancing *promesse de bonheur* – be given a proper place, a true home of one's own.

NOTES

1 Edward Saïd, *Orientalism* (Routledge & Kegan Paul, London, 1978), p. 55.
2 Gaston Bachelard, *The Poetics of Space*, tr. Maria Jolas (Beacon Press, Boston, 1960), pp. 14–15.

3 Donatella Mazzoleni, 'The city and the imaginary', *New Formations*, 12 (1990), pp. 91–104, esp. pp. 92–3.

4 Ibid., p. 97.

5 Victor Burgin, 'Paranoiac space', *New Formations*, 12 (1990), pp. 61–76.

6 Julia Kristeva, *Etrangers a nous-mêmes* (Gallimard, Paris, 1988).

7 Marguerite Duras, *Hiroshima mon amour* (Gallimard, Paris, 1960); *L'amant* (Editions de Minuit, Paris, 1984); *Le ravissement de Lol V. Stein* (Gallimard, Paris, 1964).

8 Walter Benjamin, 'Moskau', in *Gesammelte Schriften*, ed. Rolf Tiedemann and Hermann Schweppenhäuser (Suhrkamp, Frankfurt/M., 1972–89), vol. 4, ed. Tillman Rexroth (1972), pt 1, pp. 318–19.

9 Sigmund Freud, 'Das Unheimliche', in *Studienausgabe* (10 vols + 1 suppl. vol., Fischer, Frankfurt/M., 1969–79), vol. 4 (1970), pp. 241–74, esp. pp. 259–60 (author's translation).

10 André Breton, *Nadja* (Gallimard, Paris, 1928).

11 Sylvia Plath, *The Bell Jar* (Heinemann, London, 1963).

12 Christa Wolf, *Was bleibt* (Luchterhand, Frankfurt/M., 1990).

13 David Morley and Kevin Robins, 'No place like *Heimat*: Images of home(land) in European culture', *New Formations*, 12 (1990), pp. 1–23, esp. p. 19.

Part IV

Between Enlightenment and Postmodernism: The Ethics of Art and Gender

10

Popular Literature in the Third Reich

On 19 July 1937 at the opening of the 'Haus der Deutschen Kunst' in Munich, Hitler declared:

> So I wish to make it known at this time that it is my irrevocable decision likewise to do away now with this claptrap in the German art world, just as I have done away with it in the confused realm of politics. 'Artworks' which cannot be understood in themselves, but first require a pompous set of instructions to justify their existence, in order to find at last someone intimidated enough to patiently accept such stupid or impudent nonsense, from now on such works will no longer find their way to the German people.[1]

And he continued in the same vein on 7 September of the same year:

> This disgraceful regression has, however, been perpetrated by our men of letters. By persistently applying the term 'kitsch' to well-intentioned, decent, average [!] work, they have succeeded in breeding those exalted aberrations which may perhaps strike the blasé literary mind as an interesting or indeed phenomenal departure, but which in fact are a shameful step backwards, a cultural degeneration.[2]

In this context the mere word 'aesthetic' becomes suspicious to the National Socialists:

> National Socialist aesthetic? This combination of words will doubtless cause some uneasiness, for the concept of the aesthetic for us is connected with something sickly, unmanly, effeminate ... The images evoked by the sound

of the word 'aesthetic' may be different for each individual. But mentally we will always immediately adopt a defensive attitude.[3]

One would think that in a state like the Fascists', purporting to be anchored in the masses, as much attention would be paid to their cultural as to their political practices. But that would be to be taken in by ideological appearances. The wooing of the masses as the 'herd of voters'[4] is only one side of the coin, the other being the absolute scorn, indeed hatred, of the masses. 'I am no friend of the "mass man"', Hitler repeatedly stresses; 'against the "mass man" I assert the personality. Only men make history, not the masses. The masses must be led ... I am no friend of the amorphous mass, I am the deadly enemy of democracy.'[5] 'The great mass's capacity for comprehension is only very restricted, and its understanding small, but its forgetfulness, on the other hand, correspondingly large.'[6] 'The little abstract knowledge which it possesses directs its sensations more to the world of feeling ... The broad mass is just a part of nature.'[7] And since according to the Fascist conception the culturally underprivileged status of the masses is the consequence of innate inferiority, all that Hitler, with laconic cynicism, can say about these second-class human beings is:

> But what those not born to this [!] lack in their inner understanding, what they can never grasp in their hearts and souls, they must at least be moved, by deliberate education, to have an awed respect for. They must, moreover, simply learn to acknowledge these expressions of the life of one part of their people, just as the others also have to come to terms with their mentality [!] ... one has to be born to art; that is, the fundamental disposition and hence the aptitude, which lie beyond all education, are of decisive importance. This disposition, however, is a component part of the hereditary substance.[8]

Given these presuppositions there was of course no provision for further educating the masses.[9]

But it is not only innovative literature which is suspect to National Socialism in its policies on reading, but popular literature as well:

> Characteristic of this [i.e. the individualistic nineteenth-century concept of education criticized by the Fascists] is the over-valuation, ineradicable from the heads of laymen and administrators, of the *Bildungsroman* and 'novel of manners' of former times, which have produced that self-centred and frivolous kind of reading which has never found particular approval in the genuine public library. It would, however, be wrong to believe that this aesthetically diluted, irresponsible reading is only to be found in a detached upper stratum of society. No, this reading which atomizes the people, this reading removed from life, is to be found equally where the drab literature of entertainment and sensation is devoured by the undeveloped masses. It is the task of the public library neither to promote the egotistical reading of socially elevated

individuals nor to foster the mass reading of books which are only the waste products of civilization.[10]

With their idiosyncratic instinct for everything that was actually or potentially refractory, the National Socialists bracketed both kinds of literature together at a point which has remained till today the blind spot of all the theorists who cannot move beyond a split into 'high' and 'low' literature, in spite of their subjective democratic desire to do so. The ruling class 'avoids the site of the dialectical, of the concrete utopian, just as if it could see it.'[11] The Fascists did in fact see it.

Pronouncements on the reading activities of the masses are to be found not on the higher and highest levels of National Socialist cultural thinking, but, as the above quotation suggests, where the levers are being operated for the planned re-education from bourgeois to 'volkhaft' reading: in the library system and in the sphere of the censorship authorities. Since here too direct statements about *Groschenromane* (pulp novels) are very rare, the opinion of the cultural cadre can be best extrapolated from its views on the general complex of 'relaxation and entertainment' literature.

Contrary to the expectation that National Socialism would show sympathy for a mode of literature to which fascist, pre-fascist or fascistoid traits are today quickly attributed,[12] it can generally be said that its attitude to this subject is extremely ambivalent and contradictory and for the most part, indeed, unequivocally negative. Wholly individualistic and private reading as relaxation must have been abhorrent to a state which, precisely as a total state, demanded the absolute politicization of the private life of the individual citizen as well. 'The total state must be a state of total responsibility. It represents the total assumption of duty towards the nation by every individual. This assumption of duty removes the private character of the individual's existence.'[13] What is to be criticized here is certainly not the binding of the individual to a more comprehensive social frame as such, for indeed only this makes possible the development of the individual into a human being, understood as the ensemble of social relations. What is to be criticized is rather the obligation to a state which cannot legitimate itself and has to forbid the very question as to this legitimation, the question as to whether it actually is capable of realizing the happiness and dignity of the individual.

And since Aristotle in the last book of the *Nicomachean Ethics* combined the question of man's 'happiness' inseparably with the question of the 'best state', establishing 'politics' and 'ethics' as essentially inextricable (the former as the fulfilment of the latter), we have known that freedom is an eminently political concept. The real freedom of the individual existence (and not, indeed, in the merely liberal sense) is only possible in a clearly structured *polis*, in a 'rationally' organized society.

In the conscious politicization of the existential concepts, in the de-privati-
zation and de-interiorization of the liberal-idealist conception of man, the
apparent 'progress' is in fact a regression: the deprivatizing and politicizing
destroys the individual existence instead of truly superseding while preserving
it, transformed, in the 'generality'.[14]

Whatever literary escapism had survived, then, in spite of 'party-political
control of leisure-time'[15] through the 'Kraft durch Freude' ('Strength
through Pleasure') programme, was countered by the state with propaganda, controls and prohibitions. The purging of political and religious
writings as well as young people's literature was immediately followed by
the purging of 'entertainment literature' at all levels. Supported by the
indecency and obscenity laws of the Weimar Republic (of 18 and 23
December 1926), in 1934 Goebbels took over from the Ministry of the
Interior the office charged with inspecting indecent and obscene writings,
which was incorporated into the former Reichsschrifttumstelle, the bureau
for publicity and information. The purging of entertainment literature was
supervised by the Reichsschrifttumskammer (the RSK), and from 1938 by
Abteilung VIII of the Ministry of Propaganda.

From 1935 the RSK published two lists of forbidden books: (1) the 'List
of Harmful and Undesirable Writings' of 1935 (supplemented in 1938 and
through annual lists); (2) the 'List of Publications Unsuitable for Young
People and Libraries' of 1940 (modified in 1943).[16] The fight against
entertainment literature was conducted intensively up to the outbreak of
war, and directed itself in the first place against Jewish authors such as
Vicky Baum, and then later against all authors who were ideologically
suspect.[17] Exactly the same procedure was adopted as regards the mass
genres – the wild west, detective, romance and adventure novels. In 1939
Berndt, the head of Abteilung VIII, explicitly threatened the participants of
the Leipzig Booksellers' Congress with suitably strict measures by the state
in order to stem the output of these novels.[18]

Although 'these books are not destructive and degenerating in the same
sense as the above-named (of a directly political-ideological character), they
nevertheless have the effect of misleading our people spiritually, the end
result of which likewise cannot be regarded as other than pernicious' – the
books in mind being 'the "society" novels and entertainment literature in
which life and the aims of life are represented on the basis of a bourgeois
or feudal conception of life, in a superficial, untrue and mawkish manner
(e.g. Adlersfeld-Ballestrem, Stratz, Eschstruth, Heimburg, *inter al.*)'.[19] To
these must be added above all Eugenie Marlitt; and the more than 114
novels comprising the *œuvre* of Hedwig Courths-Mahler were declared
'undesirable' in 1938 by *Die Bücherkunde* (Book News), the organ of
Rosenberg's Office for the Cultivation of Literature (Schrifttumspflege).[20]

From July 1935 popular literature was subjected to strict preventative censorship. This was carried out by the Beratungsstelle (Information Centre) für Volksliteratur, which was attached to the Arbeitsgemeinschaft der Verleger für Unterhaltungsliteratur (Working Committee of Publishers of Entertainment Literature) in the RSK. The censorship was officially explained thus: 'These kinds of publication should be prevented from being printed in the first place.'[21]

The re-education of reading taste was aimed above all at the working masses and especially at those workers who, in the overwhelming majority, had remained true to the traditional workers' parties up to the end of the Weimar Republic.[22] Their alignment with the fascist regime was to be guaranteed in the long term not only by external violence but by the gradual internalization of fascist ideology. Hence the National Socialist culture of jingoism, the 'nationalistic, patriotic kitsch in literature',[23] likewise, fell victim to official condemnation. At the opening of the 'Woche des guten Buchs' in the Berliner Sportpalast in 1934 Goebbels said:

> I thus hold no brief for the kitsch and dilettantism of that army of ignoramuses who think that the great moment has come and that it must now be time to go marching in parades, waving swastika flags across the stage and the screen ... What *we* want is more than a dramatized party manifesto.[24]

And he becomes even more explicit in a speech in the Berliner Haus des Rundfunks (Radio Centre) in 1935:

> When I see a film today like '*Der Choral von Leuthen*' [The Hymn of Leuthen] then I must say: if a Communist sees this film, then he will simply leave it disgusted and repelled. But, taking the opposite case: if today a National Socialist sees the film *Battleship Potemkin*, then he will be in danger of becoming a Communist because the film is so well made.[25]

It is precisely those masses whom Goebbels has in mind here who are the readers of that broad span of unpretentious popular literature which was only partly represented in the communal public libraries and which was rather to be found comprising almost the entire reading-matter of those small, private lending-libraries which existed as one-man businesses or attached to other small shops. In the lending-library of Wedding described by Fritz Erpenbeck, which was used almost exclusively by (Communist) workers, the most-read authors were Wallace, Courths-Mahler, Sienkiewicz and Marlitt. A long way behind come Marryat, May, Sinclair and Jack London.[26]

Hence the Fascist purge hit these libraries, as well as the book trade, with full force. After the trouble-free coordination of the state public libraries,[27] these became the organizational[28] and intellectual instrument for bringing the private lending-library trade into line.[29] This process was controlled by both Goebbels' Abteilung VIII and the Beratungsstelle für das Leihbüchereiwesen (Lending Library Information Centre) in the RSK. A regulation of the year 1935 forbade all lending-libraries in department stores, and another of 1937 prohibited the opening or reopening of lending-libraries until October 1941.[30] Thus, for example, the two hundred lending-libraries in Düsseldorf (in 1933) were reduced to sixty-six (by autumn 1937).[31]

The public libraries above all were obviously delighted that, in their continual fight over the 'simple *Volksgenossen*' supposedly 'reading his way up' to 'das gute Buch', their arch-enemy, the lending-library, was having its flow of enticing wares cut off. And consequently they take to the field, in a shrill National Socialist idiom, against the traditional entertainment literature and one of its most important trade outlets:

> In considering the lending-libraries it must not be overlooked that in many cases the stocks are to this day saturated with all kinds of the most evil and pernicious sensation literature.[32]

> The government and the Führer himself in particular have turned decisively against kitsch ... So there remains past neglect to make up for, an old debt to clear: to throw out everything wishy-washy, mawkish, kitschy, soppy, apathetic, merely time-wasting and outdated ... First of all there are the old sentimental novels of love and 'high society' (the prince and the servant-girl type) ... lying tales of peasant life and salon Tyroleans; Indian stories for boys; outdated polemical novels and social-problem fiction; unrealized utopias; above all, untruthful adventure stories and the so-called detective and crime-stories which spend themselves in mere intellectual tension.[33]

> The work of education in the Third Reich is by no means helped when we keep Herzog, Stratz, Ganghofer, Bloem and the rest. Such sense of nationality as these authors have is so diluted, commercialized and sentimentalized, or created with such false pathos and so feebly expressed, that we render our people an ill service if we follow in their footsteps in our educational endeavours.[34]

And exactly *what* is undesirable about these forms is clearly stated: the stimulation of an imagination potentially capable of turning critically against the status quo because orientated towards conditions other than these which prevail.

> We will have to examine and select the adventure novels in the certain knowledge that it is not the strange, the exciting, the incredible which constitute their essential function, but their formation of the thirst for action, of the heroic man who proves himself. Thus too in the novels of peasant life we must no longer seek the idyllic and the romantic good old days, but the myth of blood and earth.[35]

These Marlitts and Courths-Mahlers with their adolescent dream-worlds ...[36]

In March 1933 the Verband Deutscher Volksbibliothekare (Association of German Public Librarians) had clearly explained its ideological task for the state:

> As regards all measures, moreover, it should be remembered that the winning of the German workers for the new German state and *Volksgemeinschaft* [people's community] is the great task of the coming years. The public library will therefore have to spare no effort to retain the trust and love of the German working community in its new form as well. It will succeed in this if it is able to convince the German worker that 'national' and 'social', in the real sense of those words, are spiritual attitudes and moral obligations which further and support one another, and that whoever neglects the one sins against the other.[37]

There was one measure, however, that even the public librarians could not carry through, namely the filling of the resultant voids. 'The withdrawal of the Courths-Mahler and Marlitt literature, whose editions ran into millions, and the exchange of the English and American crime stories and westerns for a *Volksschrifttum*, remained the wishful thinking of the NS literary policy.'[38] The problem was never solved, although the demand for a specifically National Socialist entertainment literature was made again and again.[39] This contradiction led to the paradoxical situation whereby, with the increasing pressure of demand from the population for diversion and relaxation, especially after the beginning of the war (reading during black-outs, etc.), the forbidden entertainment literature reappeared to a certain extent; and even the paper-rationing department, which was also an effective instrument of censorship in Goebbels's hands, demanded from 1942 new editions of these publications.[40]

The complete ambivalence towards the whole complex of entertainment literature is shown in the discussions between Rosenberg and Goebbels as to whether 'demanding' (Rosenberg) or 'light' (Goebbels) literature should be supplied for purposes of moral rearmament on the labour- and war-fronts.

> My welfare scheme for the submarines is running ahead in great style. The men in the subs have earned it. I am above all seeing that they get light and relaxing things to read ... There are still ideologues among us who think that when a sub-man comes out of the machine-room covered in filth and oil he prefers to reach for *Mythus des 20. Jahrhunderts*. That is pure nonsense.[41]

Thus Goebbels in his diary in 1942, although he himself in only 1940 had arranged for a renewed 'wave of purges', which caused the publishers to withdraw large quantities of 'trash literature' and 'inferior crime novels' from the market. But just how much popular literature, in spite of all the restrictions, remained in continual demand, especially later among evacuees,[42] is shown by a polemic of 1941, in which *Groschenromane* were mentioned for the first time:

> As a result of the enormously increased demand for literature purely for relaxation, we have observed with growing concern a gigantic increase, since the beginning of the war, in the production of entertainment literature, especially the cheap weekly novel series. I cannot here go into the many-sided problem of this phenomenon, which is different from the rest of the belletristic production. Let me simply say that this mass-production of cheap novels, in such an overwhelming quantity, by no means corresponds to the criteria which, while fully appreciating the necessity of lightness and readability, we must apply. Basically we welcome good entertainment literature; we reject, however, the bad, designed purely for mass consumption. It seems to us, as the aim towards which we need to develop, that the artistic entertainment literature ... can satisfy in increasing measure the demand, in itself to be welcomed, of broad strata of readers ... more comprehensive possibilities in this direction, however, still lie a long way off.[43]

It is revealing that around the same time as the problem of entertainment literature became an urgent one for the Fascists, two works appeared which for the first time deal theoretically with forms of this literature. In 'Über den Detektivroman'[44] and 'Anzengruber und wir' ('Anzengruber and us'),[45] the authors begin the kind of rudimentary research, inseparable from the prevailing kitsch, trash and filth 'theory' of popular literature, which would have been necessary for the Fascists' own production of entertainment literature.

As late as 1943, with the second, amended edition of his 'List of Publications Unsuitable for Young People and Libraries', Goebbels struck a decisive blow against the crime novel, the western and the adventure novel. This time, along with many hard-cover novels, including Agatha Christie and all the Edgar Wallace titles, numerous *Groschenromane* series were hit as well. To sum up, the policy of the Third Reich on entertainment literature oscillated continually, especially later on, between a strategy of intensified control in order to ensure the ideological coordination of the readers, and a strategy of improving the supply, especially after the beginning of the war, for purposes of emotional pacification. This wavering reflects the conflict between the total state's claim to the exclusive control of ideological indoctrination and the organization of ideological production under private property relations which themselves, however, form the indispensable economic basis of that state.[46]

On the other hand this contradiction is founded on the fact that even the total state cannot force its citizens to read for their private entertainment something dictated from above. If what is on offer doesn't please the reader, there is always the alternative of refusal, of not reading. Reading for relaxation depends precisely on its being voluntary. Hence the fundamental mistrust of reading as such, frequently found in representatives of authoritarian, repressive patterns of thinking and behaviour: 'Books are always treacherous. From books there always grows resistance against life, against reality – resistance for the sake of an idea, the tradition of resistance.'[47]

For this reason the cultural policy of the Third Reich resorted, along with explicit prohibition, to the secret control of the contents and the language of the books, a practice which, like the lists of prohibitions, was only made known to a restricted circle of insiders who were sworn to silence. How far-reaching these controls were can be seen from a few examples, which show that the surveillance extended to the least novelette.

Thus a young naval officer, who wrote adventure stories in his free time for a novelette-series, was requested to change the (non-German) nationality of a villainous opponent of his hero, since at that precise time friendly diplomatic relations with the state in question were desired and being promoted.[48]

Again, on 10 July 1941, the 'Vertrauliche Mitteilungen' (Confidential Bulletin) of the trade associations of publishers, booksellers and lending-libraries, published by the RSK, announced:

> In recent book publications, above all novels, it has happened that relationships between Germans and inferior races, which should be depicted as a racial disgrace, are written about as if such relationships were perfectly possible. The consequences of current world political events make it desirable that literature too adopt an unambiguous attitude and make a clear declaration for the National Socialist movement's thinking on race. Here too it is imperative to set the educational possibilities of literature to work. Publishers are requested to pay as strict attention as possible to these points when accepting manuscripts. In future works which do not fulfil these demands must in every instance be designated undersirable.[49]

It was these bulletins which first announced the prohibition of Herzog's *Der Graf von Gleichen* (Count von Gleichen) because its Jewish protagonist had been positively described.[50] One year later, in 1942, the following notice appeared in the press information sheet of the National Socialist Party's press office:

> Our attention is called to the fact that recently, in short stories, novellas, tales, and the novels appearing in newspapers, there are increasingly frequent descriptions of cases in which a birth takes place under the most difficult circumstances and/or even ends with the death of the mother. Such cases,

given the present standard of hygiene and medical science, are relatively rare. To give special prominence to such exceptional cases can easily have a deterrent effect and increase anxiety about giving birth. Since the desire for a healthy abundance of children is especially important in time of war, the editorial staffs are requested to see to it that the happily rare case of a mother sacrificing her life for her new-born child is not featured again in the future.[51]

Analyses of popular literature in the Third Reich, therefore, must also proceed on the assumption that the content was subject to strict control by censorship both before and after publication, and consequently to the self-censorship of the author too. From this develops one of the most important perspectives guiding the present method of analysis, a perspective, that is, concerned to articulate the tensions between (1) a form of literature which has hitherto developed through the market, that is, according to the laws of supply and demand, and which can be, indeed is, manipulated by its producers in conformity with the prevailing system – though only, let it be said, within the frame whereby it still satisfies certain legitimate and genuine needs of its readers; and (2) ideological contents which are at least partially opposed to these needs, since their aim is indeed precisely the re-education and hence the changing of those needs.

NOTES

1   Adolf Hitler, *Reden und Proklamationen 1932–45*, ed. Max Domarus (2 vols, Süddeutscher Verlag, Munich, 1965), vol. 1, p. 709.

2   Ibid., p. 718.

3   H. Arnold, *Nationalsozialistische Monatshefte* (Sept. 1936), p. 836, quoted in Joseph Wulf, *Literatur und Dichtung im Dritten Reich* (Rowohlt, Hamburg, 1966).

4   Adolf Hitler, *Mein Kampf* (Eher Verlag, Munich 1933), p. 375.

5   Extracts from Hitler's conversation with Breiting, chief editor of the *Leipziger Neueste Nachrichten*, in May and June 1931, in *Der deutsche Faschismus in Quellen und Dokumenten*, ed. Reinhard Kühnl (Pahl-Rugenstein, Cologne, 1977), p. 132.

6   Hitler, *Mein Kampf*, p. 371.

7   Ibid., p. 371.

8   Adolf Hitler, speech at the cultural conference of the Reichsparteitag of the NSDAP in Nuremberg in 1933, in *Nürnberg 1933*, ed. Wilhelm Ziegler (Zentralverlag, Berlin, 1933), p. 86.

9   See Ernst Krieck, *Nationalpolitische Erziehung* (Armanenverlag, Leipzig, 1933), pp. 98–103.

10   Franz Schriewer, 'Die deutsche Volksbücherei', *Die Bücherei. Zeitschrift für deutsche Schrifttumspflege*, 2 (1935), p. 299.

11   Ernst Bloch, *Erbschaft dieser Zeit* (Suhrkamp, Frankfurt/M., 1973), p. 289.

12 See Rudolf Schenda, *Die Lesestoffe der kleinen Leute* (Beck, Munich, 1976), pp. 132–3; Jürgen Lodemann, 'Trost für die Massen', in *Die Zeit*, 50 (1977), pp. 33–4.

13 Ernst Forsthoff, *Der totale Staat*, quoted in Herbert Marcuse, 'Der Kampf gegen den Liberalismus in der totalitären Staatsauffassung', in *Faschismus und Kapitalismus*, ed. Wolfgang Abendroth (Europäische Verlagsanstalt, Frankfurt/ M., 1974), p. 70.

14 Marcuse, 'Kampf gegen den Liberalismus', pp. 71–2 (author's translation).

15 Dietrich Strothmann, *Nationalsozialistische Literaturpolitik* (Bouvier, Bonn, 1960), p. 158.

16 Ibid., pp. 190–1.

17 Ibid.

18 Ibid., p. 192.

19 'Richtlinien für die Bestandsprüfung in den Volksbüchereien Sachsens', *Die Bücherei*, 2 (1935), p. 280.

20 Strothmann, *Nationalsozialistische Literaturpolitik*, p. 163.

21 Ibid., p. 180.

22 Cf. on the non-proletarian mass basis of fascism: K. D. Bracher, G. Schulz and W. Sauer, *Die nationalsozialistische Machtergreifung* (3 vols, Ullstein, Frankfurt/M./Berlin/Vienna, 1974), vol. 1: *Stufen der Machtergreifung*, pp. 137–90.

23 'Richtlinien für die Bestandsprüfung', p. 280.

24 Joseph Goebbels, *Goebbels-Reden*, ed. H. Heiber (2 vols, Droste, Düsseldorf, 1971), vol. 1: *1932–1939*, p. 171.

25 Ibid., p. 95.

26 Fritz Erpenbeck, 'Leihbibliotek am Wedding', *Die Linkskurve*, 7 (1930), pp. 14–15.

27 See Strothmann, *Nationalsozialistische Literaturpolitik*, pp. 139–49; Friedrich Andrae (ed.), *Die 'Waffenarsenale' der Volksbüchereien. Volksbücherei und National-sozialismus* (Harassowitz, Wiesbaden, 1970).

28 'By order of the President of the Reichsschrifttumskammer a library committee has been formed to which belong respectively three representatives of the Verband Deutscher Volksbibliothekare [Union of German Public Librarians] and Die deutschen Leihbüchereien e.V. [German Lending-Libraries Association], Section II. The work of the committees shall serve to bridge existing oppositions and bring about understanding.' *Die Bücherei*, 13 (1934), p. 75.

29 See Strothmann, *Nationalsozialistische Literaturpolitik*, pp. 158–62: 'Die Neuordnung des Leihbuchhandels'.

30 Ibid., p. 160.

31 See Walter Rischer, *Die nationalsozialistische Kulturpolitik in Düsseldorf 1933–45* (Trietsch, Düsseldorf, 1972), p. 25.

32 Karl Taupitz, 'Parteibibliotheken oder Volksbüchereien?', *Die Bücherei*, 1 (1934), p. 549.

33 Rudolf Angermann, 'Säuberung nach der Säuberung', *Die Bücherei* (1935), pp. 281–2.

34 Franz Schriewers, 'Was heisst Volkstum in der Bücherei?', *Die Bücherei*, 1 (1934), pp. 445–6.

35 Walter Hoyer, 'Grundsätze zur Auswahl der Dichtung', *Die Bücherei*, 1 (1934), pp. 268–9.

36 Hildegard Stansch, 'Was fordern wir vom Mädelbuch?', *Die Bücherei*, 8 (1941), p. 392.

37 Friedrich Andrae, *Die Waffenarsenale der Volksbücherei*, p. 53.

38 Strothmann, *Nationalsozialistische Literaturpolitik*, pp. 194–5.

39 Ibid., pp. 403–7.

40 Ibid., pp. 193ff.

41 Ibid., p. 188.

42 Rischer, *Nationalsozialistische Kulturpolitik*, p. 163.

43 Rudolf Erckmann, 'Probleme und Aufgaben unseres Schrifttums', *Die Bücherei*, 8 (1941), pp. 310–11.

44 Erich Thier, 'Über den Detektivroman', *Die Bücherei*, 7 (1940), pp. 206–7.

45 Adolf von Morze, 'Anzengruber und wir', *Die Bücherei*, 8 (1941), pp. 139–48.

46 This conflict finds clear expression in Strothmann, *Nationalsozialistische Literaturpolitik*: 'All the successes of the NS literature policy in controlling and "orientating" the book trade did not fundamentally change the private economic character and structure of these sales outlets. The same was true . . . of the lending libraries too' (p. 139).

   On the other hand: 'The RSK thus tried to put a private business at the service of NS propaganda and military training' (p. 159).

   And: 'All efforts to intervene in book production as guide and "adviser" . . . , wherever they were aimed at the bourgeois publisher . . . did not have the character of an order or a direction demanding unconditional adherence' (p. 408).

   And: 'in 1944 the Propaganda Ministry compiled a list of those publishers which were to be preserved and those which were to be closed . . . With their shutdown the last phase of the NS literature policy was to be introduced: the development of an official state and party book industry in place of a private, independent publishing system subject to the laws of the market' (pp. 124–5).

47 Hans Beyer, 'Der Widerstand in den Büchereien', *Die Tat* (June 1934), quoted in Andrae, *Die 'Waffenarsenale' der Volksbücherein*, p. 53.

48 I am indebted to Mr Rolf Schwarz of Wilhelmshaven for this information.

49 *Vertrauliche Mitteilungen für die Fachschaft Verlag*, published by the Reichsschrifttumskammer, Abtlg. III, Gruppe Buchhandel, quoted in Wulf, *Literatur und Dichtung im Dritten Reich*, p. 206.

50 Strothmann, *Nationalsozialistische Literaturpolitik*, p. 219.

51 Wulf, *Literatur und Dichtung im Dritten Reich*, p. 226.

11

Enlightenment, Sexual Difference and the Autonomy of Art

One of the central claims advanced by Adorno and Horkheimer in the *Dialectic of Enlightenment* is the following: 'Just as myth already practises Enlightenment, so too Enlightenment becomes more and more entangled with mythology with every step it takes.'[1] How is this claim to be understood? According to Adorno and Horkheimer the original sin of Enlightenment lies in a truly momentous conceptual transformation in which the initial protest against inequality turns into a programme for rendering everything universally equivalent. Thus Enlightenment cannot represent the real stage at which the moment of universality and the moment of difference interpenetrate in such a way that each side becomes the guarantee of the other. As Adorno and Horkheimer's philosophy of history construes the process, the development of Enlightenment only secures the moment of universality at the cost of repressing difference, instead of facilitating the complete realization of the latter and recognizing the right to the universality of difference.

> Anything which might be different is rendered equivalent ... The identity of everything with everything else is bought at the cost of being allowed to be identical with itself. Enlightenment undermines the injustice of immemorial inequality and the reality of unmediated domination but simultaneously perpetuates domination in the form of that universal mediation which relates each and every being to each and every other being ... Enlightenment excises the incommensurable moment of things.[2]

In the presuppositions of universalism, the intellectual process of abstraction and the linguistic process of discursive logic, Adorno and Horkheimer perceive structures of power which reproduce real objective power. 'Abstraction itself, the very instrument of Enlightenment, relates to its objects like that notion of fate which it claims to reject, namely as liquidation ... The universality of thought as articulated by discursive logic, domination in the sphere of the concept, thus erects itself upon the basis of real domination.'[3]

But at the same time Adorno and Horkheimer also make it clear that this function of abstraction and discursive logic, the universality of concept and of thought, does not inevitably arise from the processes themselves, but is itself the product of social compulsion. 'Each human being is permitted his or her own unique self quite distinct from that of everyone else in order that each may all the more easily be made equivalent to every other. But because the self was never entirely absorbed, Enlightenment still continued to sympathize with the reality of social compulsion throughout the liberal period.'[4] That appeal to the average which proclaims itself as universality is ideology and can be submitted to critical analysis as such. This insight into the ideological character of universal norms which are implicated in the interests of domination and the struggle against such norms is only possible from the perspective of those who are the victims of social compulsion. And this too is Enlightenment. As the two philosophers say: 'Thought has indeed always been able to identify its own questionableness in a concrete manner. It is the slave upon which the master cannot entirely inflict his will as he wishes.'[5]

In complete agreement with his later theory of the non-identical moment of the identical in *Negative Dialectics*, Adorno is also able to perceive non-instrumental reason at work in the very heart of instrumental rationality, in the machine itself:

> The instrument acquires independence: the mediating instance of spirit ameliorates, quite independently of the wishes of those who direct it, the immediacy of economic injustice. The instruments of domination which are intended to hold everyone in their grasp – language, weapons, and finally machines – can themselves inevitably also be grasped by everyone. Thus the moment of rationality realizes itself in domination as something which is also distinct from the latter. The objective character of the instrumental means, which makes it universally available for use, its 'objectivity' for all, already implies a critique of that domination which spawned thought as a means. As it has passed from mythology to logical calculus thought has lost the moment of self-reflection and today the machine mutilates human beings even as it sustains them. But in the shape of the machine itself we can see alienated rationality pointing towards a society in which thought as an ossified material and intellectual apparatus would be reconciled with the liberated living being.[6]

Adorno and Horkheimer recognize the original and mutual involvement of universality and difference in this dialectic of mystification and critique. 'The particular origin of thought has always been inseparably connected with its universal perspective.' And consequently, so they continue: 'Today, with the transformation of the world into industry, the perspective of the universal, the social realization of thought, is so obvious that for this very reason thought is now repudiated by the dominant interests themselves as mere ideology.'[7]

This close examination of the opening pages of the *Dialectic of the Enlightenment* reveals four important points:

1 Universality and difference cannot be divorced from one another.
2 A critique of a particular historical stage in the development of the universal must not be confused with a critique of the universal as such.
3 The category of the universal itself supplies us with a means for articulating a critical analysis of the historical stage attained by the development of the universal.
4 Theories of difference intended to supply a viable critical alternative to false universality also fall prey to ideology if they are ontologized.

Theories of difference which are applied as a virulent critique of covertly limited universality can only ever possess a rhetorical character. In other words, in the political context of the debate about gender such theories represent stylistic figures of exaggeration, of irony, of verbal contestation, which serve to reveal the inadequacies of specific historical forms of universalism. It is the antagonistic staging of difference which constitutes the stylistic function of such critiques, critiques which are explicitly aimed at those notions of equality which would like to eliminate individuality and particularity, instead of opening up equal opportunities of development to them. When women repudiate notions of equality in which they cannot recognize their own experience or from which on closer analysis they are more or less excluded and which they consequently perceive as another patriarchal means of domination, then critical appeal to an alternative model of difference seems required. But this approach is not without certain dangers of its own.

In this context the thought of difference appeals to perceived sexual difference between the genders. Adopting sexual difference as its point of departure, this approach claims to take account of other differences which also arise as a consequence in all the areas of social life in which the sexes participate. In the last analysis this approach criticizes the masculine definition of feminine needs, a definition which proclaims itself in universalistic terms but which, in the patriarchal order, is inevitably orientated to

masculine needs. But according to its own self-understanding the patriarchal order not only appeals to a universalism which is secretly coloured
by masculine bias but of course also appeals to a concept of sexual
difference that is equally motivated by reference to masculine interests. With
systems theory one could say that sexuality is a social system which operates
according to the binary code masculine/feminine and which has the reproduction of society as its essential programme. This system is autogenerative
since with every individual birth it reproduces the masculine/feminine code
both with respect to the product (daughter or son) and to the producer
(man and woman). This means that sexual difference is the central code for
the reproduction of patriarchy. I only mention this in order to emphasize
that the theory of sexual difference upon which some feminisms base
themselves is not merely argumentatively exploited by men but represents
the central systematic support of the patriarchal structure itself.

Any feminist claim which appeals to the idea of sexual difference without
specifying what is meant by this gets swallowed up and rendered invisible
by the prevailing masculine theory of sexual difference. For the latter the
feminine represents the biologically other and it is on the basis of this
biological otherness that the superstructure of the feminine as a complement
of the masculine and as a supplement to masculine domination is constructed. The masculine discourse of sexual difference legitimates the restriction of the feminine to the maternal role in the social sphere through
appeal to the biological difference that marks potential motherhood. This
means that sexual difference is ontologized, fixed and proclaimed as nature,
and thus rendered normative and unalterable. As a result we find ourselves
confronted by two universalisms, that of the masculine and that of the
feminine. There is no longer any 'man' as such, only men and women.

In what follows I would now like to show how one can employ the idea
of sexual difference without having to repudiate universalism in the process.
I will argue that we can only grasp difference as such adequately on the
basis of universalistic thought. The difficulties which arise when one
attempts to exploit the concepts of universalism and difference for social
and political action lie in the conceptual character of the ideas themselves.
These concepts form part of an abstract logical system which is linked to
the universalistic character of language. An understanding of the phenomena of the world is dependent on their simultaneous linguistic construction. It is based upon an act of identification and judgement which is the
condition of every utterance. Identification is the establishment of difference
by demarcating one phenomenon from another, but at the same time the
repression of difference by fixing the meaning of that one phenomenon.
Verbal communication is not just the repression of difference but the only
means of releasing difference into intersubjectivity and offering it to apprehension.

I want to pursue the insoluble entanglement of universalism and difference by examining aesthetics as a form of theoretical discourse directed towards the celebration of difference. What interests me especially is the concept of aesthetic autonomy (and the concurrent universalization of aesthetic discourse) and the transformation of this concept into an instrument of politically motivated critique aimed at all forms of engaged or committed art.

The question of sexual difference is already implicitly broached in this problematic issue. For autonomy is generally ascribed to the concept of the masculine, while what we could call relationality, the movement of engagement and committed identification, is generally ascribed to that of the feminine.[8] Sexual difference manifests itself in a radical form within aesthetic difference as the conventional opposition between autonomous art and sentimental kitsch.

At the same time we must recognize the paradox that it is precisely the autonomy of art which guarantees the differential value both of the language of art itself and of the theoretical discourse about art. This stress on difference against all postmodern attempts to blur the distinctions between the discourses of theory, art and ethics is not only supported by the thought of Adorno or Derrida. For the theories of modernity which take the work of Max Weber as their point of departure, like those of Luhmann and Habermas for example, perceive an irreversible progressive development in the differentiation of social subspheres and of the relevant discourses associated with them.

The validity or invalidity of the idea of artistic autonomy should be neither historicized as the opposition between modernity and postmodernity nor theorized as the polarity of ideology and truth, appearance and essence. A decision in favour of either side of this conceptual duality would lead not to an intensification of difference but to another binary opposition and a consequent loss of complexity in the analysis of the issues. Such loss of complexity accounts for the emergence of those critical approaches in which feminist or anti-racist art – engaged art in short – is disqualified by appeal to the idea of aesthetic autonomy, while hermetic art is indicted for its failure to comply with standards of everyday discourse.

A brief look at the thought of Kant and Habermas may clarify how the relationship between the autonomy and sociality of works of art articulates itself in the aesthetic speech act as a simultaneous expression of two separate levels of experience. Habermas has always insisted upon the difference of the aesthetic discourse of art against the homogenizing poststructuralist concept of textuality. For Habermas aesthetic discourse is characterized by what he calls 'illocutionary de-activation', that is, the suspension of the validity criteria which all speakers must presuppose whenever they wish to enter into communication directed towards mutual understanding.

The criterion of fictionality is thus located at a deeper level than that of the literary text, namely at the level of the reader's performative attitude. In so far as the aesthetic attitude disconnects the process of communication from immediate contact with the world, the validity criteria of truth, of truthfulness and of appropriateness are suspended. It is this disconnection which explains why art can be understood as autonomous from the viewpoint of communications theory. The autonomy of art is not a globally universal phenomenon but a specific cultural norm within particular communities. Such autonomy is actually developed and learnt from both an ontogenetic and a phylogenetic perspective. As far as the child is concerned, immediate world-related communication only differentiates itself at a relatively late stage from communication that is disconnected from immediate relation to the world. The fairy story initially presents itself to the child as a real event. It is only in societies which have developed a differentiation of realms of discourse at a particular historical moment that the institutionalization of the aesthetic attitude towards communicative acts can arise at all.

Both in classical Greece and in the culture of Western Europe during the Middle Ages aesthetic metadiscourse, that is to say, the discourse of aesthetic institutionalization, developed out of a semantics of deception, that is, from a discourse on art in which literature was still disqualified by the criteria of truth, truthfulness and appropriateness. Plato summons truth as a witness against art, although Aristotle's *Poetics* does presuppose a more discriminating aesthetic discourse without which his theory of mimesis, artistic truth, catharsis and the sublime would be impossible. Nevertheless, this discourse is closely tied to the interests of a particular social class by virtue of what it excludes. This is especially clear in Plato's *Republic* where literature, and pre-eminently the theatre, are criticized in the name of a patriarchal and aristocratic ethic.

We find a similar situation later with the poetics of the baroque age and we shall see how the historical preconditions of such poetics, the explicit isolation of a discourse upon art, is inextricable from the development of a secularizing process of rationality. In the case of Greek culture and the baroque age we find a rationality of the *polis* or a courtly rationality still tied in each case to a specific social stratum and thus to specific interests of social self-representation.

When we recognize that the explicit establishment of a discourse upon art, or in other words the emergence of aesthetic autonomy, is connected to the development of rationality, we also realize that this represents a stage in the process of civilization that cannot simply be reversed. This intrinsic bond between rationality and the autonomy of art only becomes completely clear in the work of Kant. In Kant's *Critique of Judgement* poetics turns into aesthetics. We no longer ask how a work of art is to be produced if it is to be called beautiful, but enquire rather into what transpires within ourselves when we find something beautiful. Kant's famous answer is that we experience a 'disinterested delight'.

But what does this disinterested delight in a work of art actually mean? I know that I cannot really eat the apples in the picture, that I cannot really fall in love with the hero or heroine of the novel, that I need not really fear the fatal warning pronounced in the poem, and so forth. Yet in traditional aesthetic criticism the criterion of disinterested delight is marshalled against any art that encourages sympathetic identification, engagement or pleasure. The appeal to disinterested delight stands behind all aesthetics of distance, all aesthetics of art for art's sake, all aesthetics of negativity.

Yet Kant does not develop the concept of disinterested delight with reference to art at all but rather with reference to nature and the realities of the social world. And these can certainly represent objects of our desire. In other words, it is only when we have escaped from the concern with satisfying our immediate needs that we are able to develop a disinterested delight in the objects of the world. But this in turn is only possible once a certain level of rationality in society as a whole has been attained, once the real means of sustaining human existence through the domination of nature by science and technology have been acquired. The peasant who remains caught in a more immediate relation of dependence upon nature cannot adopt the same aesthetic stance towards the latter as the city-dweller can, for whom the country is transformed into the countryside.

If we can describe nature as beautiful in any of its manifestations, then this is because we are no longer absolutely dependent upon it for our survival. And when such an urgent condition of dependence does recur, the natural necessity involved no longer appears as direct compulsion but rather as an accident or a misfortune. In liberating ourselves from the immediate sphere of natural coercion we take a step out of or back from nature, distancing ourselves from it, so that to some extent at least nature now lies over against us as an object. If we can then describe nature as beautiful, we are no longer contemplating it as nature but as a work of art.

But since we still belong to nature ourselves, through our own nature as sentient beings, Kant defines the condition of disinterested delight in which the world appears beautiful to us as a harmonious interplay of sensibility and understanding. This connection only becomes transparent when we look back at Kant's definition of the beautiful from the perspective of his subsequent discussion of the sublime. For in the feeling of the sublime the twin components of sensibility and understanding are so drastically divorced from one another that this state of crisis alone allows us to perceive the apparent harmony in the perception of the beautiful as the interplay of two forces.

In the phenomenon of the sublime it is always sensibility which is out of proportion. In the case of the mathematical sublime nature no longer offers us an intuition of cosmic ideas such as infinity or totality, although reason can think them. In the case of the dynamic sublime nature threatens to overwhelm the subject in so far as it manifests itself in tempests, hurricanes, gigantic natural formations, ravines and so forth. Yet the subject is aware of being safe from harm in such experiences. The discrepancy which arises from the collision of sensibility and reason, in which sensibility signals destruction to the subject while reason assumes salvation from annihilation, actually provokes the aesthetic pleasure we take in the sublime. Here too, in the final analysis, it is a question of mastering an essentially unmasterable power by means of reason. We could say that the tempest only becomes a possible object of sublime pleasure once the underlying laws of nature have been understood and the phenomenon has become controllable through the invention, for example, of the lightning conductor. It is only when the laws of electricity have been discovered that the fear of the tempest can be transformed into taking pleasure in its power.[9]

It is no accident that the emergence of a discourse about art takes place during the Enlightenment, the era of rationality and science. The aesthetic attitude and the discourse associated with it are consequences of the rational-scientific emancipation of man from nature and thus of the emergence of a capacity for distancing ourselves from given particular contexts.

The Enlightenment's drive towards rationality and the scientific transformation of the world possesses a universal character: all human beings can potentially share in this process, depending on their circumstances. The universal component in Kant's elucidation of the possibility of discourse about art is directly connected with this universal standard of rationality and finds expression in his theory of taste and his definition of the judgement of taste. At first glance nothing seems less universal than our judgements of taste. But in Kant's thought this is part of the paradox entailed by the judgement of taste. It is a speech act whose conceptual character implies communicability, and thus universality, but one which is grounded in a subjective response by each unique individual that cannot be universalized.

How can we show that the concept of autonomy refers us to the universal moment of theoretical aesthetic discourse? The transition from poetics to aesthetics already testifies to the historical break with the immediate relationship to the world accomplished through art. In Greek the word *aisthesis* signifies 'sensuous perception', and indeed 'sensuous perception' in general and not merely with respect to art. Sense perception represents our closest contact with the phenomena of the world because it seems to be the most direct and immediate relationship we have, as yet unformed by thought and language, the very constituents of universalizing reason. How can the term which describes our most direct contextualization of things come to characterize a process in which our immediate pragmatic relationship to the world is disconnected?

It does so, I would suggest, in so far as sense perception itself becomes an object of perception in its own right, that is, in so far as we the recipients of the work of art become aware of the presuppositions of our sensuous interaction with the world through a sensuous activity which is disconnected from the world. It is now the work of art as a substitute for the world which is presented to our sensuous perception. In this dedramatization of our immediate sensible relationship to the world the subject experiences its own act of sense perception as an intrinsic faculty or, in Kantian terms, becomes aware of the transcendental presuppositions of its own sensuous apperception.

By virtue of this abstraction from the immediate, subjective and idiosyncratic relationship to the world, one which is always shaped by our private interests, the subject is able to experience the dimension of universality which belongs even to the field of sense perception. To this extent art is always a form of objectivized sensibility. We can see, therefore, how an autonomous, that is, universalistic, theory of art can be called 'aesthetics'. The universalization of man as not merely a thinking and speaking, but a feeling and acting being is only possible through the concrete experience of a radical de-contextualization. But since sense perception represents our most immediate, and thus our most basic and subjective, relationship to the world, the process of ontological uncoupling or disconnection necessarily begins here. It is in the paradox of the 'aesthetic', in the very idea of a systematic theory of that which eludes all system, that we can recognize the profound dimension in which the universalizing movement must commence. Hence the transition from poetics to aesthetics: the break with our immediate contact with the world, certainly proceeds by means of an artefact but it cannot be represented in the artefact as such because the world from which the subject uncouples itself in the reception of art is more comprehensive than the artefact.

This argument clearly reveals how feelings, sense perception, sensibility in general, themselves depend upon certain social standards of rationality and are thus historically formed. The universal and the historical components of sensibility express themselves in the judgement of taste which declares whether or not something is beautiful. But because this is a judgement based upon sensibility, it can never be expected to lead to a consensus which could be conceptually or discursively redeemed. As Kant says, I can only await the potential 'agreement' of others with my own judgement. The universal does not speak directly for itself but can only be inferred from the resulting act of 'agreement'. To that extent the universal voice of reason is only an 'Idea'. Thus, as Kant continues, whether 'one who believes he is making a judgement of taste is in fact judging in accordance with this idea is a matter of uncertainty. But in using the word "beauty" he announces that he is referring to this idea and thus intending to express a judgement of taste.'[10] For Kant the judgement of taste expresses the *sensus communis*, a universal sense.

The possibility of an autonomous discourse about art emerges in and through this paradox. The discourse in question is autonomous because it makes universal validity claims and thus proclaims itself free from any particular interest whatsoever. Disinterested delight is thus a delight without particular interest and this is only possible by reference to a standard of rationality which belongs to society as a whole, a standard which permits me a certain distance from the immediate unconscious solidarity with nature or with the given social order. This defamiliarization is the aesthetic attitude.

Thus we see two processes of autonomization at work here. On the one hand, art becomes autonomous because a specific discourse about it arises and prescribes laws to it even though this discourse does not depend upon some other form of discourse, like those of ethics, religion or politics. On the other hand, this discourse becomes autonomous because a particular, globally ubiquitous standard of rationality has been attained, one which makes an ontology of distance possible for the first time in world history. Corresponding to this process we find a theorization of the productive side of art in terms of speech acts in which the usual validity-criteria have been de-activated.

This in principle total uncoupling of the aesthetic act from its immediate relationship to the world cannot be compared with falsehood in the sense of a lie, because the concept of 'lying' is unintelligible if the relevant validity-criteria are not in force, at least on one side of the communicative process. This defamiliarization of the aesthetic act was accomplished historically for the first time in the eighteenth century, but the fact that it can no longer be reversed, on account of its connection with a universal standard of rationality, turns it into an ontological given for us. As soon as we recognize that art as an institution has become what it is through a historical process but now exists for us as an ontological fact, it becomes clear that every attempt to reintegrate art and life is a project doomed to failure.

Art and life can now only come into closer contact with one another on a *second* level, and one which can never deny or undercut that first level of ontological separation. It is only in relation to this second level that realist criteria, appeals to aesthetic distance and negativity, the poetics of *l'art pour l'art*, or mimetic theories of art can properly be applied. The ontological level of distance can only be further intensified or weakened by this second level but it can never be completely relinquished.

The intrinsic capacity for distancing ourselves from or envisaging alternatives to the existing state of affairs constitutes the social function of the aesthetic in the world. (In the systems-theory of Luhmann the function of art consists in the production of *contingency*. In the thought of Peirce art becomes a sign for *possible objects*.) But art thereby becomes universal. The autonomy of art does not appear as a characteristic which transcends all social determination but as something which is capable of encompassing any and every aspect of social reality. The change of perspective involved here is exceptionally important. It represents a movement away from the detachment from the world towards an attitude of openness to the world. If today, in a form of aesthetic discourse which has declined since the time of Kant, the concept of 'taste' connotes arbitrariness and total freedom in the act of artistic judgement, we can see here the same loss of meaning which has taken place with the transition from 'universalization' to 'autonomization' and has led eventually to an atrophied concept of the 'autonomous'. Today the concepts of taste and autonomy conceal the dimension which they originally designated, namely the simultaneous relationship which the practice of art bore to the social and to the universal.

In this reduction of the meaning of 'universal' and 'autonomous' we can see the other side of the differentiation as a crippling shift from a local uncoupling to an act of general disconnection. Here we find the modern tendency towards the segregation of differences into ossified structures and systems incapable of movement. This ossification accompanies the clandestine exclusion of difference from the aesthetic realm, the exclusion of the feminine, of the proletarian, of the ethnically alien. This takes place less in art itself than in the theory of art, although the latter certainly reacts back in turn upon the sphere of cultural production.

Ever since Kant those forms of literature which proceed from the premise of social commitment have been ruled out of the literary canon by an appeal to the concepts of 'disinterested delight' and 'autonomy'. The values of 'solidarity', 'identification', 'feeling' and 'engagement' have been branded as 'kitsch', 'sentimentality', 'confessional literature', or 'politics', with the result that such literature has only survived as aspects of subculture.

Today, sustained by a new awareness of the value of small-scale narratives and inspired by the protest against hegemonic power, the concepts of universality, autonomy and distance have been almost unanimously rejected. This rejection represents a rhetorical excess of difference, an excess of postmodernity over modernity. If we read 'postmodernity' as a signifier for the self-enlightenment of the Enlightenment, as the reflexive moment of Enlightenment itself, then the introduction of difference represents the self-enlightenment of universalism and feminism the self-enlightenment of a patriarchal Enlightenment. This is how I would interpret Ulrike Prokop's claim that feminism is a second Enlightenment.

But why has such self-enlightenment only become possible now? If we think back to the enabling conditions of aesthetics, we could ask this question in the following way: why is it only now, since the 1970s, that we have begun asking about the possibility of developing a feminine aesthetics? In a similar fashion Nancy Chodorow asks why 'from the point of view of a hyper-gender-sensitive 1970's feminist, these women [female psychoanalysts of the 1930s] were relatively gender-blind, or unattuned to gender, regarding both their role in the profession and their profession's theory.'[11] I believe that the second Enlightenment of feminism, the feminist self-enlightenment of the Enlightenment as I have called it, is also bound up with the further development of technological rationality.

In our analysis of the sublime we saw how the emergence of aesthetics as the emancipation of sensibility from its immediate thrall to nature was entwined with the development of science and technology as a means of liberation from the realm of natural compulsion. But the traditional model of sexual difference rests on the fact of woman's greater dependence upon nature by virtue of her capacity to bear children. Feminine sensibility only becomes autonomous at the historic moment when women exchange the necessity of bearing children for the choice of doing so, the compulsion of motherhood for the option of maternity, the compulsion of heterosexuality for the discovery of sexual preference. This development has only been made possible by modern technologies of reproduction, and here I include everything from the condom to the pill, from sperm banks to *in vitro* fertilization. The fact that at the present time men are still attempting to control these technologies for economic and ethical ends is a problem that calls for political engagement and does not cancel the liberation of the feminine body which such technologies imply. Feminine sensibility becomes autonomous as soon as motherhood becomes a question of choice.

I claimed earlier that with the liberation from the immediate sphere of natural necessity in the Enlightenment, sense perception and sensibility become themselves objects of perception, and particularly in art. Hence the transition from poetics to aesthetics. In the Romantic period it was the men who emphasized and expressed their own sensibility (Rousseau, Goethe, Keats, Shelley, Constant, Baudelaire). But it is only now that this development is taking place with women. There is not only a second Enlightenment at work but also a second Romanticism, a self-enlightenment of historical Romanticism concerning the limitations of its sensibility. In this second Romanticism women are discovering and exploring their own sensibility. This is a leap which carries us from Schlegel's *Lucinde* to Elfriede Jelinek's *Lust*.[12]

From this perspective it becomes plain why masculine criticism should often find such writing alien and react to it with bafflement at best and at worst with outright hostility. It is no accident that the first famous texts produced in the name of feminine aesthetics are texts concerned with feminine sexuality, and indeed specifically with lesbian feminine sexuality, like Verena Stefan's *Shedding* or Monique Wittig's *Les Guérillères*.[13] The new *écriture féminine* with its search for the feminine body within writing, the novels of Elfriede Jelinek, the texts of Marguerite Duras, are ambitious explorations of the dark continent of feminine sensibility and its representation. The work of Sylvia Plath, by contrast, still bears witness to an agonizing struggle between the compulsive claims of reproductive sexuality and a profound desire to break free of them.

So I would now like to modify an earlier claim and put the matter this way: if a new awareness of the value of small-scale narratives and the protest against hegemonic power has led to a widespread rejection of the concepts of universality, autonomy and distance, this is only too understandable given two centuries of patriarchal sway over aesthetic discourse. Nevertheless, the partisan distortion and impoverishment of these concepts in the interests of patriarchal dominion should not be confused with the emancipatory power which these concepts articulated in the eighteenth century and which they continue to possess even today. The vital task is to resurrect this power from the by no means 'disinterested' neglect under which it has been buried.

NOTES

1 Theodor W. Adorno and Max Horkheimer, *Dialektik der Aufklärung. Philosophische Fragmente* (Querido, Amsterdam, 1944), p. 61.
2 Ibid., p. 23.
3 Ibid., pp. 24–5.
4 Ibid., pp. 23–4.
5 Ibid., p. 5.
6 Ibid., pp. 51–2.
7 Ibid., p. 52.
8 See for instance Harold Bloom, *The Anxiety of Influence* (Oxford University Press, Oxford, 1973); Susan Gubar, ' "The Blank Page" and the issues of female creativity', in *Feminist Criticism: Essays on Women, Literature and Theory*, ed. Elaine Showalter (Virago, London, 1986), pp. 292–3; Nina Baym, 'Melodramas of beset Manhood: How theories of American fiction exclude women authors', in *Feminist Criticism*, pp. 63–80.
9 See. H. D. Kittsteiner, 'Und draussen ging die Welt vorbei', *Niemandsland. Zeitschrift zwischen den Kulturen*, 3 (1989), pp. 24–42.

10   Immanuel Kant, *Kritik der Urteilskraft*, in *Werke*, ed. Wilhelm Weischedel (12 vols, Suhrkamp, Frankfurt/M., 1968), vol. 4, p. 354 (author's translation).
11   Nancy Chodorow, *Feminism and Psychoanalytic Theory* (Polity Press, Cambridge, 1989), p. 199.
12   Friedrich Schlegel, *Lucinde* (1799); Elfriede Jelinek, *Lust* (Rowohlt, Reinbek, 1989).
13   Verena Stefan, *Häutungen* (Frauenoffensive, Munich, 1975); Engl.: *Shedding*, tr. Johanna Moore and Beth Weckmueller (Daughters Publishing Company, New York, 1978).
14   Monique Wittig, *Les guérillères* (Editions de Minuit, Paris, 1969).

12

Unreal Presences: Allegory in Paul de Man and Walter Benjamin

The title of this essay names Paul de Man and Walter Benjamin, but refers also to George Steiner.[1] Steiner's book *Real Presences* gave rise, at least in Germany, to a literary debate, and prior to that caused a stir in the English media. I consider the reception of this slender volume as a sign that there is a process of reorientation in the field of ideology.

Steiner's book is a frontal attack on the textual practices of deconstruction. However, it is aimed not so much at Derrida's philosophical dismantling as at de Man's deep-rooted suspicion of ideology in literary works. Aesthetic ideology is the ostensible totalization of differential textuality by means of specific figures of speech as inventoried, for example, by classical rhetoric. Its effect is a materialization of language as an abstract medium on different levels of the literary text and its communication. In the final analysis, the materialization of language, regardless of how different the techniques may be, has always had an anthropomorphizing effect to which readers react through a process of identification. Thus, language no longer seems merely to represent, with its unbridgeable hiatus between signifier and signified, but rather manifests itself as a direct presence: the conventionality of linguistic signs disappears behind the images evoked by mimesis and figuration. In this shift in emphasis from a symbolic concatenation to an imaginary and spatial simultaneity, the subject experiences itself as identical with itself. It is secure in a bubble of truth in which sign and meaning, sign and reference concur.

It is against this *lanterna magica* of the written word, sanctioned as art, that Paul de Man's radical gesture of unmasking is directed. Although he acknowledges that the written word displays its own construction, its shortcomings in the language, its semiotic wound, for him this does not go far enough. He rips off its mask of aesthetic metaphysics resolutely and completely. George Steiner's criticism is that the face remains stuck to it. He provocatively lays claim to a discourse on truth in art which is branded as metaphysical and theological. Steiner assumes that there is no mediation between the discourses of mask and face, of aesthetic deconstruction and aesthetic experience. His book falls in a logically consistent way into two parts. The first part is an analysis of deconstruction. Steiner concludes:

> On its own terms and planes of argument . . . the challenge of deconstruction does seem to me irrefutable . . . I do not, therefore, believe that an answer to its challenge . . . can be found at all within linguistic or literary theory . . . I want to ask whether a hermeneutics and a reflex of valuation . . . can be made intelligible, can be made answerable to the existential facts, if they do not imply, if they do not contain, a postulate of transcendence.[2]

In Steiner's book there is no 'quantum leap' between 'letter', the first deconstructivist part, and 'presence',[3] the second, transcendental, or – if one prefers – metaphysical part, which is more phenomenological.

A 'quantum leap' is not a mediation in the dialectic sense, and one could let both discourses continue to exist concurrently: immediate and heteronomous. Yet aesthetics keeps a theory ready which could describe a possible leap between deconstruction as a discourse on emptiness and literature as a discourse on transcendence. That is the theory of the sublime.

The sublime is a reception category. It describes the tension within a subject which is called upon to exert all its sensory and intellectual powers as a result of the crisis in the relationship between these very same powers. In the face of a devastating eccentricity of nature, be it overwhelming in its onrush or terrifying in its non-appearance, the subject whose narcissism is threatened by his own sensuality and naturalness saves himself from downfall by using his intellect, and revels in this superiority. This power of the intellect, which Kant described as our capacity for moral ideas,[4] finds expression in positions of security, that is in the most all-encompassing sense: in our culture, in the face of threatening nature. Threatening nature can also be absent nature. And here, at the vertiginous abyss of the *horror vacui*, we see the convergence of deconstruction, allegory, melancholy and sublime.

The allegorical form occupies a central position in the linguistic theories of both Walter Benjamin and Paul de Man. Both are concerned with the existential emptiness in the linguistic sign when the divine guarantee of meaning has perished. Such an insight, conceived with a radical consistency, ought to prohibit both of them from speaking. This performative contradiction is the central argument against deconstructivist utterances.

De Man himself thematicizes this objection as a problem contained in each act of speech, even his own, an act which has to repeat precisely those procedures which it criticizes. Nevertheless, such a gesture of open modesty is supposed to disguise the fact that it is actually the performance which lends the utterance its validity, despite its contradictory status. This linguistic gesture deploys its authority by means of a rhetoric of modesty and is at the same time supported by the power of speaking. The violent positing of a performative subject makes possible the redeeming leap out of the threatening destruction of reference, meaning and subject.

The theory of the sublime is important because in comparison to the theory of the performative contradiction (both theories deal with the same phenomenon) it introduces a dimension which de Man under any circumstances has to exclude from his line of argument. This is the dimension of the psyche: the imagination and the phantasm which in his theory become the products of an antecedent language machine.

As a part of aesthetics, of course, the theory of the sublime itself falls under the verdict of aesthetic ideology if it is supposed to be merely the effect of linguistic figurality. This is the reason for the attacks on psychoanalysis,[5] the theory of which still presupposes either a subject of the unconscious, or a split subject.

De Man can only uphold the priority of language as an aesthetic subject because he takes as his starting-point two premises which are not reflected upon. The first is the subliminal preference for Freudian psychoanalysis with a Lacanian linguistic turn.

At its centre is the Oedipus complex, itself the result of the symbolic order and hence of language. This makes it possible to privilege the mechanism of language in relation to psychoanalysis. However, only a form of psychoanalysis which has incorporated the pre-Oedipal space into its approach – that of Melanie Klein or Julia Kristeva, for instance – shows that both deconstruction and Oedipal psychoanalysis can themselves be read as allegories of language as a machine.

The second premise – closely related to the first – is central to de Man's argument: namely, that the notion of language as a figure (the term used to describe rhetorical combinations of signs) is itself a metaphor. In language, of course, there is no figure, unless we think of Apollinaire's calligrams, or Benjamin's observation that the introduction of the capital letter has furthered the allegorization of abstract terms in the German language. We must ask ourselves, then, why de Man does not thematicize the figurality of language as a figure, and what the function of this metaphor might be.

What is transferred in the metaphor of rhetoric as 'figurative' speech? The aesthetic effect is transported back on to the linguistic sign, but the effect itself is not achieved by means of the trope. On the contrary, the aesthetic effect is the result of consciously actualizing the quasi-ontological difference between art and reality in the recipient. As far as the language of a text is concerned, this can never indicate a literary text, even if it seems to be literary in its rhetorical structure. The question of whether we are dealing with literature does not depend on the tropes, but on our own decision to read a particular text as a literary one. Which way the decision goes is in principle arbitrary, but it is guided nevertheless by the traditions of our culture. They cannot be simply undone; they are incorporated as inscriptions into our bodily, incarnate existence. Not only is nature always historical, but culture is always naturalized.

Aesthetic discourse is characterized in Habermas's terms by an 'illocutionary suspension of validity': that is, the reader decides on a voluntary suspension of those criteria of validity that speakers have to presuppose if they wish to enter into a process of communication geared towards understanding.

The criterion of fictionality is thus located on a deeper level than that of the text, namely the level of the performative disposition. The aesthetic disposition uncouples the act of communication from its immediate reference to the world. This suspension, thematicized by Kant as disinterested pleasure, is a capacity for distancing oneself from one's environment and therefore also one's nature, one's reality. Kant sees this capacity as an aptitude in every human being, but believes it can only be realized under certain historical conditions, such as those of science and technology, which actually loosen the attachment of human beings to nature as natural creatures with needs. It is only when the sensual relationship with the world is de-dramatized in this way that the subject can become conscious of its own sensuality as a universal capacity. Thus, in art sensuality is itself made the object of sensuality, by making the art object take the place of the world. This explains, for instance, the transition from poetics to aesthetics in the Enlightenment period.[6]

The so-called figurality of language – which can just as easily be absent in the literary text – intensifies language, but does not itself constitute grounds for fictionality or mimesis. It is, therefore, only by omitting to examine the metaphor of the 'linguistic figure' that de Man is able to privilege the *text* as the actual scene of the aesthetic event. By repressing the aesthetic as a dimension of sensuality, and consequently banishing the subject from the texts, de Man also has to make the body disappear, and psychoanalysis along with it. But it is precisely the semiotics of psychoanalysis which can tell us what is concealed behind the preference for allegory as a signifying theory. Is there perhaps an ideology of allegory as well as an aesthetic one?

Let us recapitulate: de Man is only able to insist on the exclusively linguistic semiology of the literary text because he represses the corporeality of author and recipient whose presence in the literary communication is in fact represented by the metaphor of the linguistic figure in the text. Only such a repression of sensuality rips the text so radically from its anchorage in objects and bodies that all that remains of it is the allegory of its own 'undecidability', its unreadability. The body is repressed by being castrated. Concepts such as 'mutilation', 'defacement', 'disfiguration', and 'blindness' play a central role in de Man's texts. We are familiar with castration rituals from history, grouped under the term *damnatio memoriae*, in which statues of former rulers are mutilated: their limbs are cut off, they are blinded, and their noses and ears are damaged.

This mutilation of bodies and especially the face involves destroying history, the traces of which are inscribed in the bodies. Just as the figure, the biographical and historical body of the author, is inscribed in the style of a text, and hence its figures, and just as the figure of the recipient is inscribed into the interpretation, so the disembodiment of texts involves their own castration and deprivation of meaning.

It would be a false conclusion to suggest that the loss of a centre of meaning, whether this be God or Reason or Marxism or Progress, leads to a cancellation of the contract of signs. Instead, signs and bodies bear the 'incorporated' traces of these contracts of meaning. Therefore, how violent the gaze must be of the melancholic allegorist deprived of all meaning can be seen in the vehement linguistic gestures with which the linguistic signs – arbitrary, yet composed by elective affinities – are broken up and welded together in new ways.

The Body of the Mother

The banishment of corporeality from literary communication and, as an inevitable consequence, the fragmentation of linguistic signs into signifier and signified really means the fundamental repression of the female body and in fact the mother's body. Castration devastates the presence of the body in which the memory of the mother is inscribed. De Man repeats this gesture as if by repetitive compulsion. The return of the repressed has to be repeatedly negated. Whenever the figures in the text are disfigured, the founding gesture of our Western culture – namely, the foreclosure of the feminine – is continually replayed.

Lyotard interprets Judaism's banishment of images and the amnesia of patricide as a sign of the foreclosure of castration. It is coexistent with the foreclosure of the feminine and the maternal.[7]

The comprehensive desensualization of art against the effects of ideology enacts the forgetting, denial and repression of the feminine. This is matched by the actual structure of the allegory itself. Allegories are in most cases female forms which have had a new and different meaning imposed on them. In this respect, the allegory is a figurative account of what already happens to woman within a patriarchy. Her body is made into the sign for masculine meanings.

The very fact that there is a pictorial space within which the female body can be made into the material of the allegory is itself a sign of patriarchal, and hence Oedipal, violence. However, this involves a dual mortification of the female body in the allegory: apart from its first mortification into the material of the image, the gap between image and meaning reveals the essential emptiness of the sign and the emptiness of existence. This is a consequence of the separation from the pre-Oedipal mother upon entering into language. This double mortification is described in the following quotation: 'l'écriture allégorique est écriture du figurale et destruction de tout figuratif au sens stricte'.[8]

If we project this dual destruction existing simultaneously in the allegorical image on to the temporal axis of psychography, then regression leads us back via the deathly, Oedipal interpretation of the image of the feminine, and the as yet non-sexualized mirror-image, into the emptiness of pure positionality which is only detectable later in the act of abjection. Here, where room is first created for a later self, the all-powerful pre-Oedipal mother is reduced to the abject mother. It is this dual form of murder which is expressed in the allegory and which reappears in Benjamin's remark in *The Origin of German Tragic Drama* that 'the Egyptians' had 'buried corpses in wooden images'.[9]

As a functional image, woman is always killed off anyway, since the patriarchal gaze turns the woman's body into an object, rendering it silent. Memory is linked to representations of the body and of objects, and consequently to images. The resurrection of the maternal body from the pre-Oedipal space would in any case always be the presentation of a corpse lying concealed beneath the appearance.

The Violence of Semiosis

Nevertheless, the living body of the mother has not completely disappeared. It is present in the act of violence – 'figuration' and 'disfiguration' as a process rather than its result – which all signifying practices must repeat afresh if they are intended to produce meaning. Semiosis is the 'acting out' of murder and castration within the sign. The more signifier and signified are torn apart to form hermetic constellations and hard edges, the deeper the essential abyss which opens up between them, an abyss bridged only by conventions. In this abyss, violence reveals itself as a strain on meaning.

Through its violent, unmediated construction, allegory in the form of figurative speech or emblem is the allegory of each semiotic or hermeneutic act. In Benjamin's work – just as in de Man's – an unmistakable semantics of violence plays around the allegorical form.

Allegory is allegorized as a prison, as enslaving and as exploiting. It is compared with a convulsion caused by the rebellion of its linguistic material. The allegorist is called a sadist.[10] But above all, allegory is a battlefield on which the body – especially the female body – is torn apart.[11]

The dismemberment of the body evokes the powerful fascination of the abject position in which the subject has not yet undergone the formation of a unified self-image in the mirage of the mirror and the ensuing entrance into the symbolic order with its series of separations and losses. Instead the subject is still stretched out as a *corps morcelé* in the space between the all-powerful pre-Oedipal mother and the attraction of the non-phallic father of personal prehistory, both of which enact a decisive primordial blend of fusion, absorption, space and emptiness. As argued earlier:

> The archaic pull of the abject, the simultaneous revulsion and fascination of fusion, appear in Benjamin's work as an irreconcilable juxtaposition of *Lust* ('pleasure') and melancholy in the face of the destruction of the subject and its inwardness. The reduction of the individual to a creature, a doll, an automaton, a machine, a dismembered body, the disembowelment of inner space – all are deeply enjoyed and just as deeply mourned.[12]

In the melancholic position of the (baroque) allegorist surfaces the mourning for the lost objects of a lost world. The fading of divine transcendence from the Reformation till the age of Enlightenment has emptied the world of the absolute meaning guaranteed by the promised remission of sins and salvation. The consequent erosion of the moral subject, the evacuation of things, and the hollowing of the world entail on the level of representation the loss of the aura, of narration, of *mémoire involontaire*, mimetic phenomena, whose disappearance Benjamin lamented deeply.[13]

Delight in the Destruction of the Subject

At the same time, the annihilation of the autonomy and the consciousness of the subject by ferocious acts of aggression is also perversely enjoyed. In the wake of the crisis of the transcendent certainty of salvation the body ceases to be significant as a witness and sign of divine creation. The body decays into fallen nature, becomes indifferent matter, a thing, a corpse. The allegorical furore thus swirls bodies, objects and parts of bodies indiscriminately together.

The member of the community legitimated by the assurance of salvation is now replaced by the creature in Benjamin's terminology. The creature's essential emptiness transforms the protagonists of baroque tragedy into puppets, playing-card kings, marionettes and miniatures.[14] Just as under the mortifying gaze of the allegorist the bodies of words disintegrate and their meaning trickles out till there are only syllables and letters left, so blood pours from the crushed and dismembered bodies of criminals and martyrs on the stage.

When Benjamin remarks that the court of allegory is 'l'appareil sanglant de la Destruction'[15] or when he compares allegory to the act of rape,[16] his figurative discourse betrays a sensitivity to, an affinity with the violent textuality of baroque drama. That this scenario of violence is a gendered one is more plain in Benjamin's reading of the allegorical process as an analogy of sexual violence. The allegorical intention is seen as a production of meaning in which the signifier is male and the body into which the new meaning is grafted appears to be female. The sexual excess of Benjamin's phrasing conjures up fetishistic activities just as do sadism, voyeurism and polygamy. Allegorical desire, in the arbitrariness of its choice of objects, is not 'in accord with the authority of nature', remarks Benjamin,

> but the voluptuousness with which significance rules, like a stern sultan in the harem of objects, is without equal in giving expression to it. It is indeed characteristic of the sadist that he humiliates his object and then – or thereby – satisfies it. And that is what the allegorist does in this age drunk with acts of cruelty both lived and imagined.[17]

The sexual aggression which surfaces in the rhetoric of the text finds its target in the body of the mother. Its bleeding and dismemberment point to the empty centre of allegorical imagery in its most abject form, the corpse. It is therefore symptomatic that the titles of the last chapters of *The Origin of German Tragic Drama* all bear witness to a fascination with the dead body: 'Allegorical Dismemberment', 'Dismemberment of Language', 'The Corpse as Emblem'. The uncanniness of the corpse results from its ambiguity with reference to the basic opposition dead/alive. This ambiguity, the blurring of the most fundamental categories in human life, gives rise to an abjection in which the primeval *Angst/Lust* produced by the separation of the maternal body is most intensely experienced.

But the vehement and pleasurable regression behind the screen of the mirror-image which veils the primal emptiness of existence and sign alike is only one side of this position. The other is melancholy and mourning for the lost narcissistic reflection, the precarious but necessary foundation of autonomy which is established through the pre-Oedipal distancing from the mother. In this respect, abjection gives the lie to narcissism by throwing into relief its imaginary character. But at the same time, 'abjection is a resurrection that has gone through death [of the ego]. It is an alchemy that transforms death drive into a start of life, of new significance.'[18] It is the resurrection, the ascent to new significance which is the life-enhancing dynamic within the (allegorical) production of meaning.

In this respect there is a major difference between de Man and Benjamin. De Man sets out precisely to expose images, the figural, and the aesthetic, as ideological illusions smoothing over the existential emptiness of the linguistic sign. For him, therefore, all figures of speech become fixed as allegories. For de Man at the end of the twentieth century, it is no longer possible to reassemble the shattered figures under a new light of meaning, or to lend them a fresh significance. Instead, he perseveres heroically in the limbo of emptiness and undecidability.

Benjamin, on the other hand, sets out in his work to redeem images from their traditional, corrupt meanings, and to force new revolutionary meaning out of them (as in *Das Passagen-Werk*). Therefore he too has to destroy the figures and tear apart the bodies of meaning. He does this in his book on German tragic drama. However, he then sets out to reanimate them with new meaning. He performs this resurrection, sublimation or ascension in the image of the Messiah and the 'Marxist-Sublime', as Lyotard terms it.[19] Just as, in experiencing the sublime, the (narcissistic) subject saves itself from being destroyed in sensual nature through a new impulse of reason, Benjamin maintains that the allegorist 'wakes up' in 'God's world'.

> For it is precisely visions of the frenzy of destruction, in which all earthly things collapse into a heap of ruins which reveal not so much the ideal quality of allegorical contemplation, but rather its limit ... In the death-signs of the baroque, allegorical reflection finally veers round, in a backward movement of redemption ... The spell of utter fragmentation, death and dispersion is broken ... After all, this is the essence of melancholy immersion: that its ultimate objects, in which it believes it can most fully secure for itself *that which is abject*, turn into allegories, and that these allegories fill out and deny the void in which they are represented, just as, ultimately, the intention does not faithfully rest in the contemplation of bones, but leaps forward into resurrection.[20]

However, the allegorical form is not meant to be left dead and empty, as in the baroque; instead it is to be woken up from its reified spell, and propelled into new sensuality. Whereas de Man rests faithfully in the contemplation of bones, Benjamin leaps forward completely into resurrection.

In salvaging images, Benjamin is concerned to redeem corporeality, materiality, sensuality, and hence ultimately actual or – to use perhaps a better term, coined by George Steiner – real presence. This extends into the very physis of the written signifier. 'Yet there is nothing subordinate in writing; it is not cast away in reading, like dross. It is absorbed, along with what is read, as its "figure".'[21] Here the 'figure' is not a 'figure', but rather the actual pictorial space of the letter.

Violence and Sovereignty

At the beginning of his book on German tragic drama, Benjamin refers explicitly to Carl Schmitt's concept of sovereignty. In *Political Theology* Schmitt writes:

> Sovereign is he who decides the exceptional state of emergency ... The assertion that the exception is truly appropriate for the juristic definition of sovereignty has a systematic, legal-logical foundation. The decision on the exception is a decision in the true sense of the word. Because a general norm, as represented by an ordinary legal prescription, can never encompass a total exception, the decision that a real exception exists cannot therefore be entirely derived from this norm.[22]

It is no coincidence that a theory of political power emerges in the context of a construction of allegory. As a signifying theory, allegory conceives the language of literature – and in its radicalized form, every act of speech – as an exceptional linguistic state of emergency. Interpretations can therefore no longer be grounded in procedural rules or coherent reasons. They can now only be posited by decision. The subject of semiosis which de Man has deconstructed away from the linguistic machine tacitly returns as the sovereign of power.

This possible imposition is challenged by George Steiner's book, which sets out explicitly to devise an ethics of reading. And Benjamin himself develops his methodology of dialectical images against this possibility of his own theory of allegory: a political aesthetics which presupposes a subject that not only speaks and writes, but feels and acts too.

Although feeling and action are inscribed by writing and speaking, this metabolization of the symbolic, the embodiment and secularization of language, can no longer be contained within a purely linguistic semiology or poetics. The fact that at the end of the twentieth century deconstruction has made visible the limits of the linguistic turn for a theory of the subject is its inestimable contribution. In this respect, deconstruction is the allegory of the collapse of the linguistic metanarrative.

Notes

1   George Steiner, *Real Presences: Is There Anything in What We Say?* (Faber & Faber, London and Boston, 1989).

2 Ibid., p. 134.
3 Ibid., p. 212.
4 Immanuel Kant, *The Critique of Judgement*, tr. J. C. Meredith (Clarendon Press, Oxford, 1978).
5 Paul de Man, 'Excuses', in *Allegories of Reading* (Yale University Press, New Haven, Conn., and London, 1979), pp. 278–301: 'But if her nominal presence is a mere coincidence, then we are entering an entirely different system in which such terms as desire, shame, guilt, exposure, and repression no longer have any place' (p. 289). 'Far from seeing language as an instrument in the service of a psychic energy, the possibility now arises that the entire construction of drives, substitutions, repressions and representations is the aberrant, metaphorical correlative of the absolute randomness of language, prior to any figuration or meaning' (p. 299).
6 See Helga Geyer-Ryan, 'Die Autonomie der Kunst. Zur Ästhetik Herbert Marcuses', in *Kritik und Utopie bei Herbert Marcuse*, ed. Institut für Sozialforschung (Suhrkamp, Frankfurt/M., 1992).
7 Jean-François Lyotard, 'Figure foreclosed', in *The Lyotard Reader*, ed. Andrew Benjamin (Blackwell, Oxford, 1989), pp. 69–110; p. 105.
8 Christine Buci-Glucksmann, 'Féminité et modernité: Walter Benjamin et l'utopie du féminin', in *Walter Benjamin et Paris. Colloque international 27–29 juin 1983*, ed. Heinz Wisman (Editions du Cerf, Paris, 1986), p. 418.
9 Walter Benjamin, *Ursprung des deutschen Trauerspiels*, in *Gesammelte Schriften*, ed. Rolf Tiedemann and Hermann Schweppenhäuser (Suhrkamp, Frankfurt/M., 1972–89), vol. 3, ed. Hella Tiedemann-Bartels (1972); tr. John Osborne (1977), *The Origin of German Tragic Drama* (Verso, London, 1985), p. 222.
10 Ibid., p. 200.
11 Ibid., p. 202.
12 See above, ch. 6: Abjection in the texts of Walter Benjamin', pp. 112–13.
13 Walter Benjamin, *Das Passagen-Werk*, in *Gesammelte Schriften*, vol. 5.1, ed. Rolf Tiedemann (Suhrkamp, Frankfurt/M., 1982), p. 422.
14 Benjamin, *Origin of German Tragic Drama*, pp. 138–9.
15 Benjamin, *Das Passagen-Werk*, p. 435.
16 Ibid., p. 423.
17 Benjamin, *Ursprung des deutschen Trauerspiels*, pp. 360 (author's translation).
18 Julia Kristeva, *Powers of Horror: An Essay on Abjection*, tr. Leon S. Roudiez (Columbia University Press, New York, 1982), p. 15.
19 See *Postmodernism: ICA Documents 4*, ed. Lisa Appignanesi (London 1984), p. 11, quoted in Terry Eagleton, *The Ideology of the Aesthetic* (Blackwell, Oxford, 1990), p. 231.
20 Benjamin, *Ursprung des deutschen Trauerspiels*, p. 406 (author's translation; emphasis added).
21 Ibid., p. 388 (author's translation).
22 Carl Schmitt, *Political Theology*, tr. George Schwab (MIT Press, Cambridge, Mass; and London, 1985), p. 9. (German edn first published 1922.)

13

Writing, Image, Reality

The culture of the twentieth century stands under the banner of the 'linguistic turn'. Language, previously experienced as a transparent medium for the interaction between subject and object, between man and external reality, between man and his own inner world, between one human being and another, has now been transformed into a unique machine for the production of reality. For reality in relation to man now appears as something which is always already linguistically structured. Since language is a social and intersubjective phenomenon, this has also resulted in a changed conception of the subject in our century. The new-born infant becomes a human being through its entry into a linguistically organized reality, through its subjection to an already established symbolic order, as Lacan describes such a reality. It is in this way that the infant first becomes a 'subject' in the truest sense of the word, namely something sub-jected. When Lacan says that the unconscious is structured like a language, we can clearly see the extent to which the linguistic turn has been located within the inner being of the subject. We can also see how Lacan's linguistic model has completely restructured the original Freudian model of psychoanalysis, conceived as it was in terms of mimetic representation.

The same thing has transpired in the field of philosophy. Until the twentieth century man's relationship to nature, to reality in general, to other human beings and to himself, was described in a mimetic and representational terminology. In all theses discourses concepts drawn from the semantics of vision occupy a central position, the most familiar of course being the metaphor of the mirror-image employed in all the traditional theories of reflection and representation. In these theories we are presented with a subject standing over against an object, over against objects of reality, objects which are supposedly reproduced, mirrored or reflected in the consciousness, feelings or thoughts of the subject. The subject is also capable of standing over against itself as an object, a phenomenon upon which transcendental philosophies of self-reflection, philosophies of consciousness in other words, are based.

In the twentieth century the linguistic turn has given rise to a different perspective altogether. Now the development of the new-born infant into an individual as a process of consciousness is no longer described in terms of the subject's interaction with itself, as it was for example in the period of Romanticism. We see the process of individuation as formed instead through the interaction with other individuals, and pre-eminently through linguistic communication. The subject becomes a linguistic inter-subject. Whereas in Lacan this process is described in negative terms and thus betrays a covert nostalgia for the phantasm of the absolute subject, in the later Wittgenstein the subject as essentially dialogical is liberated from the petrifaction of positivist objectivity, and similarly in Habermas from the narcissistic mirror-world of the philosophy of consciousness.

This linguistic interpretation of phenomena has also exerted an influence on the theory and practice of art and literature, and the new media of the twentieth century have encouraged this tendency. It is true that our time has been called the age of the image. Yet the invention of cinema at the beginning of the century introduced into the static, closed, objective products of photography a linguistic or textual element through its narrative structure. This dynamic character, which in the case of film is principally diachronic, proceeding in linear time, still becomes a principle of textualization in general which is not bound to specific temporal axes. At the same time as pictorial images learned to run on film, the linguist Ferdinand de Saussure in Geneva developed a linguistic theory in which signs learned to run as well. Saussure's differential model no longer allows us to interpret the signifier and the signified as fixed and given units of meaning. The arbitrary character of the relation between sound and meaning is pushed into the background through convention and context, but it never disappears. This arbitrary character has the advantage of procuring for the sign that elasticity which facilitates shifts in meaning. But this advantage also shows its down-side in the gulf that opens up between the form and content of the sign. This separation thrusts itself increasingly into the foreground the weaker the contextualization and conventionalization of the sign become. Both these elements are at their weakest in the literary text. For the function of the written word is precisely the de-contextualization of texts; and the de-conventionalization of language has belonged to the programme of literature as a central issue in the Western aesthetics of production since at least the Romantic period. Yet this self-subversion of the sign, most carefully analysed by Derrida, does not stop at the limits of literary discourse. It merely becomes most obvious at this point. The self-subversion which Derrida calls 'différance' threatens every semiotic practice in principle. When does this threat become an acute one?

I have said that the gulf between signifier and signified is rendered invisible through convention, that is through a quasi-naturalization of the sign, and through its embeddedness in context. As written word and as linguistic innovation literature programmatically neglects these conditions, and that is why the process of interpretation can never be completed once and for all. The same effect is obtained when certain conventions enter into crisis and the supporting mechanisms for particular semiotic practices begin to collapse as a result. This occurred in a dramatic fashion in the period of the First World War. The collapse of the value-system which had prevailed in the nineteenth century and the revelation of its function of domination shattered the faith of writers in the possibility of linguistic communication based upon a universal consensus. The literary avant-garde turned this rupture of communication into an aesthetic programme for the destruction of language. And indeed the scepticism about the communicative capacities of language at the close of the nineteenth century, the bohemian character and marginalization of artists and writers, the increasing obscurity of the written word – all these things anticipated the phenomenon of the historical avant-garde movement.

This situation arose once again during the 1960s and still prevails today. Yet the crisis of convention has spread much further for now the theoretical discourses which previously organized our existence in the world have also been drawn into the confusion of semiotic instability. As a result the concept of reality itself has become critical.

In *The Postmodern Condition* Lyotard reveals the literary character of the social-philosophical theories which we have inherited from the nine-teenth century and through which we have hitherto attempted to orientate the meaning of our social practices. Lyotard shows that the ideas of rational enlightenment, of progress, of social-biological evolution, and of Marxist revolution, have exactly the same narrative structure as that with which we are otherwise familiar only in literature. Since these grand narratives, as Lyotard calls them, organize our understanding of reality, both contemporary and historical, this reality can claim no other status than that of fiction. The fictional character of these narratives is underlined by the fact that their own global themes of enlightenment, progress, evolution or revolution can hardly be said to have been realized if we consider the barbarities of the twentieth century. The suspicion aroused by such narratives has been directed with particular effect at the discourses of philosophy and history, but even the language of science, and thus science itself, has not escaped the charge of metaphoricity (Mary Hesse), narrativity (Lyotard) and contingency (Kuhn). The interpretation of reality as a linguistic construct, which was already claimed by structuralism, has undergone a further radicalization in postmodernism: even the privileged status of scientific language with its claim to truth, a status to which structuralist discourse itself aspired, is now put into question. Structuralism itself becomes in post-structuralism and postmodernism another fiction too. Thus the linguistically structured character of reality is now transposed into a reality structured by its literary character.

Yet long before the advent of twentieth-century linguistic philosophy literature itself had already thematized the constructed character not only of its own language but of texts in general. The possibility of the self-reflection of language is constitutively bound up with the novel. For in the novel, by virtue of its very form, we are confronted by a multiplicity of narrative voices which automatically relativize the diverse interpretations of reality which these narratives express. This is one reason for the perennial suppression and control of the novel by conservative institutions. For polyphony, pluriformity and heterology are an affront to all authoritarian systems, for which there can only be one correct language, one exclusive interpretation of reality. Bakhtin has defined the novel through his concepts of dialogism, polyphony and heteroglossia and thus projected a theory of the novel appropriate to our linguistically orientated century. But in Bakhtin's work language in general, as spoken language right down to its finest semantic elements, is always already dialogical and polyphonic in character. In his theory every word bears the traces of all the social and ideological contexts in which it has been employed. These social, ideological and historical shadows cast by the linguistic elements of speech, this *doppelgänger* haunting the words themselves, constitute the dialogical character inherent in language. Every word is embedded in the dissemination of its social contexts and has absorbed these contexts into itself.

Bakhtin exempts the lyric from this model of a language that is already fissured. It is true that the linguistic elements of the lyric are also ultimately dialogical, in so far as it also employs the structures of language in general, but the lyric principally aims to push this dialogical quality into the background through the use of its own special poetic techniques. The poem presents itself as a linguistic unity in its own right, like something self-created at a stroke. In this way for Bakhtin the language of the lyric can serve to throw the language of the novel into contrasting relief. The monological orientation of the poem turns it into something closed in on itself, something static and quiescent, resembling a product or an object rather than a text. By virtue of its object-like character the poem seems to require representational or mimetic theories rather than text-oriented theories for its understanding and interpretation. It presents itself as an image, a reflected image of the inner life of a subject which remains identical to itself in its relationship to the world. Yet the more critical and problematic the concept of identity becomes, along with that of the world and of the subject as well, the more lyrical speech also finds itself exposed to crisis and disturbance. That is why the speech of the dominant trend of European lyric poetry tends increasingly towards the cessation of speech in silence.[1] Yet this is only a radicalization of the problematic of language that began as far back as the Romantic period, that is in the period which witnessed the culmination of lyrical expression in general. What actually finds utterance here is the verbal art of an idiosyncratic subjectivity which projects itself in absolute and autonomous terms. In such language the ego expresses its own state of being in the world, while the heterogeneous and centrifugal dynamics of the world are focused and filtered through a synthesizing and unifying linguistic centre. Behind all this we can see the construction of an autonomous and absolute subject. Its function is to homogenize the social multiplicity of language in the world. The technique employed by this subject of lyrical speech relies upon exclusion.

Just as the idea of the subject presupposes a substantive monadic conception of the self, so too the idea of the lyric is predicated on monological interiority. The subject thus presents itself as precisely delimited from other selves. In such lyrical speech the linguistic multiplicity of the world, in passing through the soul, is supposed to find purified expression in a unique and authentic voice.

In the course of the twentieth century, with its crisis of identity thinking in every area and its preference for theories of negativity, heterology, dialogism and intersubjectivity, poetry has also reflected this development towards polyphony. Thus we see the beginning of a consistent self-subversion of the unity of lyrical speech. In the following poems by Bertolt Brecht and Tony Harrison the unified character of language in general, and thus of their own poetic language, is actually exhibited as an ideological construct serving the interests of particular power relations.[2]

Fragen eines Lesenden Arbeiters

Wer baute das siebentorige Theben?
In den Büchern stehen die Namen von Königen.
Haben die Könige die Felsbrocken herbeigeschleppt?
Und das mehrmals zerstörte Babylon –
Wer baute es so viele Male auf? In welchen Häusern
Des goldstrahlenden Lima wohnten die Bauleute?
Wohin gingen an dem Abend, wo die Chinesische Mauer
fertig war
Die Maurer? Das grosse Rom
Ist voll von Triumphbögen. Wer errichtete sie? Über wen
Triumphierten die Cäsaren? Hatte das vielbesungene Byzanz

Nur Paläste für seine Bewohner? Selbst in dem sagenhaften Atlantis
Brüllten in der Nacht, wo das Meer es verschlang
Die Ersaufenden nach ihren Sklaven.

Der junge Alexander eroberte Indien.
Er allein?
Cäsar schlug die Gallier.
Hatte er nicht wenigstens einen Koch bei sich?
Philipp von Spanien weinte, als seine Flotte
Untergegangen war. Weinte sonst niemand?
Friedrich der Zweite siegte im Siebenjährigen Krieg. Wer
Siegte ausser ihm?

Jede Seite ein Sieg.
Wer kochte den Siegesschmaus?

Alle zehn Jahre ein grosser Mann.
Wer bezahlte die Spesen?

So viele Berichte.
So viele Fragen.
> (Bertolt Brecht, *Svendborger Gedichte*: Chroniken)

Questions from a worker who Reads

Who built Thebes of the seven gates?
In the books you will find the names of kings.
Did the kings haul up the lumps of rock?
And Babylon, many times demolished.
Who raised it up so many times? In what houses
Of gold-glittering Lima did the builders live?
Where, the evening that the Wall of China was finished
Did the masons go? Great Rome
Is full of triumphal arches. Who erected them? Over whom
Did the Caesars triumph? Had Byzantium, much praised in song
Only palaces for its inhabitants? Even in fabled Atlantis
The night the ocean engulfed it
The drowning still bawled for their slaves.
The young Alexander conquered India.
Was he alone?
Caesar beat the Gauls.
Did he not have even a cook with him?
Philip of Spain wept when his armada
Went down. Was he the only one to weep?
Frederick the Second won the Seven Years' War. Who
Else won it?

Every page a victory.
Who cooked the feast for the victors?

Every ten years a great man.
Who paid the bill?

So many reports.
So many questions.

(trans. Michael Hamburger)

The Ballad of Babelabour

> This Babylonian confusion of words results from
> their being the language of men who are going down.
> (Bertolt Brecht)

What ur-𝔖prache did the labour speak?
ur ur ur to t'master's 𝔖prache
the hang-cur ur-grunt of the weak
the unrecorded urs of gobless workers

Their snaptins kept among their turds
they labour   eat and shit
with only grunts not proper words
raw material for t'poet

They're their own meat and their own dough
another block   another
a palace for the great Pharaoh
a prison for their brothers

Whatever name's carved on those stones
it's not the one who labours
an edifice of workers' bones
for one who wants no neighbours

Nimrod's nabobs like their bards
to laud the state's achievements
to eulogize his house of cards
and mourn the king's bereavements

The treasurer of 𝔖prache's court
drops the bard his coppers

He knows that poets aren't his sort
but belong to the ur-crappers

Ur-crappers tongueless bardless nerks
your condition's shitty
no time for yer Collected Works
or modulated pity

but ur ur ur ur ur ur urs
sharpened into 𝕾prache
revurlooshunairy vurse
uprising nacker starkers

by the time the bards have urd
and urd and urd and 𝕾prachered
the world's all been turned into *merde*
& Nimrod's Noah'sarkered

sailing t'shit in t'ship they urd at
no labour can embark her
try and you'll get guard-dog grrred at
the shitship's one class: 𝕾prache

Bards & labour left for dead
the siltworld's 𝖓𝖊𝖚𝖊 𝖓𝖊𝖚𝖊
bard   the HMV doghead
in that *negra negra* Goya.
(Tony Harrison, *The Bonebard Ballads*)

The lyric deconstruction of the language of history in Brecht and of the language of poetry in Harrison are the reflexive themes of the texts. The poems refer directly to the conditions of their own production, which in this case include the privileged position of the writer in a capitalist society characterized by the division of labour. This position harbours the danger that the interest in maintaining such privilege may secretly continue to govern the production of texts which nevertheless present themselves as disinterested. Whereas this critique of language on the poem's narrative level draws the speakers of different social classes into a kind of linguistic struggle, the issue also finds itself reflected on the formal level as heteroglossia. Both Brecht and Harrison incorporate the most various sociolects into their texts. In this way they build into their way of writing protective mechanisms to counter the dangers which they represent on the semantic level as a threat to their own linguistic practices.

It is only now, from the sharpened perspective of a radically self-critical consciousness of language, that we can see that the unified character of earlier lyric forms also rests upon an act of violence. Or, expressed more precisely, it is not the form of the lyric itself, but the discourses produced about the lyric by aesthetics, poetics, criticism and literary theory which force the mask of homogeneity upon the poem. These discourses are characterized by the idea of providing a final definitive interpretation.

Ode on a Grecian Urn

I

Thou still unravished bride of quietness,
    Thou foster-child of silence and slow time,
Sylvan historian, who canst thus express
    A flowery tale more sweetly than our rhyme:
What leaf-fringed legend haunts about thy shape
    Of deities or mortals, or of both,
        In Tempe or the dales of Arcady?
    What men or gods are these? What maidens loth?
What mad pursuit? What struggle to escape?
        What pipes and timbrels? What wild ecstasy?

II

Heard melodies are sweet, but those unheard
    Are sweeter; therefore, ye soft pipes, play on;
Not to the sensual ear, but, more endeared,
    Pipe to the spirit ditties of no tone:
Fair youth, beneath the trees, thou canst not leave
    Thy song, nor ever can those trees be bare;
        Bold Lover, never, never canst thou kiss,
Though winning near the goal – yet, do not grieve;
    She cannot fade, though thou hast not thy bliss,
        Forever wilt thou love, and she be fair!

III

Ah, happy, happy boughs! that cannot shed
    Your leaves, nor ever bid the Spring adieu;
And happy melodist, unwearièd,
    Forever piping songs forever new;
More happy love! more happy, happy love!
    Forever warm and still to be enjoyed,
        Forever panting, and forever young;
All breathing human passion far above,

That leaves a heart high-sorrowful and cloyed,
  A burning forehead, and a parching tongue.

IV

Who are these coming to the sacrifice?
  To what green altar, O mysterious priest,
Lead'st thou that heifer lowing at the skies,
  And all her silken flanks with garlands dressed?
What little town by river or sea shore,
  Or mountain-built with peaceful citadel,
    Is emptied of this folk, this pious morn?
And, little town, thy streets for evermore
  Will silent be; and not a soul to tell
    Why thou art desolate, can e'er return.

V

O Attic shape! Fair attitude! with brede
  Of marble men and maidens overwrought,
With forest branches and the trodden weed;
  Thou, silent form, dost tease us out of thought
As doth eternity: Cold Pastoral!
  When old age shall this generation waste,
    Thou shalt remain, in midst of other woe
Than ours, a friend to man, to whom thou say'st,
  'Beauty is truth, truth beauty, – that is all
    Ye know on earth, and all ye need to know.'
                                        (John Keats)

My Last Duchess (Ferrara)

That's my last Duchess painted on the wall,
Looking as if she were alive. I call
That piece a wonder, now: Frà Pandolf's hands
Worked busily a day, and there she stands.
Will't please you sit and look at her? I said
'Frà Pandolf' by design, for never read
Strangers like you that pictured countenance,
The depth and passion of its earnest glance,
But to myself they turned (since none puts by
The curtain I have drawn for you, but I)
And seemed as they would ask me, if they durst,
How such a glance came there; so, not the first
Are you to turn and ask thus. Sir, 'twas not

Her husband's presence only, called that spot
Of joy into the Duchess' cheek: perhaps
Frà Pandolf chanced to say 'Her mantle laps
Over my lady's wrist too much,' or 'Paint
Must never hope to reproduce the faint
Half-flush that dies along her throat:' such stuff
Was courtesy, she thought, and cause enough
For calling up that spot of joy. She had
A heart – how shall I say? – too soon made glad,
Too easily impressed; she liked whate'er
She looked on, and her looks went everywhere.
Sir, 'twas all one! My favour at her breast,
The dropping of the daylight in the West,
The bough of cherries some officious fool
Broke in the orchard for her, the white mule
She rode with round the terrace – all and each
Would draw from her alike the approving speech,
Or blush, at least. She thanked men, – good! but thanked
Somehow – I know not how – as if she ranked
My gift of a nine-hundred-years-old name
With anybody's gift. Who'd stoop to blame
This sort of trifling? Even had you skill
In speech – (which I have not) – to make your will
Quite clear to such an one, and say, 'Just this
Or that in you disgusts me; here you miss,
Or there exceed the mark' – and if she let
Herself be lessoned so, nor plainly set
Her wits to yours, forsooth, and made excuse,
– E'en then would be some stooping; and I choose
Never to stoop. Oh sir, she smiled, no doubt,
Whene'er I passed her; but who passed without
Much the same smile? This grew; I gave commands;
Then all smiles stopped together. There she stands
As if alive. Will't please you rise? We'll meet
The company below, then. I repeat,
The Count your master's known munificence
Is ample warrant that no just pretence
Of mine for dowry will be disallowed;
Though his fair daughter's self, as I avowed
At starting, is my object. Nay, we'll go
Together down, sir. Notice Neptune, though,
Taming a sea-horse, thought a rarity,
Which Claus of Innsbruck cast in bronze for me!

                                        (Robert Browning)

The above poems by Keats and Browning also thematize the act of reception and the act of production. Just as in Brecht the worker reading the poem addresses his questions to the text from a certain social distance, so too the lyrical ego in Keats addresses an object from the remote historical past. And just as the hermeneutical crisis of incomprehension reveals to both question-ers violence, exclusion, enforced silence and death in the objects as the ground of semiotic practice, so too the lyrical subjects in Browning and Harrison describe the homogenization of the material which occurs in the creative act as murder.

Nevertheless there are certain decisive differences between the poems of the nineteenth century and those of the twentieth. The later poems reflect their own praxis as texts. The earlier lyric poems reflect upon themselves through the medium of the material artefact. Brecht and Harrison, in the century of the linguistic turn, speak about the relationship between text and reality, text and truth, and thus speak about epistemological questions concerning art, epistemology understood here precisely as a theory of communication. Keats and Browning speak about the relationship between art and life, and thus about ontological questions concerning being in the world. And they could do so because their poems still possessed an object-like, representational and internally closed character.

Their linguistic form is strongly unified through the use of rhyme and rhythm, their sociolect is a timelessly literary one and thus not dialogical. On the semantic level they present us with objects of art, the picture and the urn, objects which themselves already possess iconic meaning: as a portrait and as a scenario. They also present us with the primal scenes of life, with the essence of the imaginary: sacrifice, sexuality, narcissism and power, the murder of woman and the exhibition of her body. As a medium of self-reflection these texts thematize not a textual practice, like the act of reading or writing in the poems by Brecht and Harrison, but rather the gaze. But this gaze is double-edged. It makes something present (in opposition to the re-presentation involved in a text) and it transfixes it, devitalizes it. That is why the texts speak unflinchingly about the preservation of life in art at the same time as speaking about death.

Nevertheless the gaze, even with that danger of literal mortification which we need to examine more closely, does capture something which escapes a purist theory of textuality: the corporeal, material feel of reality. In the context of philosophical, semiotic and linguistic debates this aspect has been subordinated to the question of the subject of sign production. I cannot go into these debates here but I would like to mention the discussion of 'Semiotics and Experience' in the book by Teresa de Lauretis, *Alice Doesn't*. In contrast to the prevailing metaphysics of the sign which has developed in the wake of the linguistic turn (whether this is based on the concept of difference as in Derrida, of the signifier as in Lacan, of the sign itself as in Eco, or of communicative action as in Habermas) Teresa de Lauretis insists, in the context of a feminist reading of the semiotics of Peirce, upon the equal importance of language, the body and social action. It is true that the body and action are fields for the inscription of meaning which are not independent of language but they are not exhausted by language. She writes:

> But the significance of the sign could not take effect, that is to say, the sign would not be a sign, without the existence of the subject's experience of a social practice in which the subject is physically involved ... The intimate relationship of subjectivity to practices is recognized by psychoanalysis and semiotics in the expression 'signifying practice(s)', but seldom analysed outside of verbal or literary textual practices, cinema being the notable exception. The dominance of linguistic determination in theories of the subject, and the objectivist or logico-mathematical bias of most semiotic research have made the notion of signifying practice restrictive and over-specialized, forcing it into what amounts to theoretical obsolescence.[3]

The lost dimension of corporeality and of social action in the theories of the linguistic turn is still preserved in the privileged position of the image, of the object in the two poems from the nineteenth century. Yet the problematic status of the representation of this dimension manifests itself in the aura of death and loss. We must insist upon the fact that both of these poems are also permeated by language, just as the poems of Brecht and Harrison also incorporate images into themselves. The polarization of text and image is a theoretical construct which serves to clarify and underline certain issues. But it is only in theory that we are presented with a static opposition between the textual and the mimetic, between the allegorical and the symbolic. The literary products themselves deconstruct such rigid oppositions. The extent to which the images involved only exist in turn by virtue of the meanings which are ascribed to them is made very clear through the questions with which the urn is addressed and through the sibylline couplet 'Beauty is truth, truth beauty, – that is all / Ye know on earth, and all ye need to know'. The couplet reflects once again the hermeneutic problem of the urn, since we do not know who is saying this to whom, just as the urn itself can no longer tell us anything about its own original context.

Similarly the whole of the dramatic monologue 'My Last Duchess' can be read as the response of the Duke of Ferrara to the implicit question of his addressee about the history of the first duchess and her picture. The hermeneutic crisis of sense, the continuous slippage of meaning on account of the ontological arbitrariness of the sign, is arrested in both poems by the body. The poem alerts us to the crucial somatic dimension which precedes language and the dimension of action which lies beyond language. In this way the gap opened up within the sign, through which socially stabilized meaning constantly threatens to leak is plugged: 'if the chain of meaning comes to a halt, however temporarily, it is by anchoring itself to somebody, some body, an individual subject.'[4] It is here, therefore, in the aesthetic fusion of language and image, of spirit and matter, that the existential division of the human being is healed. It is this compensation in art for the deficiency of language in life which the deconstructionists identify in the objects of their study as aesthetic ideology. But in this respect the poems are fractured and divided within themselves. They do offer reconciliation through the contemplation of meaning, but only at the cost of a double frustration. Firstly: the meaning always points up its own precarious status (the questions about the sense of the object in Keats, the narrative excess in Browning). Secondly: the body in which meaning is anchored and which must guarantee the fantasy of reconciliation and wholeness is the female body. In this respect the poem closely accommodates itself to a patriarchal reality. For in such a reality the body of the woman becomes a sign for the phallus. She becomes a fetish, for as a sign of male sexual and social power she conceals the consciousness of that ontological castration which man and woman alike undergo with the separation from the mother and the entry into language. In the symbolic order the body of the woman is 'the guarantor of fantasy', of an 'imaginary fantasy of coherence', the sign for the fantasy of the male's own wholeness. But the poems do not just blindly reproduce the patriarchal ideology in which the woman becomes a sign for the phallus. Both of the poems narrate that history of violence which transpires behind the production of the female as a phallic sign and behind the arrest of the production of meaning as a process. In Keats a semantic field of violent sexuality is unfolded and allegorically connected with the hermeneutic violence inflicted upon hermetic artefacts. Browning blends the lethal taming of the unconventional duchess, the murderous production of the discourse of power and the mortification of life in art. Thus we are only offered a reconciliation which has incorporated its own radically opposed other, that deadly division accomplished through the fatal exercise of power, and has openly exhibited this process.

The image, the object, always has something rigid and petrified about it because it constitutes itself through the look or gaze. The danger of mortification by the gaze only threatens, moreover, when the gaze is that of power and domination. This is what the poems of Keats and Browning tell us. It is against this gaze of domination, against a mimesis of power, that the stylistic strategies of Brecht and Harrison are directed as strategies of textuality. Their poems pit the critical force of social polyphony against the hegemony of a single correct discourse. But they also go beyond this. In Brecht the act of textual reception is thematized, in Harrison the act of production. Both texts work into themselves the communicative presuppositions of their own function and thus their own textuality. But in what way are they to be distinguished from texts of the nineteenth century which also reflect upon themselves as works of art? In Keats and Browning the self-reflection of the text transpires through its metaphorical translation into a pictorial image. This reveals the mimetic, reproductive character of art in so far as it can represent the pre-linguistic and post-linguistic components of reality. But the twentieth-century texts assert the processual character of reality against the potential dangers of a world represented in terms of images and objects.[5] This is expressed in the self-consciousness of the text as text. If we suppose that reality is represented in texts in such a way that it not only registers the contingency of reality but also produces it for the first time, then in encountering a text within a text we find a text within (fictional) reality. But that means that the text which reflects itself as a text refers us to a reality in which it has already been taken up as a text, and thus as a production of signs, as a production of a new reality. The text is always already in advance of the reality in which it emerges in so far as it has already assimilated the reality which will have absorbed it in turn. This dynamic of an infinite spiralling semiosis between text and reality has been described with a phrase from André Gide as a 'mise en abîme'. Brecht's text encourages us to address the same questions towards it which the reader addresses towards the historical text in the poem itself. But our way of reading the poem must always reckon with the reader who presents our text with precisely the same questions in turn, and so on. At each new level of questioning the reality itself changes within which text and questioning engage with one another. If we wish to describe this endless production of signs and meaning then ironically enough we must turn back to the old metaphor of mirroring. (Thus Lucien Dällenbach supplies his investigations of the 'mise en abîme' with the title 'Le récit spéculaire' or *The Mirror in the Text*.[6]) Let us now return to our interpretation of reality as a literary construction. 'Construction' can have two meanings: the result of the process of construction or the act of constructing itself. The first meaning would correspond to the idea of the pictorial image, of the object. It would grasp reality as a totality which is divided into static structures. It is only construction in the second sense, in its processual character, which can do justice to the resolutely changing dynamics of reality. And I understand by dynamics here both the polyphonic constellations of social heteroglossia and the infinite number of different narrations. Such dynamics involve the intrinsically endless production of meanings which, since they incessantly transform the reality from which they emerge, also produce a new reality.

But as the poems of Keats and Browning suggest, it is not yet enough to say this. The textuality of such a reality can only manifest itself through something which is not itself textual. If everything is a text then the concept of the text becomes meaningless. In opposition to Eco, Lacan, the later Lyotard and Paul de Man, the semiotic theories of the later Roland Barthes,

Julia Kristeva and Teresa de Lauretis, all of whom write from the perspective of psychoanalysis, proceed from the pre-linguistic reality of the body, as does the anti-Freudian theory of Deleuze and Guattari. The American pragmatists Peirce and Rorty attempt to construct a still more effective bridge between the body and social action via language. If textuality must be anchored in the body, in order that linguistically competent subjects can learn to speak, then it is also the body which tests the validity of the different texts of reality against one another. Only those texts which respect the integrity of the body are legitimate texts. Torture, hunger, lynching, the destruction of nature, forced labour, can be suppressed or rationalized in texts. But if meanings are enacted by people in reality, then it is human bodies which interpret the texts by experiencing them. Can the opposition between death and life be deconstructed?

NOTES

1 See for instance George Steiner, *Language and Silence: Essays 1958–1968*, ed. George Steiner (Penguin, Harmondsworth, 1969), esp. 'Silence and the Poet', pp. 57–76; Christiaan Hart Nibbrig, *Die Rhetorik des Schweigens. Versuch über den Schatten literarischer Rede* (Suhrkamp, Frankfurt/M., 1981).

2 Cf. my article 'Heteroglossia in the poetry of Bertolt Brecht and Tony Harrison', in *The Taming of the Text: Explorations in Language, Literature and Culture*, ed. Willie van Peer (Routledge & Kegan Paul, London, 1988), pp. 193–221. Hamburger's translation of the Brecht poem published in Bertolt Brecht, *Poems*, ed. John Willet and Ralph Hauheim (Eyre Methuen, London, 1981).

3 Teresa de Lauretis, *Alice Doesn't: Feminism – Semiotics – Cinema* (Macmillan, London, 1984), p. 183.

4 Ibid., p. 178.

5 It is significant in this respect that the central figure of the *Künstlerroman* is normally a painter in the nineteenth century and a writer in the twentieth.

6 Lucien Dällenbach, *Le récit spéculaire. Essai sur le mise en abîme* (Seuil, Paris, 1977); tr. Jeremy Whitely with Emma Hughes, *The Mirror in the Text* (Polity Press, Cambridge, 1989).

14

From the Dialectic of Force to *The Dialectic of Enlightenment*: Re-reading the *Odyssey*

In the 'entanglement of enlightenment and myth',[1] Adorno and Horkheimer saw both the cause and the effect of the reduction of reason to instrumental reason. Yet this interweaving is dependent on other entanglements which are taken for granted by them in a much more tacit way: that of the philosophy of history with literature and that of hermeneutics with the male viewpoint. It is no longer considered outrageous to say that the discourses of philosophy and literature (and even of the natural sciences) are not strictly delineated. The process of their interbreeding is, depending on where one stands, an obvious truth or a subversive introduction to the deconstruction of logical and theoretical texts which – on the pretence of being non-narrative and non-metaphorical – press their claim to discursive truth. Even the awareness that social and psychological perspectives are inevitably inscribed in texts and readings is no longer the source of iconoclastic interpretative gestures, but rather of a constantly renewed caution and reflexivity on the part of the reader. For Adorno and Horkheimer it is only the identification of identifications which, in terms of the philosophy of history, produces the *tabula rasa* upon which only instrumental reason remains decipherable.

Yet this concept of instrumental enlightenment seems mythical to us, and not simply because it appears so total as to preclude the possibility of its critique and transformation. It is also because it is never quite clear how the concept of instrumental enlightenment was constructed. When Adorno and Horkheimer were writing the *Dialectic of Enlightenment* in exile in the USA in the early 1940s, they were caught in a paradoxical situation which called their cultural and political identity into question. Moulded by bourgeois liberal and Marxist traditions of thought, which converge in the demand for the liberation and emancipation of the individual,[2] they now found themselves confronted with a counter-trend in world politics charac-terized by irrationality and inhumanity which culminated in German fasc-ism. In their view, the emphases within the dialectic of instrumental reason and disinterested reason are so radically tilted towards instrumentality that manifestations of a more impartial reason can scarcely be detected any longer. Of course, Adorno and Horkheimer are thereby making their own enlightening voices heard nevertheless, but for them reason is only present in the critical speech act with no hope of finding a point of practical reference in the historical process. In the tradition of Nietzsche and de Sade, Adorno and Horkheimer also become musicians playing back to history its own dark melody in the vain hope of teaching it to dance. In order to prove the 'circularity of historical progress',[3] they go back to the written origins of Western culture and demonstrate, in a hermeneutic *tour de force*, that the fascistic catastrophe of modern Western culture is prefigured in its narrative beginnings in Homer's *Odyssey*.

It is an inescapable fact that one approaches a temporally remote docu-ment from the perspective of one's own time. But in reflecting this fact, being aware of the controlling influence it has and exposing it through argument in order to identify one's starting-point and focus of interest, one can at least make one's own blind spots visible. Adorno and Horkheimer do not do this in the *Dialectic of Enlightenment*. The book's sweeping, monolithic arguments, partly justified in subjective terms by the monstrosity of the world around them at that point in history, leave no room either for considering 'counterfactual' alternatives in the past (in Benjamin's sense), or for sounding out contradictions in the present, from which they them-selves plainly profited (having been given sanctuary as exiles).

If the theory of the global triumph of instrumental rationality depends on proving that it has always existed, then the essay on the *Odyssey* forms the cornerstone of the *Dialectic of Enlightenment*. But if a re-reading of the epic from a present point of view produced a different interpretation, then the fatal link between the genesis and effect of instrumental rationality which Adorno and Horkheimer trace back to the *Odyssey* could be broken. This would dissolve the strict determinism which causes Adorno and Horkheimer to view Western history as a headlong rush towards fascism, compelling them to prophesy that the 'course of the avalanche'[4] would not be diverted by defeating fascism. To contest their account of the *Odyssey* would not, of course, be to imply that the catastrophic experiences of fascism, the Second World War, Stalinism and the current nuclear and ecological threats could simply be erased from the world; yet it might help point towards the potential for resistance, a potential which generates the pathos of the *Dialectic of Enlightenment* itself, even though with the theoretical tools at their disposal the writers can no longer conceptualize it.

In the current situation, this hidden reservoir of a more disinterested reason can be tapped using the means provided by the concept of communicative rationality, as well as by research along feminist lines. Applying the methods and perspectives of the most diverse disciplines, such as psychoanalysis, philosophy, history, anthropology, literary criticism and theology, in a different way, as feminists have done, opens up undreamt-of opportunities to deconstruct and reconstruct dominant cultural discourses. Admittedly, Adorno and Horkheimer also demonstrate that the violence of instrumental reason is closely bound up with the repression of women; yet even so in the *Dialectic of Enlightenment* women appear only as victims or as collaborators with men.

The *Odyssey* as *Bildungsroman*

As they work towards their philosophical conclusions, both Adorno and Horkheimer make no secret of the fact that they take their tools from aesthetic discourses. While the contemporary metatheories of Derrida, Irigaray, Lyotard, Hayden White or Foucault leave no stone unturned to show how metaphors, power interests and narrative structures invisibly direct and visibly bolster such apparently pure theoretical discourses as philosophy, history and natural science, Adorno and Horkheimer are an almost perfect example of how metatheory clings mimetically to the literary blueprint.

According to Adorno and Horkheimer, the identity of Odysseus, the density of his being, is wrought by the suppression of external and internal nature. That is to say, in the course of historical development, the external sacrifices which man uses to barter with nature are increasingly internalized. The control and suppression of his own instincts, fantasies and desires is the price man pays for conquering nature with science. This process further involves the repression of man's communicative nature, which devalues him from being an end in himself to being a means to an end. All that remains are arid gestures of dominance mimed by a monadic and monological subject. Odysseus' voyage describes the 'trajectory of the subject'.[5] The writers see the mythical dimension of natural forms in the subject-matter of the adventure, while through the teleological organization of the narrative, 'enlightenment' evolves from the mythical darkness of the grottoes, caves and underworlds. The narrative thread, seen as a process of breaking free and escaping, is analogous to the process of enlightenment seen as an ontogenetic and phylogenetic process. Here we can clearly detect the interweaving of literature and philosophy.

Yet that is not the point of my critique. There seems to be no human knowledge that can be attained without narration.[6]

Scientific knowledge cannot know and make known that it is the true knowledge without resorting to the other, narrative, kind of knowledge, which from its point of view is no knowledge at all. Without such recourse it would be in the position of presupposing its own validity and would be stooping to what it condemns: begging the question, proceeding on prejudice.[7]

But what Adorno and Horkheimer do not see as a problem is the fact that they are using a quite specific model of narration, one of several possible models, to analyse the *Odyssey*. It is the evolutionary model set out in Hegel's *Phenomenology of the Spirit*, by way of the *Theory of the Novel* by Lukács. Ironically, in doing so they project back on to the *Odyssey* a structural model which is itself constructed on the basis of a reading of the *Odyssey*. Of the *Phenomenology* Walter Kern says: 'it is the very logbook of the odyssey of the spirit' ... 'the transposition of the great *Bildungsromane* of the time, such as Goethe's *Wilhelm Meister*, into the broader philosophical dimension of human consciousness in general.'[8] However, it should be added that in the *Dialectic of Enlightenment* the circumstances are changed: the progress towards the best of all possible worlds becomes the regress towards the triumph of disaster.

Adorno and Horkheimer argue in both a Hegelian and an anti-Hegelian way. The Hegelian element is the use of a biological model of development, a model which moves towards a climactic aim. Lukács applies this model, which according to Hegel is just one of the manifestations of the world spirit, to the historical succession of epic and novel itself. For Hegel, after the epic of antiquity, which is an ideal justified in terms of the philosophy of history, narrative art sinks to the trivial level of the 'novelesque'. The world spirit moves on in the form of law, religion and philosophy. Lukács, on the other hand, rescues the philosophical dignity of post-epic narrative by interpreting it as the appropriate form of expression for a changed world. Whereas in Hegel the evidence of the world spirit in a changing world is accounted for by a change in the discursive manifestations of that spirit, Lukács sees art itself as a representation of that spirit and traces the course of this artistic spirit through history in the changing art forms, in this case the sequence of epic and novel. Thus Hegel's spirit is reflected once again on a secondary level in Lukács's major narrative categories. (There is no equivalent English term for 'Bildungsroman'. Normally, it is translated as 'educational novel'.)

Given these choices, Adorno and Horkheimer selected the *Bildungsroman* construction showing personal development rather than that of the adventure novel, which, according to Lukács, would have been just as good and more appropriate to the *Odyssey*. For political reasons they prefer the organic model, since the biographical form is the only path along which both world spirit and novel (in the form of the *Bildungsroman*) can move.

The anti-Hegelian element is evident in the way in which Hegel's writing is transformed into a phenomenology of the demonic spirit which now, projected back on to the *Bildungsroman*, leads to a degeneration into the sly, selfish and power-conscious subject. And this model of the perverted *Bildungsroman* hero is reapplied to the hero of Homer's epic.

Hegel (and Lukács) saw the essence of the epic in the effortless integration of individual and society:

> The conditions of moral life must have come about, established themselves and developed, but on the contrary not yet thrived to the point of becoming general imperatives, duties and laws with a validity of their own beyond the living subjective particularity of individuals and with the power to keep individuals from exercising their free will ... The conditions of objective morality must already be sought after and realized, but only by way of the acting individuals themselves and their character.'[9]

In the epic, the life world and the system world (to use Habermas's terms) have not yet been separated; in the novel the two clearly stand in opposition to one another: 'The epic individual, the hero of the novel, arises from this alienated attitude towards the external world.'[10]

In Adorno and Horkheimer, Odysseus becomes an ultrarationalistic Wilhelm Meister, a fact which is consistent with Novalis's view of him as 'prosaic' or the commonplace critical description of him as 'bourgeois'. But the inappropriateness of identifying the *Odyssey* with Goethe's *Bildungsroman* becomes apparent in their suppression of the aesthetic potential for resistance in epic and novel. The sensitivity to alienation acquired by the novel's protagonists over centuries of artistic development disappears in their account, as does the human community of the epic into which the excessive violence of the hero is safely reabsorbed. All that is left of the two forms for Adorno and Horkheimer is a power-broking monster as hero and a society transformed into a burial-ground. Lukács says of the novel: 'The novel tells of the adventure of interiority; the content of the novel is the story of the soul that goes out to find itself, that seeks adventures in order to be proved and tested by them and, by proving itself, to find its own essence.'[11] The Frankfurt theorists turn the *Odyssey* into a black allegory of a kind of 'spirituality' which is perverted into instrumental rationality.

The *Iliad* and the Male View

In order to reinterpret the *Odyssey* in this way, Adorno and Horkheimer are forced to suppress two important factors: the existence of the *Iliad* as an earlier text and the fact that their own viewpoint is a male viewpoint. The two factors are interconnected. This may seem paradoxical in view of the fact that there are strong affinities between male fantasies and a preference for the *Iliad*.[12] Yet the *Iliad* lacks something which is perhaps even more fundamental for the constitution of a male subject than wielding power and violence, and that is the possibility of a genesis, a primal origin.[13] The *Iliad* begins in the middle of things: not with the start and the causes of the Trojan War but with the wrath of Achilles.

Nor is the *Odyssey* a text describing an origin, as the *Iliad* precedes it both temporally and in terms of subject-matter. Although universal creation myths are not a feature of Greek mythology – in contrast to monotheistic religions – Adorno and Horkheimer impute their own obsession with origins to the *Odyssey*, an obsession which is a product of their own time. It is this male perspective which suppresses the *Iliad* in reading because it does not speak of origins and which reads the epic as a novel. For in its theoretical and cultural institutionalization the novel is primarily a male literary form. Adventure stories, picaresque novels, romances of chivalry, *Bildungsromane*, *Künstlerromane* (novels with an artist as the main protagonist) and social novels are all essentially stories by men about men. Lukács states this over and over again quite openly: 'The novel is the art form of virile maturity in contrast to the normative childlikeness of the epic';[14] 'the novel is the art form of virile maturity'.[15]

The basic form of the (male) novel is the quest. It begins with the adventure novel and ends with the increasingly vain search for the essence of self, its language and its meaning in the modern age. In addition to his physical birth, the male creates for himself the occasion to be born once again in the realm of transcendence. Thus for Lukács the quintessence of the novel is found in the statement 'I go to prove my soul', and, he continues, 'if this marvellous line is out of place, it is only because it is spoken by a dramatic hero' (Browning's *Paracelsus*).[16]

Nina Baym examines the misogynistic tradition of the American novel in her study 'Melodramas of beset manhood: how theories of American fiction exclude women authors'.[17] The particular nature of white conquest in America allowed the notion of a free land 'as the medium on which he [the man] may inscribe, unhindered, his own destiny and his own nature'.[18] The notion persisted far longer than in Europe, where the relatively early division of the land to be conquered sent the voyagers off in search of the dark continents of their souls: man as a God. But the materials from which the statue of the godlike self-creator is hewn, growing ever higher with every obstacle, are the women left behind on the way.[19] 'In the course of his individualization, the man (father) will persevere by *assimilating* the other and the external into himself and for himself. In this way he will consolidate his vitality, his irritability, his activity, experiencing a particular feeling of triumph at the moment when he absorbs the other into himself.'[20]

From being the substance, the material, the mother, the matrix which man incorporates and then releases from himself as his own, women in the novels become the embodiment of the social. The man must pass through his social sphere and the social through him so that he can leave it behind as the waste product of his self-creation.

> In these stories the encroaching, destroying society is represented with particular urgency in the figure of one or more women ... For heterosexual men, these socializing women are also the locus of powerful attraction ... This attraction gives urgency and depth to the protagonist's rejection of society. To do it, he must project onto the woman those attractions that he feels, and cast her in the melodramatic role of temptress, antagonist, obstacle – a character whose mission in life seems to be to ensnare him and deflect him from life's important purposes of self-discovery and self-assertion. (A Puritan would have said: from communion with Divinity.) As Richard Case writes in *The American Novel and its Tradition*: 'The myth requires celibacy.'[21]

With the movement towards self-referentiality in the modern novel, the hero's quest (now as a writer) is rewarded with the creation of the text. The modern creator is the author. 'One can see ... the transference of the American myth from the Adamic hero *in* the story to the Adamic creator *of* the story, and the reinterpretation of the American myth as a metaphor for the American artist's situation.'[22] Yet here the so-called American experience can very clearly be seen as an overall male occupation of the novel and – perhaps even more so – of novel theory in the Western world. 'Americanness has vanished into the depths of what is alleged to be the universal male psyche.'[23]

This seems to apply so well to the *Odyssey* that one wonders whether the epic is not indeed a (male) novel and whether, this being the case, Adorno and Horkheimer give it an entirely appropriate reading after all. Lukács describes the difference between epic and novel metaphorically as the difference between childlike (naive) and male. But the 'childlike' aspect is precisely the experience of being securely embedded in society, which becomes so problematic in the 'male' novel. And it is exactly this dimension which is suppressed in Adorno and Horkheimer's reading. Although Odysseus is the central figure in the epic, he never becomes a monument of masculinity, growing ever more erect the more isolated it appears to be in its weariness of society. Odysseus is not the superhero – he is neither the highest in rank (Agamemnon) nor the strongest and most splendid (Achilles). Rather he is the embodiment of the average hero in the sense used by Walter Scott. His story is not an account of the moulding of a rational subject from the material of nature or of a transcendent being from the material of society. On the contrary, Odysseus' story is the tale of his laborious reintegration from the a-social theatre of war into the society of Ithaca and his painful re-education from warrior into human being.

So if the crucial concept of instrumental reason in their philosophy of history depends on Adorno and Horkheimer's reading of the *Odyssey*, and this is a reading which can be described for various reasons as patriarchally 'prejudiced' (in Gadamer's sense), then a feminist reception of Homer's epic could also produce a different evaluation of the current state of instrumental reason.

For interpretation and the philosophy of history are subject as narratives to the same possibilities of 're-emplotment' as historical narrative in general. 'The important point is that most historical sequences can be emplotted in a number of different ways, so as to provide different interpretations of those events and to endow them with different meanings.'[24]

A female philosopher was reading Homer at around the same time as Adorno and Horkheimer. She too as a Jew was under threat from German fascism and she too was reading in a war context: Simone Weil's brilliant essay on the *Iliad*, 'L'Iliade ou le poème de la force', appeared in winter 1940/41.[25] From the viewpoint of one oppressed on three counts – as a woman, as a Jew and as a French citizen under German occupation – the inhuman aspect of the bellicose machismo is demonstrated with utmost clarity by a text which is a key document of the Western cultural tradition. It is an aspect which has either been overlooked or euphemistically distorted by the predominantly male exponents of the discourse of classics.

In Simone Weil's case, pity and fear, the Aristotelian components of poetic identification, are nourished by the direct experience of a threat to herself from her social and political surroundings. For the true victims of the Trojan War are the women. Yet the hero cult with its central devices of honour and glory serves solely to found a male subjectivity which lives on even after death. (The immortality which Calypso offers Odysseus he of course turns down. It is not linked to his name and it comes from a more powerful woman.) Self-creation and immortality of the name are part of the mania of omnipotence. Occupying space in the memory of later generations guarantees an eternal mirroring of one's own image. Whereas the male ascends in this way to the level of transcendent subject, the women are reduced to the level of things. They are raped, dragged off into slavery and killed.

Nowhere is Benjamin's statement about the empathy of those who control culture with the historical victors so clearly demonstrated as in the male critical views of Homer. Kakridis, for example, sees the warning voices of the Trojan women as being 'reactionary' and calls it their duty to endure the fate thrust upon them by the men with absolute passivity, although 'when a town was conquered, women and children fell into slavery'.[26] The following quotation from Kakridis is further proof of Nina Baym's theory that women in fiction are merely tests on the road to self-apotheosis.

> It is the main poetic mission of a woman in the *Iliad* to consciously exert this restraining power over men, trying to avert them from doing their duty as they feel they should. The poet presents to us this reactionary attitude of women not because he has any interest for psychological analysis: he has no interest in stressing the difference between the two sexes. He presents that attitude because man is the central hero in his work, and it is him the poet wants to hold up by placing a woman in his way who attempts to stop him.[27]

On the *Odyssey* Kakridis says: 'And Odysseus; it is not only savages, terrible beasts and sea-storms he must conquer; it is also the love that three women, Calypso, Circe and Nausicaa consciously or unconsciously offer him. But here, too, as a man he will triumph over the trial and he will come out of it free.'[28]

C. R. Beyle goes one decisive step further. He admits from the start that both Homer's texts and the commentaries of male researchers are equally indebted to the universality of the male viewpoint. 'The generations of male critics apparently did not know how to accommodate women into the epic tradition.'[29] According to him, this viewpoint is demonstrated in the *Iliad* as being the one side of an ideal of woman, namely the absolute possession of her as a thing which is passed from one male hand to another with no will of its own. In the *Odyssey*, on the other hand, there is an expression of both the need for women and the fear of them. For that reason, he says approvingly, the *Odyssey* is also devalued by male critics.

> Critics tend to leave the *Odyssey* alone. A very intelligent critic talks of the preponderance of women in the poem and prefaces those remarks with the statement that the *Odyssey* is like a novel, almost a sentimental novel, an altogether light work compared to the *Iliad*. This seems to be an example of the common attitude. The *Odyssey* has not been given the same serious criticism or estimation which the *Iliad* elicits. Is this because of the large part which women play in the poem? Or is the very recently but often heard notion true, that the militaristic *Iliad* which says no to life and yes to death, and out of an abiding spiritual desperation sets the highest value on a kind of macho-competitiveness, speaks more directly to us [the men's club of classicists?] in the twentieth century than the *Odyssey* which seems to have to do with

psychic integration, sensitivity, awareness, an affirmation of life and the one-to-one male-female confrontation?[30]

Yet it is not the men in the *Iliad* who now stand condemned but women. While the men speak directly to 'us' (does that include Simone Weil?) in the twentieth century on account of their violence, Penelope and Clytemnestra show 'two ways for women to resolve the repressed rage of a woman deserted . . . The pair is there to give expression to both sets of feelings, but the one, murderous rage, is so anti-social that its expression must be coupled with condemnation.'[31]

But the misogynistic traits of researchers' fantasies are most clearly seen when the latent homosexuality of the heterosexuals and the open homosexuality of gay interpreters appraise the relationship between Achilles and Patroclus which draws its *raison d'être* from the sexualization of male force and the sodomization of male sexuality, both libidinal formations of a culture centred on the degradation of women. Yet although the *Iliad* invites us to perceive these two spheres as interdependent, for most male critics it remains the most sublime expression of masculinity.[32]

The *Iliad* and the Female View

For Simone Weil, the blood of the *Iliad* cannot be expunged either by Clytemnestra's murder of Agamemnon or by the realization that 'the first great love story of world literature . . . is a love story between men.'[33] 'The true hero, the true subject, the centre of the *Iliad* is force.'[34] Neither the Trojans nor the Greeks escape this force and its terrible consequences. There are no victors, only losers on both sides. No one involved in this archetypal slaughter escapes dehumanization.

> Force is as pitiless to the man who possesses it, or thinks he does, as it is for its victims; the second it crushes, the first it intoxicates. The truth is nobody really possesses it. The human race is not divided up in the *Iliad*, into conquered persons, slaves, suppliants, on the one hand, and conquerors and chiefs on the other. In this poem there is not a single man who does not at one time or another have to bow his neck to force.[35]

The heroes of the *Iliad* become killing machines with the inevitability of natural forces. In the similes of the *Iliad*, Weil decodes a second language which compares the warriors with fire, flood and wild animals.

The most powerful image in this connection is the Trojan Horse. It is animal and machine at the same time; like a tank it encloses its human substance, the warriors who have become blind, deaf and dumb appendages of their own destructive creation. Yet in Weil's view, the *Iliad* gives cause neither for admiration nor contempt but merely for sorrow that human beings can be so transformed.

From here there is a direct connection to the *Odyssey*. For the Greeks who set off on the journey home after the destruction of Troy are those fighting machines. Upon them will be wrought the revenge of the gods, the nemesis for the violation of human society. 'This retribution, which has geometrical rigour, which operates automatically to penalize the abuse of force, was the main subject of Greek thought. It is the soul of the epic.'[36]

In the *Iliad* the cosmic consequences of violating creation by human force is elucidated. Grillparzer put this idea into words in a striking manner in the nineteenth century. In *König Ottokars Glück und Ende* the (anachronistic) hero, Ottokar, expounds this law of creation which he has violated, in wonderful verses:

> My ways upon Thy earth have not been good,
> Almighty God! Like tempests, like a storm,
> I swept across Thy peaceful fields.
>
> .   .   .   .
>
> And Man, whom Thou hast put here for his joy,
> A unit, end, a world within the world –
> Him, Thou hast made a wonder of Thy hand:
> His forehead, high; his neck, erect and proud,
> And robed him fair in beauty's festal robe,
> With wonders wondrously encircling him.
> He hears and sees and feels, knows pleasure.
> Once food and drink have furnished him with strength,
> Creative energies begin their work,
> And weave untiringly through tissues, nerves and veins
> To build his house, his frame. No king's abode
> Can be compared with such a human form,
> But I threw them away by thousands at a time,
> To satisfy a folly, please a whim,
> As one would scatter refuse from a door.
> No single one of all those left for dead,
> But had a mother who, on bearing him in pain,
> Pressed him with pleasure to her mother breast,
> A father who regarded him with pride,
> And brought him up, instructed him for years.
> When he did merely graze his finger-tip,
> They ran to him and washed and bound the cut,
> And watched that it would surely heal aright.
> All for a finger-tip, a bit of skin!
> But I cast them aside like wisps of straw,
> And for unbending iron cleared a path
> Straight through their pulsing warmth.[37]

It is precisely in this point that the Greeks are at fault, despite their victory.

We see men in arms behaving harshly and madly. We see their sword bury itself in the breast of a disarmed enemy who is in the very act of pleading at their knees. We see them triumph over a dying man by describing to him the outrages his corpse will endure. We see Achilles cut the throats of twelve Trojan boys on the funeral pyre of Patroclus as naturally as we cut flowers for a grave. These men, wielding power, have no suspicion of the fact that the consequences of their deeds will at length come home to them – they too will bow the neck in their turn.[38]

Nemesis gets to work at the point where even the strongest have a weakness. For the strong forget that they also have weaknesses and the weak that they also have strengths. The Greeks want everything from Troy, no longer just Helen, but 'they forget one detail, that *everything* is not within their power, for they are not in Troy.'[39] And so, as the death of Hector was but a brief pleasure for Achilles and the death of Achilles was a brief pleasure for the Trojans, so also the fall of Troy is a brief pleasure for the Achaeans.

This is where the connection between the *Iliad* and the *Odyssey* lies from a non-male perspective. The *Odyssey* does not recount the story of a subject freeing itself from the bonds of nature, but rather the ever-precarious reconciliation of a subject with its environment. It is an account of the nemesis of the gods upon the Greeks, and at the same time a story of the rehumanization of a fighting machine. In *Man is Man*, Brecht shows us how a man is dismantled and rebuilt into a fighting machine. Homer depicts the reverse process: the deconstruction of a fighting machine and the remodelling of it into a man.

Odysseus' Adventure

The pivotal point of *Man is Man* and the *Odyssey* alike is the hero's denial of his own name, which he is forced to do in order to survive, and thus the extinction of his status as a subject. The instability of the name implies the questionable nature of the subject who believes himself to be autonomous. Both plays are therefore anti-heroic. For the hero in the traditional sense is at the same time social and a-social. He is the object of his society's desire for meaning but, for this very reason, he himself becomes the absolute subject of power. The mythical aspect of the hero is his loneliness, the aura of emptiness and silence around him. It is only through this process of isolation that his emergence as a hero is possible.

The *Odyssey* moves its hero back into populations, and, because of this, his stature dwindles. Yet the diminution of Odysseus does not only stem from the enhancement of the figures around him, but also from his much more frequent confrontations with strong and independent female figures. In the *Iliad*, where the men brand their mark on the defenceless bodies of female objects like signatures (Chryseis, Briseis, Cassandra, Polyxena, Helen, Andromache, Hecuba), and where authorship and individuality become more clearly defined, the more completely destroyed and marked are the victims left behind them. By contrast, in the *Odyssey* the women no longer reflect man's image, or at least only reluctantly and in a fragmentary way. Admittedly, as far as accentuation, the dominant narrative perspective and the settings are concerned, the *Odyssey* is still a text in the patriarchal context. But just as art, in the form of mimesis, must as a rule always also articulate the other which is suppressed in the discourses of theory, as a kind of counterpoint which makes action and conflict possible in the first place, so the matricentric threads are visible in the patriarchal text.[40]

Admittedly the patriarch is at the end reinstated as king of Ithaca – with limitations which become apparent later – but on the road to that destiny his hero's armour is stripped from him piece by piece. He does not, as Adorno and Horkheimer think, internalize the sacrifice by suppressing his own nature in order to dominate external nature. In order to make good the violation of the cosmos perpetrated in the *Iliad*, Odysseus himself becomes the victim, driven once more through the various historical stages of mankind until he is again allowed to take his appointed place, cut down at the last to human size.

Already in the *Odyssey* pure nature no longer exists. The work does not furnish us with images which could be read as representations of the first divisions between nature and consciousness, nature and culture, and nature and society.[41] All the figures and settings of Homer's epic are already suffused with the light of history. It is only from later viewpoints that earlier historical stages are interpreted as nature.

Even the man-eating Laestrygonians and the Cyclops portray stages of human history which, to a later consciousness, may appear as bestial or barbaric as they did to Homer himself.[42] Thucydides suspects, for example, that both peoples lived in Sicily and were then overrun by the Sicani.[43] Others perceive them as a patchwork of different social characteristics: 'la peinture de leur attitude, de leurs moeurs et des lieux où ils vivent est faite de traits réellement observés chez divers peuples ou en diverses parties de l'univers connu du poète.'[44] Even Scylla and Charybdis and the Aeolian winds are 'natural' phenomena which only assume historicity in a signifying context, when apprehended by a population who already practise seafaring.[45] That these first sailors felt sailing the sea to be sacrilegious may explain why, in this case too as a sacrifice, Odysseus is plunged into the elements.[46]

Odysseus is thrown into various historical contexts, integrated into them for a while, dissolved, rescued and brought a little closer to home. Yet this slow, phased return to Ithaca cannot be achieved by means of domination and power strategies but only by using a more empathetic form of reason.

The supposedly autonomously emerging subject must be able to lose itself in the other, and it can only be rescued once it is able to do so.

On the way to making good there lurk on one side the dangers of total self-renunciation, and on the other the risk posed by the rigidity of autonomous and violent subjectivity. The first category is represented by the enticements to forget the homeland: the Lotus Eaters, the Sirens, Circe, Calypso, Nausicaa. The second is characterized by the threat from the Bulls of Helios, Aeolus' bag of wind, Polyphemus, Scylla and Charybdis.

It is precisely the inhuman qualities cultivated by Odysseus and his comrades for their military functions which are their undoing in the adventures which form the second category. The attack and pillaging of the Cicones immediately after the destruction of Troy had already reduced the returning warriors by half. It is the same marauding behaviour which causes the Greeks to slaughter the forbidden Bulls of Helios for food and to open Aeolus' bag of wind, because they suspect it contains the booty Odysseus has set aside.

The self-denying negation of one's own name is intolerable for the classical hero, and it is this which finally induces Odysseus to say his name in the Polyphemus episode. Not only must he first deny his own name and call himself 'Nobody' in the presence of the giant, but he can only escape by adopting the shape of a beast, by stealing out of the cave clinging to the belly of the leading ram in Polyphemus' herd. Yet survival 'in one's smallest form',[47] which Brecht saw as the only chance for the individual in a hostile environment, is anathema to the hero of antiquity. In good heroic tradition, after blinding Polyphemus, Odysseus triumphantly shouts out his name, origin and descent. It is only this hubris which enables Poseidon to take revenge for the mutilation of his son because now he knows who the culprit is.

When Odysseus decides to fight Scylla with his sword instead of fleeing (unheroically) on Athene's advice, the goddess says:

> So you are not prepared to give in even to immortal gods? I tell you, Scylla was not born for death: the fiend will live for ever. She is a thing to shun, intractable, ferocious and impossible to fight. No: against her there is no defence, and valour lies in flight. (12. 116–20)[48]

Poseidon's revenge hounds Odysseus across the Mediterranean for ten years. The sacrificial journey thus lasts as long as the siege of Troy, and just as the Trojans fell then, so now Odysseus' comrades perish to a man. From this voyage of death the bloody shadow of the Trojan slaughter rises and falls now upon the Greeks themselves. There are no victors any more. Odysseus survives because after the débâcle with Polyphemus, he learns to accommodate himself to the other, not to pit himself against it but to give himself over to it. This other dimension is defined by the female figures, and here we find the fragmentary reminders of a form of society organized on matriarchal lines. They can be seen in certain matrilinear and matrilocal phenomena in the *Odyssey* and in the scattered gestures of female independence and female-defined sexuality. In his contacts with women and when he is thrown into their spheres, the hero is increasingly robbed of his heroic stature and reduced to purely generic definitions.

In the storm after the slaughter of the Bulls of Helios, Odysseus loses all his comrades and thereby his social dimension. Charybdis destroys his ship too, and with it the last cultural artefact. Odysseus, as organic matter within organic matter, 'clung like a bat to the branches of a fig-tree' (12. 433), culture is exiled into the imaginary sphere of the simile used to describe the moment when Charybdis spits out the ship which has now been reduced to matchwood. He relates:

> However, I stuck grimly on until such time as she should spew me up my mast and keel once more. My hope was justified, though they came up very late, in fact not till the time when a judge with a long list of disputes to settle between obstinate litigants rises from court for his evening meal. (12. 439–41).

He barely manages to escape with his life to the island of Calypso. For seven years Odysseus remains in the realm of a woman who, as a goddess, is more powerful than he. And although she must ultimately obey Zeus, it is clear that she dates back to pre-Olympian and pre-patriarchal times.

When Hermes delivers Zeus' command to let Odysseus go, she rebels against male control and the restriction of her desire, moved by the spirit of a repressed gynocentric culture:

> A cruel folk you are, unmatched for jealousy, you gods who cannot bear to let a goddess sleep with a man, even if it is done without concealment and she has chosen him as her lawful consort. You were the same when Rose-fingered Dawn fell in love with Orion. Easy livers yourselves, you were outraged at her conduct, and in the end chaste Artemis rose from her golden throne, attacked him in Ortygia with her gentle darts and left him dead. And so again, when the lovely Demeter gave way to her passion and lay in the arms of her beloved Iasion in the thrice-ploughed fallow field, Zeus heard of it quickly enough and struck him dead with his blinding thunderbolt. And now it is my turn to incur that same divine displeasure for living with a mortal man – a man whom I rescued from death as he was drifting alone astride the keel of his ship. (5. 118–31)

It is symptomatic that the autonomy of female sexuality can only be conceptualized in a male-dominated world as the prerogative of goddesses and is always interpreted in critical commentaries as 'prostitution'. As a result, genuinely female sexuality is once again bound up in a phallocentric linguistic system. In the concept of the hetaira or prostitute, one facet of the female, precisely that which is not linked to motherhood, is neutralized by being given the function of mirroring desire which may not be marital desire, yet which is in its extramarital form exclusively male. Adorno and Horkheimer are no exception here: 'It is this non-differentiation ... which constitutes the nature of promiscuity: the essential quality of the courtesan, reflected still in the prostitute's look.'[49] More than forty years later, Karl Markus Michel in the same tradition of thought describes Circe as a witch who really is a goddess.[50]

But with Circe, too, Odysseus undergoes a traumatic reduction. Even before he comes to Calypso in book 12 as somebody stripped of all social and cultural definitions, Circe has sent the former hero to Hades in book 11 to the absolute zero-point of existence.

Hades marks the anti-heroic fulcrum of the *Odyssey* in three senses. First, it is the structural and spatial link between the killing at Troy and that at Ithaca. It is the transitional domain in which the desecration of Troy, the annihilation of the Greeks and the murder of the heroic young men of Ithaca are brought together. Here, in book 11, Odysseus encounters Agamemnon, Achilles and Ajax, the outstanding individual figures in the Greek army. Achilles perished at Troy; Agamemnon was slain by Clytemnestra solely because of events arising from his warrior role (the sacrifice of Iphigenia for better wind, his long absence and his bringing back Cassandra to be a Trojan concubine); Ajax drowned in the sea because Athene took revenge on him for the desecration of her priestess, Cassandra, in her temple at Troy. Here Odysseus meets Elpenor, one of his companions on the journey back, who fell from Circe's roof where he was sleeping, when they started for Hades. There can only be one explanation for this episode, which is entirely unconnected with the rest of the story, and for the fact that Odysseus only realizes Elpenor has died when he meets him in Hades: Elpenor represents all the other companions who are still alive but who will be killed in book 12. Book 24 will present Hades again in extraordinary detail spread over 201 lines. Once more, the characters from the first Hades scene appear, but this time they are confronted with the suitors who have been slain meanwhile. In the portrayal of this encounter and, above all, in the convergence of their different experiences of death, the profound reciprocity of the killings in Troy and in Ithaca is demonstrated. For the suitors tell of their misfortune in response to questions which project the fate of Troy on to them. Agamemnon asks:

> Amphimedon, what catastrophe has brought you down into the bowels of the earth with this chosen band of men of your own age, as carefully picked as

though one had gone round and taken the very flower of some city's best? Did Poseidon catch your ships in a gale and overwhelm you in the heavy seas? Or did you fall to some hostile tribe on land as you were lifting their cattle and their flocks, or fighting with them for their town and women? (24. 106–13)

Second, in his encounter with Achilles, the Greek superhero, the gruesome void of the heroic ethic of honour and glory in the face of the loss of life is revealed to him. Odysseus is praising the power of Achilles:

Achilles, the most fortunate man that ever was or will be! For in the old days when you were on the earth, we Argives honoured you as though you were a god; and now, down here, you are a mighty prince among the dead. For you, Achilles, Death should have lost his sting. (11. 482–6).

Achilles' answer is completely disillusioning:

My lord Odysseus, spare me your praise of Death. Put me on earth again, and I would rather be a serf in the house of some landless man, with little enough for himself to live on, than king of all these dead men that have done with life. (11. 488–91).

Third, the Hades episode is overlaid with a network of female power and dominance. In Hades Odysseus meets his mother and an array of the most famous women of antiquity whose experiences in life all call into question the institution of marriage as a way of organizing female sexuality within patriarchy. Moreover, the Hades scene is inserted after the Circe episode and before the encounter with Calypso, which is preceded by the events which reduce Odysseus to a purely physical existence. This passage is contained once more within a framework of female power because Odysseus recounts this episode at the court of the Phaeacians who are ruled by Queen Arete. And it immediately follows his encounter with Calypso.

The link between the two areas of female autonomy is established by the goddess Leucothea. The ship built when Odysseus is with Calypso is also destroyed by Poseidon in the storm. At Leucothea's behest, Odysseus must let go of even its last timber and only manages to get to the Phaeacian shore wrapped in the nymph's own veil. Now he is nothing more than a body. Even his skin is stripped away on the sharp reefs. But he is clothed and rescued by the other, the female, the potency of which, in a patriarchal context, can once again only be identified with the superhuman. At this point, Odysseus does indeed become part of the elements to the extent that it is impossible to distinguish him from them. His accommodation of himself to natural matter and to the female reaches its extreme at the lowest point in his orbit as a hero.

He clung there groaning while the great wave marched by. But no sooner had he escaped its fury than it struck him once more with the full force of its backward rush and flung him far out to sea. Pieces of skin stripped from his sturdy hands were left sticking to the crag, thick as pebbles that stick to the suckers of a squid when he is torn from his hole. (5. 428–35)

It is like a second birth. He is washed back and forth, out of the water, swathed in the lanugo-like bluish veil of the nymph, and later finds himself in the postnatal slime of the mud on the shore, from the bushes of which he bursts forth like a new-born child.

So the gallant Odysseus crept out from under the bushes, after beaking off with his great hand a leafy bough from the thicket to conceal his naked manhood. Then he advanced on them like a mountain lion who sallies out, defying wind and rain in the pride of his power, with fire in his eyes, to hunt the oxen or the sheep, to stalk the roaming deer, or to be forced by hunger to besiege the very walls of the homestead and attack the pens. The same urgent need now constrained Odysseus, naked as he was, to bear down upon these gentle girls. Begrimed with salt he made a gruesome sight, and one look at him sent them scuttling in every direction along the jutting spits of sand. (6. 127–38)

The dissolution of Odysseus into the elements surrounding him, into overlapping spheres of the female, could not be clearer than here, where even the similes explicitly underline his assimilation of the natural.

From the court of the Phaeacians onwards his reconstruction as a subject begins, but it is now as a relational subject. Yet even the Phaeacians, with the central figures of Arete and Nausicaa, are merely the projections of what really awaits him in Ithaca. There he starts once again from the bottom. In Ithaca he relives the new beginning in purely physical survival which he experienced with Calypso and the Phaeacians. He awakes from his slumbers on the sand: Athene girds him in the night. No one recognizes him; he does not recognize his fatherland. His reintegration begins painfully slowly, and when it begins it begins at the very bottom of the social ladder, with the swineherd Eumaeus.

Odysseus' Homecoming

If we disregard the section dealing with Telemachus, the story of Odysseus himself can be divided into two parts: the adventures and the homecoming. The homecoming begins in book 13, exactly in the middle of the epic. In the course of the adventures, the heroic stature of Odysseus is diminished. It is ground down by the forces of nature, by the societies representing various historical stages, by the power of women. Odysseus is broken and this happens in the realm of the imaginary with its pretence of a unified, radiant self. The fantasies of omnipotence the warrior cherished have been smashed along with the fortress of the ego and the armour-plated self. The corresponding element in the adventure section is the imaginary geography which researchers have located in the western Mediterranean around Sicily. This is where we find the dark continents of natural forces, of female potency, of pre-literate cultures. They all liquefy the solid self of the *Iliad* from which a new social self now emerges. The imaginary geography stands in contrast to the real geography alluded to in Ithaca. Its landmarks were at the beginning Troy, Lesbos, Sparta and Pylos, and now they are Ithaca, Crete and Rhodes in the fictional accounts of his journey which Odysseus tells before he is recognized in his homeland.

The similes from the natural world in the imaginary section now make way for historical reminiscences about the Trojan War. Just as in the imaginary part nemesis drags the body of the abdicated hero through the world, so this body now casts the shadow of the Trojan War over its own social world. We have seen how Hades becomes the crucial connection between the two worlds in three senses. Since Ithaca can no longer exist without reflecting the bloody Trojan War, Odysseus' homecoming cannot be a true homecoming any more.

In Hades, Teiresias foretells that Odysseus must journey on after killing the suitors, until he finds a people who do not know the sea, salt and the oar. There he must make a sacrifice to Poseidon and, back in Ithaca, to the other gods. Then he will die of natural causes in old age. This narrative excess will be the wound in the body of the text, allowing no closure of the narrative. The end is deferred indefinitely as the point of rest now lies beyond the text.

Just as Agamemnon's homecoming was aborted by Clytemnestra's fatal blow, so Odysseus' homecoming is a slow, agonizing and bloody process. The atmosphere in Ithaca is unpredictable and dangerous from the start. Odysseus does not recognize the island. He is afraid for the gifts given to him by the Phaeacians. He is a beggar at the swineherd's and a beggar in his own house. The triangular story of Agamemnon, Clytemnestra and Aegisthus is inscribed by inference in his own situation like mirror-writing. Any reading of the events in Ithaca must take this other story into account. In Penelope's dream we can still recognize at least a trace of that gynocentric desire which expressed itself so openly in Clytemnestra's actions. Penelope recounts her dream:

Let me ask you to interpret a dream of mine which I shall now describe. I keep a flock of twenty geese in the place. They come in from the pond to pick up their grain and I delight in watching them. In my dream I saw a great eagle swoop down from the hills and break their necks with his crooked beak, killing them all. There they lay in a heap on the floor while he vanished in the open sky. I wept and cried aloud, though it was only a dream, and Achaean ladies gathering about me found me sobbing my heart out because the eagle had slaughtered my geese. But the bird came back. He perched on a jutting timber of the roof, and breaking into human speech he checked my tears. 'Take heart,' he said, 'daughter of the noble Icarius. This is not a dream but a happy reality which you shall see fulfilled. The geese were your lovers, and I that played the eagle's part am now your husband, home again and ready to deal out grim punishment to every man among them'. (19. 536–51)

The return of the repressed matricentric element in a situation where patriarchal control is weakened is clear also in the confrontations between Penelope and Telemachus over who holds sway in Odysseus' house and in the aspirations of the suitors who seek her hand and the throne of Ithaca.

The crowning moment of the return, the moment of recognition, is missing. Penelope does not recognize Odysseus. She denies him his identity, her mirror is blind. Only after testing him three times does she acknowledge him. The supposed key scenes of anagnorisis are inhibited and fragmented. The dog Argos dies at the very moment it recognizes its master. The nurse Euryclea and Odysseus have to disown each other for tactical reasons instead of rejoicing, as do Odysseus and Telemachus. The only happy moment of recognition, that between Odysseus and his father Laertes, is postponed for too long, only to be immediately overshadowed by the imminent revenge of the Ithacans for the murder of their sons.

Before Odysseus can move into his house he must kill the flower of the young heroes of his kingdom. The reunion with Penelope takes place literally on the pile of corpses which has been hidden for the night beneath the anteroom. The renewal of the marital alliance is really a blood wedding, for while the suitors are being slain inside the house, music plays outside to let the Ithacans think that Penelope is about to marry one of them. The maids too, who have fraternized with the suitors, are mercilessly put to death. Thus Odysseus, in the heart of his own land, perpetrates the same terrible deeds against the Greeks which the Greeks perpetrated against the barbarians, the Asians of Troy. The mirroring process is clear: in book 22 of the *Iliad* Achilles slays Hector and drags his body around the town; in book 22 of the *Odyssey* Odysseus kills the suitors and the maids in Ithaca.

One could say that the resocialization of Odysseus leads him back to the very old categories which he is supposed to have abandoned. But the protagonist appears here not so much as a subject powerful in himself but rather as an instrument of the gods. Every step he takes is prepared and controlled by Athene, and the manifestations of divine intervention come thick and fast during the homecoming episode. Odysseus is victim and avenging angel in one: by taking revenge on his own people he becomes a victim too.

Many researchers are irked by the fact that the *Odyssey* does not end after the reunion between Odysseus and Penelope. For if it did, it would be a homecoming in the fullest sense. It is interesting in this connection that, in his essay on Lévinas, Derrida, the enemy of homecoming *par excellence*, mentions this French philosopher's aversion to the *Odyssey* because he reads it as a happy homecoming story, as a return to the same while excluding the other. Derrida says:

> But Lévinas does not care for Ulysses, nor for the ruses of this excessively Hegelian hero, this man of *nostos* and the closed circle, whose adventure is always summarized in its totality ... 'To the myth of Ulysses returning to Ithaca, we would prefer to oppose the story of Abraham leaving his country forever for an as yet unknown land, and forbidding his servant to take back even his son to the point of departure' (*La Trace de l'Autre*). The impossibility of the return doubtless was not overlooked by Heidegger: the original historicity of Being, the irreducible wandering all forbid the return to Being *itself*, which is nothing.[51]

Yet Odysseus does not arrive either. At the very moment when he climbs into the marital bed with Penelope, the moment when the private and royal alliance is renewed, the process of restoration is ruptured once again and left open. Odysseus tells her of the imminent fight with the families of the slain suitors and the prophecy of Teiresias, which drives him on beyond Ithaca as soon as he has set foot on the island after an absence of twenty years.

When does this homecoming happen exactly? When he sets foot on the island? When he recognizes it? When he falls in with Eumaeus, the swineherd? In the recognition scene with Telemachus? When he enters his own house as a beggar? The recognition scene with the dog Argos? With the nurse Euryclea? With Penelope? With his father Laertes? Does it begin when scores are settled with the suitors? In the final armed conflict with the families of the suitors? Is it the renewed alliance with the gods?

The new alliance with the gods marks the end of the story, but this too is undermined by Teiresias' prophecy. We have, then, an end-point which could also be a starting-point, and yet is neither, because the story goes on beyond it. So far, philologists and critics have found no explanation for Teiresias' prophecy which fits into a coherent exposition. It is the surplus of meaning which, on a textual level, makes a homecoming impossible.

In his work *Die unendliche Fahrt*,[52] Manfred Frank describes the *Odyssey*, as Hegel and Lukács did before him, as a textualization of a consciousness for which existence still appears to be immediately meaningful. In Lukács's understanding of this notion, this consciousness is vouchsafed a 'transcendental refuge' in which home and homecoming are still possible. In contrast, the modern consciousness, starting with the Romantics, no longer manages to find immediate meaning in existence. *Die unendliche Fahrt* works both on the narrative level and in the chain of signifiers which continues to shift and therefore defies any attempt to give it definitive meaning. According to Derrida, though, this is a mark of language in general, not only of language in the modern period.

If we now take Manfred Frank's metaphorical path in the other direction and apply the impossibility of giving a text a definitive meaning to the *Odyssey*, then a homecoming would be impossible from this angle too. This is confirmed on the level of the plot. Teiresias' prophecy constantly conveys Odysseus, the guarantor of meaning, beyond any place where we might believe him to have finally arrived. The vision of the future does not allow Odysseus' definitions of identity to be consolidated on Ithaca after they have become so fluid during his adventures.

Homecoming – just like repetition – is impossible. For time and the passing of time continue to be written back into the very point of departure, with the result that there is no longer any origin to come back to. This is apparent in the *Odyssey* from Athene's continual attempts to rejuvenate the royal couple so that they recognize and desire each other. Yet traces of the other, the effects of passing time, are indelibly etched on the consciousness and the memory. Penelope summarizes this with painful words: All our unhappiness is due to the gods, who couldn't bear to see us share the joys of youth and reach the threshold of old age together' (23. 210–12).

Even the *Odyssey* no longer gives us an origin (*Ursprung*) in the sense of origination (*Ent-springen*), but only the result of the leap (*Sprung*), the trace of what is broken (*Zersprungen*). Texts, the *Odyssey* included, are always the evidence of the rupture which they themselves hide and seek so untiringly.

The Dialectic of Enlightenment

From what has been said so far it should be impossible to read the *Odyssey* as an allegory of instrumental reason. On the contrary: at the dawn of Western culture there emerges a text which questions the prerequisites and consequences of a concept of the human subject as autonomous and severed from natural and communal ties. When the nurse wishes to rejoice at the slaying of the suitors, Odysseus urges her to show a new communal kind of reason:

> Restrain yourself, old dame, and gloat in silence. I'll have no jubilation here.
> It is an impious thing to exult over the slain. These men fell victim to the hand

of heaven and their own infamy. They paid respect to no one who came near them – good men and bad were all alike to them. And now their insensate wickedness has brought them to this awful end. (22. 411–16).

The homogeneous narrative structure, which Adorno and Horkheimer wish to construe as reflecting the trajectory of the subject, does not exist. For the narrative thread of the *Odyssey* is just as meandering and convoluted as the contexts into which Odysseus is moulded again. It is not without contradiction either. If we set out to measure the logic of a story by its lack of contradictions, then the story is illogical at important points. If such a logic is defined as predominantly male, because in the troughs between the narrative peaks the female is left behind, like Circe and Calypso on their islands, then we can detect the traces of female power in the contradictions and unresolved meanings of the story-line: for example, the text's indecision regarding the rival claims to power of Penelope and Telemachus; the matriarchal figure of Arete in a patriarchal context at the court of the Phaeacians; the dominance of Helen at the court of Menelaus compared with the weak position held by women at the court of Nestor; the help given by Leucothea and Eidothea against Poseidon and Proteus; and the weak position of Laertes in Ithaca.

These recalcitrant elements of a submerged female tradition and of a subjectivity defined by communication and relationship are inserted into the narrative in such a way as to forbid any definitive historical victory, whether of patriarchy or of instrumental reason, to be reconstructed.

Domination can never definitively establish itself and must constantly reinforce itself in all areas. The assumption that it is possible for hegemonic power to be defeated is part, however, of just such a view of history as domination. Adorno and Horkheimer do not share this view. The monolithic force of their determinism forges origin and telos together into a henceforth unbreakable circle – a form of thinking which can only be imposed upon the *Odyssey* by brute constraint. In the *Dialectic of Enlightenment* women consistently appear in two variations of a final repression: they are either helpless victims or the cynical accomplices of male power.

Our different view of the *Odyssey* also involves a different view, not only of the historical state of instrumental reason reflected in the *Dialectic of Enlightenment*, but also of the quality of reason itself. It has been shown that nemesis struck a male warrior caste which drew its power and force from a principle of autonomous self-absorption which was ethically transposed into the concepts of honour and fame. The re-education of Odysseus transforms this self into a relational one. In order to achieve this, Odysseus becomes both the tool and the object of retribution: the tool in the world of the Ithacan Greek men: the object in the world of women. The distinctive features of this new Odysseus, which point to a different kind of subject and reason, are expressions of pity, solidarity, concern and love.

Relational reason manifests itself most clearly in the low social world of the swineherd. It is only in the Eumaeus episode that Homer uses the familiar form of address, which is immediately directed at the swineherd in the form of a lyrical 'thou'. It is only in this chapter of the Odyssey that we find a situation of affection and trust which is not between members of the same family. It is Eumaeus who says: 'Yet the blessed gods don't like foul play' (14. 83).

The critique of war also puts forward the case for a relational ethic. Only the illusion of an autonomous self can assume that the murder of another does not affect one's own life in a profound way, that such destruction and violation does not become an act of self-destruction. This is made clear again at the end of Homer's epic. After murdering the suitors, Odysseus has to confront their families with a small army. Everyone who speaks on these final pages tells the truth, yet it is not the whole truth. Thus the father of Antinous speaks against the murderer of his son: 'I denounce Odysseus as the inveterate enemy of our race. Where is the gallant company he sailed away with? Lost by him, every one; and our good ships lost as well! And now he comes home and slaughters the very pick of the Cephallenians!' (24. 425–9).

The old seer Halitherses speaks against the call to battle against Odysseus:

> Ithacans, I beg you for your attention. Your own wickedness, my friends, is to blame for what has happened. You would not listen to me or your leader Mentor, when he urged you to check your sons in their career of folly. They threw all restraint to the winds, and in plundering the estate and insulting the wife of a prince whom they counted on never seeing here again, they were guilty of a flagrant offence. I hope therefore that you will be persuaded by me when I propose that we should take no action; or else I fear that some of you may bring your own doom on your heads. (24. 453–61)

Only the gods can break this bloody round of murder and suicide. And they do so in the name of relational reason. In response to Athene's question: 'Are you planning to prolong this strife, with the horrors and turmoil it entails, or to establish peace between the warring sides?' (24. 474–5) Zeus replies:

> Since the admirable Odysseus has had his revenge on the suitors, let them make a treaty of peace to establish him as king in perpetuity, with an act of oblivion, on our part, for the slaughter of their sons and brothers. Let the mutual goodwill of the old days be restored, and let peace and plenty prevail. (24. 481–5)

Whereupon Athene cries: 'Ithacans, stop this disastrous fight and separate at once before more blood is shed! ... Noble Odysseus, hold your hand

and bring this civil strife to an end lest you offend Zeus, the god of thunder!'
(24. 531–2, 541–3). Only a divine act of social amnesia can break the lethal
circle which never produces victors, only losers.

The *Odyssey* provides an answer to the question posed by Adorno and
Horkheimer, but which they thought could not be answered. Ironically,
they arrived at this conclusion through their reading of the Homeric text.
That question is: how can secular reason alone argue the case that murder
is abhorrent even if it serves one's own cause? Viewed in the light of
relational reason, murder is suicide; that is the answer the *Odyssey* gives us.

NOTES

1 Theodor Adorno and Max Horkheimer, *Dialektik der Aufklärung. Philosophische Fragmente* (Querido, Amsterdam, 1944), p. 61 (author's translation).
2 Ibid., p. 7.
3 Ibid., p.49.
4 Ibid., p. 262.
5 Ibid., p. 61.
6 For the connection between history and narration see for example Paul Ricœur,
Hermeneutics and the Human Sciences, ed. and tr. John B. Thompson (Cambridge University Press, Cambridge, 1981), esp. the chapter 'Narrative function'.
7 Jean-François Lyotard, *The Postmodern Condition: A Report on Knowledge*,
tr. Geoff Bennington and Brian Massumi (Manchester University Press, Manchester, 1986), p. 29.
8 Walter Kern, 'Die Phänomenologie des Geistes', in *Kindlers Literaturlexikon*
(25 vols, Deutscher Taschenbuch Verlag, Munich, 1974), vol. 17, p. 7428.
9 Georg Wilhelm Friedrich Hegel, *Ästhetik* (2 vols, Deutsche Verlagsanstalt,
Frankfurt/M., 1955), pp. 413–14 (author's translation).
10 Georg Lukács, *Die Theorie des Romans. Ein geschichtsphilosophischer Versuch über die Formen der grossen Epik* (Luchterhand, Neuwied, 1962), p. 64
(all quotations author's translations).
11 Ibid., p. 89.
12 See Hubert Fichte, 'Patroklos und Achilleus', *Merkur*, 5 (1986), p. 369.
13 See Luce Irigaray, *Speculum of the Other Woman*, tr. Gilliam C. Gill (Cornell
University Press, Ithaca, NY, 1985), p. 23: 'It seems . . . that one might be able
to interpret the fact of being deprived of a womb as the almost intolerable
deprivation of man, since his contribution to gestation – his function with
regard to the origin of reproduction – is hence asserted as less than evident, as
open to doubt. An indecision to be attenuated both by man's "active" role in
intercourse and by the fact that he will mark the product of copulation *with
his own name.* Thereby woman, whose intervention in the work of engendering
the child can hardly be questioned, becomes the anonymous worker, the
machine in the service of a master-proprietor who will put his trademark upon
the finished product. It does not seem exaggerated, incidentally, to understand

quite a few products, as a counterpart or a search for equivalents to woman's function in maternity. And the desire that man here displays to determine for himself what is constituted by "origin", and thereby eternally and ever to produce him (as) self, is a far from negligible indication of the same thing.'

14 Georg Lukács, *Die Theorie des Romans*, p. 69.
15 Ibid., p. 88.
16 Ibid.
17 Nina Baym, 'Melodramas of beset manhood: How theories of American fiction exclude women authors', in *The New Feminist Criticism: Essays on Women, Literature and Theory*, ed. Elaine Showalter (Virago Press, London, 1986), pp. 63–80.
18 Ibid., p. 71.
19 See Barbara Johnson, 'Is female to male as ground is to figure?', in *Feminism and Psychoanalysis*, ed. Richard Feldstein and Judith Roof (Cornell University Press, Ithaca, NY/London, 1989), pp. 255–68.
20 Irigaray, *Speculum of the Other Woman*, p. 221.
21 Baym, 'Melodramas of beset manhood', p. 73.
22 Ibid., p. 77.
23 Ibid., p. 79.
24 Hayden White, *Tropics of Discourse: Essays in Cultural Criticism* (Johns Hopkins University Press, Baltimore, 1978), pp. 84–5.
25 Simone Weil, 'The *Iliad*: A poem of force', in *The Pacifist Conscience*, ed. Peter Mayer (Rupert Hart-Davis, New York/London, 1966), pp. 292–316.
26 Johannes T. Kakridis, 'The role of the women in the *Iliad*', *Eranos*, 54 (1956), pp. 21–7, esp. p. 23.
27 Ibid., pp. 24–5.
28 Ibid., p. 26.
29 Charles Rowan Beyle, 'Male and female in the Homeric poems', *Ramus*, 3 (1974), pp. 87–101, esp. p. 93.
30 Ibid., p. 94.
31 Ibid., p. 97.
32 See Beyle, 'Male and female in the Homeric poems', pp. 88–9; Fichte, 'Patroklos und Achilleus'.
33 Fichte, 'Patroklos und Achilleus', p. 375.
34 Weil, 'The *Iliad*', p. 292.
35 Ibid., p. 297.
36 Ibid., p. 300.
37 Franz Grillparzer, *King Ottocar: His Rise and Fall*, tr. E. Burkhart (The Registrar's Press, Yarmouth Port, Mass., 1962), p. 142.
38 Weil, 'The *Iliad*', pp. 299–300.
39 Ibid., p. 301.
40 Cf. Kaarle Hirvonen, *Matriarchal Survivals and Certain Trends in Homer's Female Characters* (Annales Acad. Scient. Fennicae, Helsinki, 1968), pp. 54, 74, 76–8, 106–9, 133, 150.
41 See Jacques Derrida's criticism of Lévi-Strauss in the chapter on the writing lesson in his *Of Grammatology*, tr. Gayatri Chakravorty Spivak (Johns Hopkins University Press, Baltimore, 1976), 'The violence of the letter'.

42   See for example Hayden White on the characterizations of the original inhabitants of America by the European imperialists: 'The noble savage theme as
fetish', in *Tropics of Discourse*, pp. 186–7.

43   L.C. Pocock, *The Sicilian Origins of the Odyssey* (New Zealand University
Press, Wellington, 1957), p. 3.

44   Roger Dion, *Les anthropophages de l'Odyssée. Cyclopes et Lestrygons* (Librairie Philosophique J. Vrin, n.p., 1969), p. 59.

45   The assumption that behind the many-headed Scylla with her ring of barking
dogs a giant sea-monster is hidden is enhanced by the observation of marine
biologist Claude Morris: when the giant squids are taken out of the water, the
sounds they make are reminiscent of the barking of young dogs. (Oral communication, Clare Hall, Cambridge, 1987.)

46   Cf. W.B. Stanford, *The Odyssey of Homer*, edited with general and gramma-
tical introduction, commentary and indexes, 2nd edn (2 vols, Macmillan,
London, 1959), p. 353.

47   Bertolt Brecht, *Gesammelte Werke* (20 vols, Suhrkamp, Frankfurt/M., 1967),
vol. 2, p. 602.

48   The *Odyssey* is quoted from the translation by E.V. Rieu (Penguin, Harmondsworth, 1946).

49   Adorno and Horkheimer, *Dialektik der Aufklärung*, p. 88.

50   Karl Markus Michel, 'Die Stunde der Sirenen', *Kursbuch*, 84 (1986), p. 1.

51   Jacques Derrida, *Writing and Difference*, tr. Alan Bass (Routledge & Kegan
Paul, London, 1978), p. 320.

52   Manfred Frank, *Die unendliche Fahrt. Ein Motiv und sein Text* (Suhrkamp,
Frankfurt/M., 1979).

Index